Interpreting
Puzzling Texts
in the
New Testament

Interpreting Puzzling Texts in the New Testament

Robert H. Stein

Baker Books

A Division of Baker Book House Co.
Grand Rapids, Michigan 49516

Published by Baker Books
a division of Baker Book House Company
P.O. Box 6287, Grand Rapids, MI 49516-6287

First hardcover edition published under the title *Difficult Passages in the New Testament:
Interpreting Puzzling Texts in the Gospels and Epistles*, 1990
Third printing, August 1991

First paperback edition published 1996

Printed in the United States of America

Library of Congress Cataloging-in-Publication Data

Stein, Robert H. 1935–.
    Interpreting puzzling texts in the New Testament / Robert H. Stein
       p. cm.
    Compilation of three previously published works: Difficult passages in the Gospels. 1984. Difficult sayings in the Gospels. 1985. Difficult passages in the Epistles. 1988.
    Includes bibliographical references.
    ISBN 0-8010-2102-2
    1. Bible. N.T. Gospels—Criticism, interpretation, etc. 2. Jesus Christ—Teachings. 3. Bible. N.T. Epistles—Criticism, interpretation, etc. I. Title.
BS2361.s.S74 1990
225.6—cd20   89-29148

For information about academic books, resources for Christian leaders, and all new releases available from Baker Book House, visit our web site:
http://www.bakerbooks.com/

To my loving parents,
William and **Ella Stein**

To **Florence** and **LeRoy Thatcher**

And to **Bill** and **Syl,**
Duane and **Helen,**
Ann, Jan and **Jim**

Contents

Preface

Several years ago this writer was approached by the *Standard*, the monthly periodical of the Baptist General Conference, to do a series of articles on problem passages in the New Testament. This resulted in a series of twenty-nine articles which appeared in the *Standard* over a period four years dealing with various passages in the Gospels. These were then brought together and published in 1984 by Baker Book House under the title *Difficult Passages in the Gospels*.

A few of the difficult passages discussed in *Difficult Passages in the Gospels* dealt with the presence of hyperbole and overstatement in Jesus' teachings. I had earlier referred to Jesus' use of such exaggeration in *The Method and Message of Jesus' Teachings* (Westminster, 1978). However, whereas I had demonstrated the fact that Jesus used this literary genre, I had not dealt in any systematic way with how one might be able to determine if a saying of Jesus was hyperbolic or an overstatement. Throughout the history of the church the main means by which individuals determined if a passage contained hyperbole or overstatement seems to have been intuition. Generally such intuition proved useful and correct, but the history of the church also contains numerous examples where, sometimes quite tragically, Jesus' use of exaggeration was interpreted literally. In dealing with this problem, thirteen canons, or rules, were formulated for determining whether a passage contained exaggeration. After the detection of such exaggeration, the next need was to arrive at how such language functions and thus how exaggeration is to be interpreted. The result of this investigation was *Difficult Sayings in the Gospels,* published by Baker Book House in 1985.

After the series on difficult passages in the Gospels, it was quite natural to do a series for the *Standard* on difficult passage in the Epistles of the New Testament. Since this involved a different literary form, a new set of hermeneutical issues were involved. This series ran in the *Standard* over a period of four years and was published by Baker Book House in 1988 under the title *Difficult Passages in the Epistles.*

There are numerous people who need to be thanked for the part they played in the publication of these three works. These involve Aletta Whittaker, Laurie Dirnberger, and above all Gloria Metz for their help in preparing the various drafts for submission to the publisher; my teaching assistants Cory Dahl and Daniel Nold and my colleague, Tom Schreiner, for reading the various manuscripts; Donald E. Anderson, the editor of the *Standard* for the invitation to begin the series which led to this work and for his editorial insight and suggestions during the series; my wife, Joan, for having read, critiqued, and made suggestions throughout the reading of all three works; and finally to Baker Book House for having published these three volumes and for now bringing them together under a single cover.

Unless otherwise stated all biblical quotations come from the Revised Standard Version. Parallel passages in the Synoptic Gospels come from either the *Synopsis of the Four Gospels* (United Bible Societies, 1982) or *Gospel Parallels* (Nelson, 1967).

Introduction

Within the New Testament we encounter four distinct literary forms. These are historical materials, or to be more exact, historical narrative (the Gospels and Acts), epistles or letters (the Pauline and most of the General Epistles), wisdom literature (James), and apocalyptic literature (Revelation). Within these four distinct literary forms we also find different literary genres as well. For instance, within the Gospels we encounter not only such historical materials as miracle stories but also poetry, parables, prophetic and apocalyptic sayings, proverbs, puns, hyperbole, etc. Within the epistolary materials we find such genres as greetings, prayers, thanksgivings, confessions of faith, hymns, salutations, careful theological argumentation, along with historical materials, poetry, parables, prophetic and apocalyptic sayings, proverbs, puns, hyperbole, etc. And within the wisdom and apocalyptic books of the New Testament we also find present various other literary genres.

In order to interpret these various literary forms and genres correctly, we must understand the hermeneutical rules that govern them. In other words, to understand what the authors of Scripture were seeking to convey in their writings, we must understand the literary rules and principles under which they worked. This is evident for they based their choice of words and literary forms on the assumption that their readers would interpret them according to the accepted norms governing those words and genres. As a result, if we are unaware of the norms and principles which govern these words and forms, we shall interpret them differently than the way the author intended and misinterpretation cannot help but take place. In a similar way if one seeks to interpret a basketball game by the rules that govern soccer or a football game by the rules that govern hockey, confusion can only result. As a result, if we seek to interpret a parable as if it were an historical account or an historical account as if it were a parable, this will cause an incorrect interpretation in each instance. Likewise, to interpret hyperbole in the same way that one interprets a carefully worded theological argument such as Romans 13:1-7, or vice versa, can only lead to confusion. Numerous difficult passages in the Bible can be explained rather easily when they are interpreted in light of the particular genre found in those passages and by the rules that govern those genres.

The present work consists of three distinct volumes that have previously been published separately. They have been brought together into one volume due to the similarity of content. All deal with difficult passages in the New Testament. The first volume deals with some of the problems encountered in the reading of the Gospels. One such problem involves the fact that we encounter numerous parallel accounts in the various Gospels. Careful comparison of these accounts, however, reveals that at times the order of these accounts as well as their wording differ in different Gospels. The first section of this volume deals with such problems. What really happened? (If one wanted to use more technical terminology, we could reword this, What actually occurred in the first *Sitz im Leben?*) How can these differences be explained and reconciled? Two other problems that we encounter in the Gospels, and which are discussed next, involve the difficulty created by some of Jesus' sayings and actions. At times some of them seem to raise moral and theological problems and some of them appear to contradict what Jesus says or does elsewhere! The final area that is discussed involves several prophecies of Jesus which appear unfulfilled or untrue.

The second volume is devoted to the particular form of Jesus' teachings that has caused the most confusion and difficulty. This involves the presence of hyperbole and exaggeration in his teaching. Whereas over the centuries such exaggeration has been recognized intuitively by Christians, the major section of this volume is devoted to establishing certain canons, or rules, by which such exaggeration can be detected. Thirteen canons are suggested and discussed. This is followed by a short discussion of the differences between "referential" and "commissive" language and how hyperbole and exaggeration, as examples of commissive language, function. Instead of being considered unimportant or less important than referential language, which seeks primarily to convey information, it is suggested that we are better able to detect within Jesus' use of hyperbole and exaggeration more than anywhere else what was especially near and dear to his heart.

The third book deals with some of the problems that are encountered in the study of the epistolary materials of the New Testament. Here we are seldom concerned with historical kinds of questions. Such questions as what actually happened or why there are differences in the various parallel accounts are important concerns in Gospel studies but are of minor importance in the study of the New Testament Epistles. Here we are more concerned with literary issues, i.e., with the task of understanding what the authors sought to convey by their words. To accomplish this we must first of all understand what the authors meant by the basic building blocks or words which they used. Next we must seek to understand what these individual words mean in combination with other words. Thus we turn secondly to study the part that grammatical syntax plays in seeking to understand the authorial meaning. Whereas individual words possess a range of possible meanings, as any dictionary or lexicon clearly reveals, within the grammatical context which an author gives in his writing, the range of possibilities narrows down to a singular particular meaning. The simplest grammatical context involves the phrase or sentence in which the author has placed the word. After discussing the importance of this simpler context in interpretation, we look at the larger context provided by the individual author in his Letter or Letters. By understanding the larger context in which an author placed his words, the reader is better able to interpret the smaller portions found in this context. Thus the third section in this book deals with the role that this larger authorial context provided by his other writings plays in interpretation and how certain difficult passages can more easily be explained when interpreted in light of this larger context. Next, we look at the even larger canonical context and note why and how the canonical context assists in understanding the meaning of certain difficult passages. Finally, we look at two difficult passages in the Epistles which serve as examples for this entire hermeneutical process.

It is hoped that through the discussion of specific difficult passages found in the Gospels and Epistles of the New Testament the reader will not merely come to "solve" specific difficult passages but to develop a comprehensive methodology of interpretation that can be applied to other passages as well.

Part 1

Difficult Passages in the Gospels

Introduction to Part 1

The New Testament contains four works called Gospels. These Gospels deal with the life and teachings of Jesus of Nazareth, who in the opinion of each of the writers is the "Christ, the Son of God." The fact that the New Testament has four such works is a cause for great joy. How much more blessed is the church by this fourfold testimony to her Lord than if she possessed only one such work.

Yet this very richness is also a cause for consternation. For example, some Gospels speak of a virgin birth and resurrection appearances in Galilee, some do not. The wording of Jesus' sayings varies in the four Gospels. Some place certain events in Jesus' life in a different order. It becomes clear that three of them—Matthew, Mark, and Luke—highly resemble each other both in the order of events and in their wording, whereas the other—John—does not.

As early as the second century A.D. an attempt was made by Tatian in his *Diatessaron* (A.D. 150–170) to combine the four Gospels into a single, comprehensive account. In the third century A.D. Ammonius reportedly utilized the term *harmony* for the first time. His work consisted of the text of the Gospel of Matthew with the parallel passages in the other Gospels listed alongside. The work of Ammonius formed the basis of the famous Canons of Eu-

sebius. Eusebius, bishop of Caesarea (A.D. 260–340), using
the work of Ammonius, provided a useful table to help the
reader find the parallel materials in the various Gospels.
The various manuscripts of the Greek New Testament and
numerous printed editions of the Greek New Testament
use it extensively.

Eusebius's table contains ten "canons" or tables of lists.
The Gospels are divided into sections: Matthew contains
355; Mark, 233; Luke, 342; and John, 232. The sections are
numbered consecutively. The first canon lists material
common to all four Gospels. Thus, the first entry is
Matthew—8; Mark—2; Luke—7; John—10. This indicates
that the eighth section of Matthew has a parallel in the
second section of Mark, the seventh section of Luke, and
the tenth section of John. All sections deal with the same
event: the baptism of Jesus. The second canon treats
material common to Matthew, Mark, and Luke; the
third, material common to Matthew, Luke, and John; the
fourth, material common to Matthew, Mark, and John;
the fifth, material common to Matthew and Luke; the
sixth, material common to Matthew and Mark; the seventh, material common to Matthew and John; the eighth,
material common to Luke and Mark; the ninth, material
common to Luke and John; and the tenth contains four
subsections and lists material unique to each Gospel.

The terms *harmony* and *synopsis*, which are frequently
used to describe such works, tend to be misunderstood.
Frequently they are used interchangeably. Even more
confusing is the fact that some writers name their works
harmonies when they would more accurately be termed
synopses. The reverse has also been true. Although an
absolute distinction between the two cannot be made, the
term *synopsis* is best used for works in which the parallel
accounts in the Gospels are placed side by side, usually in
columns. The primary purpose is to place similar materials
side by side for comparison. A harmony seeks to arrange
the material in the four Gospels in an historical order.

Thus it interweaves the various material and places it in chronological order.

Some works utilize both techniques and do not fall neatly into either category. In such instances it is best to classify the work according to its primary purpose. If the aim is to present an historical arrangement of the gospel materials, it is a harmony; if it is primarily for purposes of comparison, it is a synopsis. Thus, the work of Tatian could be termed a harmony, while the works of Eusebius and Ammonius (despite his use of the term harmony) are best called synopses. The term *harmonize* frequently is used to describe an attempt to reconcile different and apparently conflicting accounts and teachings.

One of the problems encountered when a harmony of the Gospels is attempted is that the exact order of the events recorded in the four Gospels cannot always be ascertained. Events and sayings which seem to be identical are located in different places in the Gospels. It sometimes appears that the Evangelists were not interested in the exact order of various events or sayings when they wrote their Gospels. In synopses, even more significant problems arise. Parallel events and sayings often appear with significant variations. How does one deal with such problems?

From the beginning of the Christian Church to the present time various men and women have sought to explain these variations in the context of the inspiration and infallibility of the Scriptures. One of the first and most notable defenders was the greatest theologian of the early church, Augustine. Augustine is known primarily for his theological contributions. But, he was not only a great theologian, he was also a fine New Testament exegete. Around A.D. 400 he wrote *De Concensu Evangelistarum (On the Harmony of the Evangelists)*. Augustine compares the four Gospels and seeks to harmonize them. He tries to demonstrate that ". . . the writers in question [Matthew,

Mark, Luke, and John] do not stand in any antagonism to each other."[1] Augustine later states:

> For this reason let us now rather proceed to examine into the real character of those passages in which these critics suppose the evangelists to have given contradictory accounts . . . ; so that, when these problems are solved, it may also be made apparent that the members in that body have preserved a befitting harmony in the unity of the body itself, not only by identity in sentiment, but also by constructing records consonant with that identity.[2]

Augustine was neither the first nor the last churchman who attempted to defend or harmonize the Gospels. John Calvin states:

> There is no disagreement, first, that one can make no intelligent or apt comment on one of the three Evangelists without comparing the other two. For this reason faithful and skilled commentators have expended most of their efforts on reconciling the three accounts.[3]

Similar purposes lie behind most of the early harmonies. Certainly this is true of Andreas Osiander's *Harmoniae Evangelicae*(1537). Due to his a priori understanding of truth, he believes that the same saying or incident in the life of Jesus must be worded identically and must occur in the same sequence in each Gospel. Any variation in the wording or sequence of parallel accounts means that even virtually indistinguishable passages refer to different sayings or incidents in the life of Jesus. As a result, Osiander argues that Jesus raised Jairus's daughter from the dead on a least two occasions, that Jesus was crowned with thorns at least twice, and that Peter warmed himself at a fire four times. Augustine and Calvin believe that a high view of the inspiration and trustworthiness of the Scriptures does not require such a radical view. William Newcome's *An Harmony of the Gospels in Which the Text is Deposed*

After Le Clerc's General Manner, also attempts to harmonize the accounts. He states, "I have here attempted, after many others, to shew the consistency of the evangelists, and to fix the time and place of the transactions recorded by them."[4] Other works have been written which seek to explain the apparent conflicts found in the Gospels.[5]

The terms *harmonize* and *harmonization* have fallen into disrepute. Some of this may be due to the farfetched and unconvincing harmonizations made in the past by certain scholars. This writer still remembers attending a graduate seminar at a famous German university where a student's explanation was rejected on the grounds that *"Das ist nur Harmonizierung!"* ("That is simply a harmonization!") To reject an explanation because it harmonizes difficult gospel passages is certainly as prejudicial as to accept an explanation on the grounds that it harmonizes these passages. The correctness or incorrectness of an explanation is not dependent on whether or not it harmonizes the disputed passages. It depends on whether that explanation correctly interprets the authors' meanings and logically illustrates that these meanings do not conflict with each other.

This book attempts to follow in the tradition of such scholars as Augustine and Calvin and seeks to establish, if at all possible, a harmony in the passages discussed. This purpose is served best by a forthright openness to the textual data. A prejudicial handling of the data for the sake of establishing the harmony of the Gospels (or for establishing a disharmony) is neither commendable nor, in the case of the former, devout. The Word of God is to be treated reverently even by those who would seek to defend it. The Word of God can and always will defend itself! The evangelical task is, first of all, to understand the meaning of the text. When this is accomplished, the demonstration of its harmonious nature is relatively simple. Newcome states the same thing in the Preface to his harmony: ". . . by thus entering into the manner of the

evangelical writers [I take this to mean the authors'
meanings], I have endeavoured to make them their own
harmonists."[6]

This book contains various representative passages
which present certain kinds of difficulties and demonstrates a methodology to deal with them. The first chapter
treats the difficulties that arise due to variations in parallel
accounts in the Gospels. First, the variations found in
parallel accounts of Matthew, Mark, and Luke are discussed. Then the difficulties which result between the
parallels in the Synoptic Gospels and the Gospel of John
are treated. Chapter two deals with certain difficulties
found in the teachings of Jesus. How can some of the
sayings of Jesus which seem to conflict at times with what
he teaches elsewhere, with his own actions, and with the
teachings of the rest of Scripture be explained? Chapter
three treats difficulties created by certain actions of Jesus,
and chapter four covers selected sayings or predictions of
Jesus that do not appear to have come to pass.

The reader should be aware that the author makes no
claim of being completely original in his solutions. He is
heavily indebted to the work of scholars before him, some
of whom have already been mentioned. The numerous
references to and quotations of Augustine and Calvin in
this work demonstrate this point. An original interpretation or explanation may be offered, but this is not done in
order to be original, but simply to deal honestly with the
data. On occasion the reader may be disappointed that the
author has not found a convincing explanation. This
should not be construed as a lack of confidence in the
Word of God on the part of the author. Rather it should be
interpreted as indicating that the Christian in this life can
only "know in part" (I Cor. 13:12). The lack of a satisfactory explanation may be due not to absence of confidence in
the Scriptures but to a lack of confidence in possessing
sufficient data to resolve the issue. In the majority of
instances hopefully the reader should find help and

assistance in understanding not only the specific passage or passages discussed, but also in developing a methodology which he or she can extend to similar passages.

1

Parallel Passages

One of the most valuable tools for the study of the Gospels is a synopsis. In a synopsis, parallel materials are placed side-by-side for comparison. When a synopsis is studied, in the original Greek or in a good translation, it becomes apparent that similar gospel accounts and sayings are seldom identical. Although the differences between the accounts are frequently insignificant and unimportant, at times they appear to present an apparent conflict. How should these differences be treated? Should it be concluded that every parallel incident or saying occurred as many times as the number of parallel accounts?

The material in this chapter deals with ten examples of this type of problem. Seven examples involve differences between parallel accounts in the Synoptic Gospels and three of them treat differences between parallel accounts found in the Synoptic Gospels and the Gospel of John. Each instance deals with both the sayings of Jesus and various events in his life.

Difficult Parallel Passages in the Synoptic Gospels

The Voice from Heaven at Jesus' Baptism

Matthew 3:17	Mark 1:11	Luke 3:22
. . . and lo, a voice from heaven, saying, "This is my beloved Son, with whom I am well pleased."	. . . and a voice came from heaven, "Thou art my beloved Son; with thee I am well pleased."	. . . and a voice came from heaven, "Thou art my beloved Son; with thee I am well pleased."

These parallel accounts present an apparent conflict. This variance does not present any insuperable problem but does illustrate a major principle in the treatment of minor conflicts. The basic issue involves the exact words which were spoken from heaven during the baptism of Jesus. Did the voice say, "Thou art my beloved Son; with thee I am well pleased," as recorded in Mark and Luke, or did the voice say, "This is my beloved Son, with whom I am well pleased," as recorded in Matthew? Or, was the voice addressed to Jesus (Mark and Luke) or to the crowds (Matthew)? That problem is minor, but if it is believed that the Gospels give exact, tape-recorded accounts of what the voice from heaven said, then a problem does exist. However, did Matthew, Mark, and Luke seek to write perfect, tape-recorded accounts of exactly what the voice said?

It may be helpful to note that biblical scholars have wrestled with such questions for many centuries. For example, Augustine was probably the greatest mind in the Christian church between the time of the apostle Paul and the Reformers. Around A.D. 400 Augustine wrote *De Concensu Evangelistarum* (On the Harmony of the Evangelists). Augustine compares the four Gospels and discusses the various parallel accounts in order to harmonize any of the apparent conflicts and discrepancies. This work is still profitable reading both from the perspective of observing Augustine's reverential treatment of the Gospels as well as for his many suggestions on how to harmonize various problems found in the accounts. Many solutions remain convincing today.

Augustine states that "the heavenly voice gave utterance only to one of these sentences. . . ."[1] In other words, Augustine does not seek to resolve the issue by claiming that the voice from heaven spoke both "Thou art my beloved Son . . ." *and* "This is my beloved Son. . . ." (Nor does he seek to resolve the issue by stating that the Greek text of Matthew or Mark and Luke is inaccurate, so that originally all three gospel accounts were alike.) It is not hard to agree with Augustine. To postulate that the voice spoke both statements is not a convincing way to resolve this problem. Second, Augustine points out that despite the differences in wording, each account conveys the same meaning.

> If you ask which of these different modes represents what was actually expressed by the voice, you may fix on whichever you will, provided only that you understand that those of the writers who have not reproduced the self-same form of speech have still reproduced the identical sense intended to be conveyed.[2]

Third, Augustine points out that when an evangelist does change the wording of the voice from heaven, he does so in order to help the reader understand the meaning of those words.

> From this it becomes sufficiently apparent, that whichever of the evangelists may have preserved for us the words as they were literally uttered by the heavenly voice, the others have varied the terms only with the object of setting forth the same sense more familiarly. . . .[3]

Augustine's treatment of this passage has much to teach not only about this particular account but also about other instances in the Gospels where variations occur in the parallel accounts. The facts that the Gospels were written in Greek and that the voice from heaven would have been in Hebrew or Aramaic, the native language of Jesus and the crowds, indicates that no gospel writer was interested in producing a tape-recorded account of the incident.

Augustine also points out that there is no real difference in the accounts. All give the same meaning. If the question were asked, "What did the voice from heaven say at Jesus' baptism?" would not the following answer be perfectly acceptable to all? "It said that Jesus was the Son of God and that God was very pleased with him." Surely the purpose of each Evangelist is to have his readers understand that this Jesus, who was baptized by John, is the Son of God and that God was very pleased with all he did and taught.

If the voice from heaven actually addresses Jesus, this means that Mark's and Luke's accounts are closer to the actual words and that they allow their readers to realize that this Jesus is indeed God's Son. This means that Matthew sought to help his readers by making this application for them. There is no diversity in meaning. Augustine's solution of fifteen centuries ago is still valuable and convincing.

"Blessed are the poor. . . ."

Matthew 5:3	Luke 6:20
"Blessed are the poor in spirit, for theirs is the kingdom of heaven."	"Blessed are you poor, for yours is the kingdom of God."

The Gospels of Matthew and Luke contain two sets of beatitudes. The more famous is found in the opening words of Matthew's Sermon on the Mount (Matt. 5:1–12). Less well known is the parallel account in Luke's Sermon on the Plain (Luke 6:17–23). These passages contain a number of differences. Only one difference is discussed, but in so doing principles will be used that will be helpful for dealing with the other differences.

The term *differences* is used to describe the variations in the two accounts. This term is chosen carefully. Critical scholars tend to use terms such as *discrepancies* or *contradictions* to describe these variations. Such terms prejudge the situation, however, and ought to be avoided. This is especially true at the beginning of an investigation.

The first beatitude, Luke 6:20, reads, "Blessed are you poor, for yours is the kingdom of God." Matt. 5:3, however, reads, "Blessed are the poor in spirit, for theirs is the kingdom of heaven." One explanation frequently used is to state that the two accounts represent two separate speeches by Jesus given at two different times and at two different places. In this instance, Augustine tends to favor this interpretation.[4] This type of explanation, however, has been abused. A sixteenth-century scholar, Andreas Osiander, tends to resolve every minor difference in the Gospels in this manner and as a result argues: Jairus's daughter was raised from the dead on two separate occasions; Jesus was twice crowned with thorns; and Peter warmed himself at a fire four separate times.[5] Luther and Calvin reject these explanations. Yet it cannot be denied that at times such explanations are possible. In this instance the different settings given to the beatitudes (a mountain in Matt. 5:1 and a plain in Luke 6:17) make the possibility of two separate sermons an attractive solution for some.[6]

A fundamental issue that will determine how to view these two accounts involves how the relationship of the Synoptic Gospels to one another is viewed. How can the similarities or "look-alike" character of Matthew, Mark, and Luke be explained? To claim that this is due to God's inspiration does not really answer this question. The Gospel of John is also inspired by God and it is not similar to Matthew, Mark, and Luke! Its vocabulary, content, and form are quite different.

Another attempt to answer this question is to say that Matthew, Mark, and Luke are similar because they record,

in chronological order, the events of Jesus' life. Yet it
becomes clear that this is not a sufficient explanation.
Much of the material in the Synoptic Gospels is arranged
on a topical rather than a chronological basis. Mark
1:21–45, for instance, consists of four healing miracles;
Mark 2:1–3:6 consists of five pronouncement stories; and
Mark 4:1–34 consists of five parables. Matthew arranges
the teachings of Jesus into five main sections (5–7; 10; 13;
18; 24–25) that all end in a similar manner.[7] It would
appear that topical considerations (placing parables together; listing various miracle stories together; and placing
similar teaching material together) are utilized in the
Gospels. Augustine states:

> And furthermore, who can fail to perceive that the ques-
> tion as to the precise order in which these words were
> uttered by the Lord is a superfluous one? [The passage
> being discussed is Matt. 12:38–42 and the parallel in Luke
> 11:16, 29–32, but this would also apply to a passage such as
> the one presently under discussion.] For this lesson also
> we ought to learn, on the unimpeachable authority of the
> Evangelists,—namely, that no offence against truth need
> be supposed on the part of a writer, although he may not
> reproduce the discourse of some speaker in the precise
> order in which the person from whose lips it proceeded
> might have given it; the fact being, that the mere item of
> the order, whether it be this or that, does not affect the
> subject-matter itself.[8]

A commonly accepted explanation for the similarity of
the Synoptic Gospels is that the Evangelists made use of
common written materials. This should not cause any
difficulty because the author of Chronicles clearly uses
1 and 2 Samuel and 1 and 2 Kings and Luke (Luke 1:1–4)
specifically refers to his investigation of both oral and
written materials. Without entering into a total explanation of the "Synoptic problem," it should be pointed out
that a commonly accepted explanation of Matthew's and

Luke's similarities in their teaching material and beatitudes is that one used the other (usually Luke used Matthew or, more probably, that both used a common source (which scholars have termed "Q"). If either explanation is accepted (this would not be a rejection of or weakening of the belief that the Gospels of Matthew and Luke are inspired of God) then the explanation of the differences in their beatitudes cannot be explained as two different sermons.

What about this difference between the first beatitude in Matthew and in Luke? Does it not appear that the blessing in Matthew is pronounced on those possessing a spiritual attitude ("being poor in spirit") whereas in Luke it appears to be pronounced on a particular economic strata ("poor")? Some even argue that Matthew "corrupts" Jesus' teaching (which originally, according to Luke, blessed the "poor") and makes it more acceptable to a middle-class church with members not "poor," but "poor in spirit!" Such a negative conclusion is unwarranted.

The basic issue that must first be addressed is the definition of the term *poor* in Luke 6:20. Does it mean economically poor without any additional qualification? Does it mean spiritually poor in the sense of being humble? Does it refer to those who are believers and are economically poor? Before it is proposed that an irreconcilable difference exists between the two beatitudes, it is necessary to understand what the term *poor* meant in the first century A.D.

In the Old Testament the term refers to an economic status and it also is used metaphorically to refer to a spiritual attitude. Psalm 40:17 states, "As for me, I am poor and needy; but the Lord takes thought for me." In Psalm 86:1 and 109:22 the psalmist uses the same two terms to describe himself.[9] It is clear in these instances that the term *poor* is not an economic term because these are "Psalms of David," and the readers of such psalms understood that David, the king, was not economically

poor, so that the term should be understood metaphorically. This term is also used in this metaphorical sense in
Proverbs 3:34, where it is the opposite of being scornful
and is translated humble; Proverbs 16:19, where it is the
opposite of being proud and is translated poor; and in 2
Samuel 22:28, where it is the opposite of being haughty
and is translated humble. The term *poor* could be and is
used in the Old Testament to describe a spiritual state of
being humble.[10]

The terminology of translation may assist at this point.
It is quite likely that Jesus used the term *poor* without
qualification. Luke's use of *poor* is then an exact formal
equivalent or a word-for-word translation of this term.
Matthew, on the other hand, uses a dynamic equivalent or
a thought-for-thought translation. He knew that Jesus
metaphorically used the term *poor* for "humble" or "poor
in spirit."

Therefore the terms *poor* and *poor in spirit* do not conflict
but are two different ways of expressing the idea of
humility. However, each Evangelist gives his own emphasis to the term. Luke, more than any other Evangelist, is concerned for the poor and aware of the danger of
riches. (This is apparent from Luke 1:53; 6:24; 12:16–21;
16:19–31; 18:18–26; and Acts 4:32–37.) Luke is also aware
that the blessedness of the kingdom of God is not
exclusively reserved for the economic poor. Zacchaeus,
too, shall enter the kingdom (Luke 19:9) even though
he is not poor. (Note how Zacchaeus is distinguished
from the poor in Luke 19:8.) Luke also mentions
rich women (Luke 8:3) and men (Joseph of Arimathea,
Luke 23:50–56) who followed Christ. Even the apostle
Paul is far from poor according to Acts 28:30 (see also
Acts 24:26).

For Luke, however, the term *poor* well designates the
blessed followers of Jesus, since many church members
come from the lower economic classes (Cf. 1 Cor. 1:26–31;
James 2:5; Gal. 2:10 and Rom. 15:26). That the beatitude is

addressed to the Christian poor, or the humble believers in the lower classes, is evident from Luke 6:20 (see also Matt. 5:1) where Jesus addresses the beatitudes to the disciples and Luke 6:22 (see also Matt. 5:11) where the blessing is addressed to those hated "on account of the Son of man."

Clearly it is the believing poor, those who are "poor in spirit," who are blessed. Luke's beatitudes are especially precious for such people even as they would be for the disadvantaged and oppressed believers of any age. They are blessed for God gives to such humble people, who trust in Him, the kingdom. But woe to the rich who in their haughtiness, arrogance, and unbelief oppress those poor for there is coming a day of judgment (Luke 6:24)! Matthew chooses not to emphasize this particular aspect of the beatitude.

Rather than seeing a conflict or discrepancy between Matthew's and Luke's accounts of the first beatitude the terms *poor* and *poor in spirit* should be seen as equivalent translations of the term Jesus uses. Each Evangelist emphasizes the particular aspect of Jesus' meaning most needed in his situation. Calvin states, "The metaphor in Luke is unadorned, but . . . Matthew expresses Christ's mind with more clarity."[11] Augustine in dealing with a similar issue, the difference between the form of Jesus' saying in Matthew 12:28 ("But if it is by the Spirit of God that I cast out demons, then the kingdom of God has come upon you.") and in Luke 11:20 ("But if it is by the finger of God that I cast out demons, then the kingdom of God has come upon you.") states:

And the circumstance that Luke here designates the Spirit of God as the finger of God, does not betray any departure from a genuine identity in sense; but it rather teaches us an additional lesson, giving us to know in what manner we are to interpret the phrase "finger of God" wherever it occurs in the Scriptures.[12]

Today many scholars would argue that Luke is closer to the actual words of Jesus, and that Matthew designates in his account what Jesus meant by "the finger of God." However, Augustine's insight remains. There is no "departure from a genuine identity in sense" when one Evangelist gives us "an additional lesson" by his inspired interpretation of what Jesus meant.

One problem remains. This involves the different settings given to the beatitudes by Matthew and Luke. It is possible that Matthew remembers a particular incident in which Jesus taught his disciples on a mountain and uses this scene to form his first collection of Jesus' teachings (Matt. 5–7). Luke may have used another particular incident in which Jesus taught his disciples on a plain for his first collection (Luke 6:17–7:1). This is essentially the view of Calvin who states:

> It should be enough for reverent and humble readers that here, before their eyes, they have set a short summary of the teaching of Christ, gathered from many and various discourses, of which this was the first, where He spoke with His disciples on the true blessedness.[13]

The Healing of the Centurion's Servant

Matthew 8:5–13	Luke 7:1–10
As he entered Capernaum, a centurion came forward to him, beseeching him and saying, "Lord my servant is lying paralyzed at home, in terrible distress." And he said to him, "I will come and heal him."	After he had ended all his sayings in the hearing of the people he entered Capernaum.
	Now a centurion had a slave who was dear to him, who was sick and at the point of death. When he heard of Jesus, he sent to him elders of the Jews, asking him to come and heal his slave. And when they came to Jesus, they besought him earnestly, saying, "He is worthy to have you do this for him, for he loves our nation, and he built us our synagogue." And Jesus went with them. When he was not far from the house, the centurion sent friends to
But the centurion answered him,	

"Lord,
I am not worthy to have you come
under my roof;

but only say the word, and my
servant will be healed. For I am a
man under authority, with soldiers
under me; and I say to one, 'Go,'
and he goes, and to another, 'Come,'
and he comes, and to my slave, 'Do
this,' and he does it." When Jesus
heard him, he marveled, and said to
those who followed him, "Truly I say
to you, not even in Israel have I
found such faith.

"I tell you, many will come from
east and west and sit at table with
Abraham, Isaac, and Jacob in the
kingdom of heaven, while the sons
of the kingdom will be thrown into
the outer darkness; there men will
weep and gnash their teeth."

And to the centurion Jesus said,
"Go; be it done for you as you have
believed." And the servant was
healed at that very moment.

him, saying to him, "Lord, do not
trouble yourself, for I am not worthy
to have you come under my roof;
therefore I did not presume to come
to you. But say the word, and let my
servant be healed. For I am a man
set under authority, with soldiers
under me: and I say to one, 'Go,'
and he goes; and to another, 'Come,'
and he comes; and to my slave, 'Do
this,' and he does it." When Jesus
heard this he marveled at him, and
turned and said to the multitude that
followed him, "I tell you, not even in
Israel have I found such faith."

And when those who had been
sent returned to the house, they
found the slave well.

The two previous passages deal with differences in the
various sayings found in the Synoptic Gospels. At this
point some of the differences found in various narrative
accounts that resemble each other will be discussed. The
first example is found in the parallel accounts of the
healing of the centurion's servant in Matthew 8:5–13 and
Luke 7:1–10. A careful reading of the text raises the
question, "Who actually spoke to Jesus? Was it the centurion as Matthew 8:5–9 records or was it the elders of the
Jews and the friends as Luke 7:3 and 6 claim? These two
accounts of the incident appear to teach contradictory
things.

An approach used to harmonize such difficulties has
already been mentioned: to claim that these accounts are
two different, but similar, incidents. There is little doubt
that Jesus often repeats his teachings at different times and

places and that he varies them to fit the need of the situation. It is quite possible that similar situations reoccur in the ministry of Jesus. Perhaps Matthew 8:5–13 and Luke 7:1–10 refer to two separate, but similar, incidents in which a servant near death is healed by Jesus.

It seems unlikely that this can be the case. For the circumstances are too similar. In both accounts: the location is Capernaum; a servant of a centurion is involved; Jesus is stopped from entering the centurion's house; Jesus is told, in effect, "Simply say the word and my servant will be healed"; the centurion (or his friends) says "I am a man under authority . . ."; and Jesus marvels at his faith and says, "Not even in Israel have I found such faith." These similarities and the nearly exact wording make it highly unlikely that there are two separate accounts. How could two different centurions even live in Capernaum at the same time? (A centurion was a commander of one hundred soldiers.) One is surprising. Finding two with sick servants, who both have faith and say the same things, seems quite improbable.[14]

If Matthew and Luke contain two versions of the same incident, then who actually spoke to Jesus? The problem can be resolved by the use of a present-day example. If a conversation between the President of the United States and the Premier of Russia, were reported, it could be described in at least two ways. First, the president says in English to his interpreter, "A." The interpreter then says in Russian to the premier, "A." The premier says in Russian to his interpreter, "B," and the interpreter says in English to the president, "B." Second, the president says to the premier, "A," The premier responds "B."

Both descriptions are correct! The last account, which every newspaper report follows, chooses to omit for brevity's sake the role of the interpreter. The other account includes it. It is possible that the Gospel writers follow a similar procedure. Matthew excludes any reference to the elders, whereas Luke includes them in his account.

There is a saying that "As the king—so the messenger." This saying explains that in biblical times a king's messenger was considered an extension of the king. His words were the king's words. His treatment, therefore, was in effect the treatment of the king. With this in mind, it is easier to understand Acts 9:4 ("Saul, Saul, why do you persecute me?"); Matthew 25:37 ("Lord, when did we see thee hungry and feed thee, or thirsty and give thee drink?"); and many others. The messengers, or friends, of the centurion are an extension of him. Their words are the words of the centurion. Thus, the problem dissipates when it is realized that Matthew chose for the sake of brevity, to omit any reference to the intermediate messengers.

This view is confirmed by a careful analysis of the Greek in Luke 7:3 and 6. In Luke 7:3, the text should be translated as follows, "Hearing [singular] concerning Jesus he [the centurion] sent elders of the Jews to him *asking* [singular]. . . ." It should be noted that whereas the elders will speak to Jesus, the participle "asking" is singular. In Luke's mind, although the elders are the ones who actually speak to Jesus, it is the centurion who really asks. In understanding Luke and Matthew, it is the centurion who asks Jesus to heal his servant. Luke 7:6 also should be translated, ". . . the centurion sent [singular] friends saying [singular] to him. . . ." Here again the singular of saying indicates that, in Luke's mind, the centurion says these words to Jesus through the lips of these friends.

The apparent disagreement between Matthew's and Luke's versions disappears when it is understood that Matthew eliminates the reference to the messengers from his account. Calvin comments, "Matthew quite reasonably attributes to him [the centurion] what was done at his request and in his name."[15] Matthew may have done this for the sake of brevity. He had other materials that he wanted to include in his Gospel. The length of a papyrus scroll was limited. (A normal scroll was about 31–32 feet long. Both Matthew and Luke would take up an entire scroll.) Luke, on the other hand, included a reference to them.

Which is correct? Both are correct, for both accurately report what happens between the centurion and Jesus. To be disturbed by Matthew's omission would be to require greater historical exactness in this account than in present-day reports. Neither Matthew nor Luke err in their reports of this incident. It is important to understand how they tell their story of this incident and not demand that they do so in a specific format. After all, they both were inspired of God; we are not.

The Raising of Jairus's Daughter

Matthew 9:18–19, 23–25	Mark 5:21–24, 35–43	Luke 8:40–42, 49–56
	And when Jesus had crossed again in the boat to the other side,	Now when Jesus returned,
While he was thus speaking to them,	a great crowd gathered about him; and he was beside the sea. Then	the crowd welcomed him, for they were all waiting for him. And
behold, a ruler came in	came one of the rulers of the synagogue, Jairus by name; and seeing him, he fell at his feet, and besought him, saying,	there came a man named Jairus, who was a ruler of the synagogue; and falling at Jesus' feet he besought him to come to his house, for he had
and knelt before him,		
saying,		
"My daughter has just died; but come and lay your hand on her,	"My little daughter is at the point of death. Come and lay your hands on her, so that she may be made well	an only daughter, about twelve years of age, and she was dying.
and she will live." And Jesus rose and followed him, with his disciples.	and live." And he went with him.	As he went, the people pressed round him.
	While he was still speaking, there came from the ruler's house	While he was still speaking, a man from the ruler's house came

And when Jesus came
to the ruler's house,
and saw the flute
players, and the crowd
making a tumult,
                    he said,

"Depart; for the girl is

      not dead but sleep-
ing." And they
laughed at him.

But when the crowd
had been put outside,

he went in
                    and took
her by the hand,

and the girl arose.

---

some who said, "Your
daughter is dead. Why
trouble the Teacher any
further?" But ignoring
what they said, Jesus
said to the ruler of the
synagogue, "Do not
fear, only believe."

And he allowed no one
to follow him except
Peter and James and
John the brother of
James.
When they came to the
house of the ruler of
the synagogue, he saw
a tumult, and people
weeping and wailing
loudly. And when he
had entered, he said to
them, "Why do you
make a tumult and
weep? The child is not

dead but sleeping."
And they laughed at
him.

But he put them all
outside, and took the
child's father and
mother and those who
were with him, and
went in where the
child was. Taking her
by the hand he said to
her, "Talitha cumi";
which means, "Little
girl, I say to you,
arise."

And immediately the
girl got up and walked
(she was twelve years
of age), and they were
immediately overcome
with amazement. And

---

and said, "Your
daughter is dead; do
not trouble the Teacher
any more." But Jesus
on hearing this
answered him, "Do not
fear; only believe, and
she shall be well." And
when he came to the
house, he permitted no
one to enter with him,
except Peter and John
and James, and the
father and mother of
the child.

And all were
weeping and bewailing
her; but
                    he said,

"Do not
                    weep; for she
is not dead but
sleeping." And they
laughed at him,
knowing that she was
dead. But

                    taking her
by the hand he called,
saying,

"Child, arise." And her
spirit returned, and she

got up at once; and he
directed that something
should be given her to
eat. And her parents
were amazed;

he strictly charged	but he charged them to
them that no one	tell no one what had
should know this, and	happened.
told them to give her	
something to eat.	

In seeking to understand why the wording in one account is different from the parallel account in another Gospel, it is helpful to understand not only the theological emphases of the Evangelists but their literary style as well. An example of this is the account of the raising of Jairus's daughter. In Mark's account and in Luke's parallel, a ruler of a synagogue comes to Jesus and asks him to heal his daughter. On the way messengers inform the ruler that she has died, but Jesus encourages the ruler and raises his daughter from the dead. In Matthew's account a ruler comes to Jesus and asks him to bring to life his daughter who has died. Jesus proceeds to his home and raises her from the dead. That this is the same incident is evident not only by the similarity of the stories but by the fact that between the two halves of the story is the account of Jesus' healing of the woman who hemorrhaged for twelve years.

The problems that Matthew's account raises can be resolved once the literary style of Matthew is recognized. If Matthew's treatment of other parallel accounts is compared to Mark's, Matthew's style in telling the story of the raising of Jairus's daughter is better understood. The first account is the healing of the woman who was hemorrhaging. In Mark, the account consists of ten verses (153 words in Greek), whereas in Matthew, the account consists of three verses (48 words in Greek). Matthew obviously abbreviates the story by omitting the following details: the woman spent all her money on doctors, Jesus sensed that healing power had left him, Jesus asked who touched him, the disciples replied that everyone was touching him, and the woman's fear that she would be discovered.

Another example of this tendency of Matthew is found in the account of Jesus' healing of the paralytic. Mark's account consists of twelve verses (196 words in Greek), and Matthew's consists of eight verses (126 words in Greek). Again, Matthew abbreviates the account by leaving out that a crowd had gathered in the home and that the friends had to dig up the roof in order to lower the paralytic before Jesus (which was why Jesus saw their faith). Matthew left out material that, while important, is not essential in recounting the miracle.

A final example is found in Luke 7:1–10 and Matthew 8:5–13. The story of the healing of the centurion's servant consists of ten verses (186 words in Greek) in Luke and nine verses (124 words in Greek) in Matthew. (This total excludes verses 11 and 12, which contain a saying of Jesus that Matthew adds at this point but is found elsewhere in Luke.) In order to abbreviate the account Matthew omits the role of the centurion's servants and the Jewish elders.

It is clear that Matthew has a tendency to abbreviate the various accounts he incorporates into his Gospel. Often he omits material that is of considerable interest and value but that is not absolutely essential. In his desire to include additional material Matthew was concerned with the limitation of his scroll. Our present Gospel of Matthew contains about as much material as a single scroll could contain. In order to include the birth accounts, the Sermon on the Mount, and various resurrection appearances Matthew abbreviated or eliminated some of the material he found in Mark or his other sources. His abbreviation of the three passages, which total 237 words in Greek, enabled him to include additional material such as Matthew 5:1–18 (251 words). The issue for Matthew was simple: abbreviate these stories or eliminate something like Matthew 5:1–18.

In light of Matthew's tendency toward abbreviation we can better understand what has happened in Matthew 9:18–19, 23–25. Matthew summarized the story of Jesus' raising of Jairus's daughter. He records that a ruler of the synagogue comes to Jesus for help concerning his daughter and that Jesus goes to his home and raises her from the dead. What he omits are various interesting but unnecessary details such as that when Jairus first arrives his daughter is not yet dead. It is interesting to compare the statements of Augustine and Calvin on this passage. Augustine writes:

> But as it was Matthew's object to tell the whole story in short compass, he has represented the father as directly expressing in his request what, it is certain, had been his own real wish, and what Christ actually did.[16]

Calvin states:

> . . . Matthew aiming at brevity mentions in one breath what the others space out more accurately, as it took place. . . . Matthew . . . set down as occurring at the very beginning, what actually happened with the passing of time.[17]

Matthew's account is an inerrant summary of Jesus' raising of Jairus's daughter. Difficulties are encountered if the details of this summary are pressed in a way that Matthew never intended.

The Healing of the Paralytic

Matthew 9:1–8	Mark 2:1–12	Luke 5:17–26
And getting into a boat he crossed over and came to his own city.	And when he returned to Capernaum after some days, it was reported that he was at home. And many were gathered together, so that there was no longer room for them, not even about the door; and he was preaching the word to them.	On one of those days, as he was teaching, there were Pharisees and teachers of the law sitting by, who had come from every village of Galilee and Judea and from Jerusalem; and the power of the Lord was with him to heal.
And behold, they brought to him a	And they came, bringing to him a	And behold, men were bringing

paralytic, lying on his bed;

and when Jesus saw their faith he said to the paralytic, "Take heart, my son; your sins are forgiven." And behold, some of the scribes

said to themselves,

"This man is blaspheming."

But Jesus, knowing their thoughts,

said,

"Why do you think evil in your hearts? For which is easier, to say, 'Your sins are forgiven,' or to say, 'Rise

and walk'?

But that you may know that the Son of man has authority on earth to forgive sins"—he then said to the paralytic—"Rise, take up your bed and go home."

paralytic carried by four men.

And when they could not get near him because of the crowd, they removed the roof above him; and when they had made an opening, they let down the pallet on which the paralytic lay. And when Jesus saw their faith, he said to the paralytic,

"My son, your sins are forgiven." Now some of the scribes were sitting there, questioning in their hearts, "Why does this man speak thus? It is blasphemy! Who can forgive sins but God alone?" And immediately Jesus, perceiving in his spirit that they thus questioned within themselves, said to them, "Why do you question thus in your hearts? Which is easier, to say to the paralytic, 'Your sins are forgiven,' or to say, 'Rise, take up your pallet and walk'? But that you may know that the Son of man has authority on earth to forgive sins"—he said to the paralytic—"I say to you, rise, take up your pallet and go home."

on a bed a man who was paralyzed, and they sought to bring him in and lay him before Jesus; but finding no way to bring him in, because of the crowd, they went up on the roof and let him down with his bed through the tiles into the midst before Jesus.

And when he saw their faith he said,

"Man, your sins are forgiven you." And the scribes and the Pharisees began to question, saying, "Who is this that speaks blasphemies? Who can forgive sins but God only?" When

Jesus perceived their

questionings, he answered them, "Why do you question

in your hearts? Which is easier, to say, 'Your sins are forgiven you.' or to say 'Rise and walk'?

But that you may know that the Son of man has authority on earth to forgive sins"—he said to the man who was paralyzed—"I say to you, rise, take up your bed and go home."

And he rose	And he rose, and	And immediately he rose before them, and
and went home. When the crowds saw it, they were afraid, and they glorified God, who had given such authority to men.	immediately took up the pallet and went out before them all; so that they were all amazed and glorified God,	took up that on which he lay, and went home, glorifying God. And amazement seized them all, and they glorified God and were filled with awe,
	saying, "We never saw anything like this!"	saying, "We have seen strange things today."

Each Synoptic Gospel contains an account of Jesus' healing of a paralytic. It is evident that these are parallel accounts of the same incident rather than two or three separate but similar incidents. First, Matthew and Mark both locate their accounts in Capernaum (see Matt. 9:1 with 4:13). Second, the wording in all three accounts is similar, especially the words of Jesus.[18]

Finally, all three Gospels follow this incident with the account of Jesus' calling of Matthew-Levi and with the question of why Jesus' disciples do not fast. In Mark and Luke these last two accounts are followed then by the accounts of Jesus' disciples plucking grain on the Sabbath and Jesus' healing of the man with the withered hand. It is clear that these three accounts refer to the same incident in which Jesus healed a paralytic in Capernaum. Calvin states, "There is no doubt that the same incident is being told by the three, though there is a slight variation on points of detail between them.[19]

The main issue is the apparent conflict between Mark 2:4, "And when they could not get near him because of the crowd, they removed the roof above him; and when they had made an opening, they let down the pallet on which the paralytic lay"; and Luke 5:19, "but finding no way to bring him in, because of the crowd, they went up on the roof and let him down with his bed through the tiles into the midst before Jesus."

The type of roof described in these two accounts presents a problem. Luke clearly refers to a tile roof by stating that the paralytic is lowered "through the tiles." In Mark, however, the paralytic's friends "removed the roof" (literally—"unroofed the roof") and "made an opening."

The conflict is not as evident in the RSV ("made an opening") as it is in the NIV ("digging through it"), NEB ("had broken through"), and NASB ("had dug an opening"). In the Greek, however, the phrase "made an opening" literally translates "dig or gouge out." The term *exoruxantes* frequently is used in Greek literature to refer to gouging out someone's eye, digging a trench, tunneling, or digging a grave (Judg. 16:21; 1 Sam. 11:2; Jos ANT. 6.71; Plutarch, ARTAX. 14,10; Herodotus 2,150; 7, 23; 8, 116; etc.). The verbal root (the verb minus the preposition *ex* which means "out of") is used in Matthew 21:33; Mark 12:1; and Isaiah 5:2 to describe the digging of a winepress in the ground; in Matthew 25:18 to burying one's talent; and in Psalm 94:13 (LXX) to digging a pit.

Mark's use of this term makes it evident that he envisions a typical first-century Galilean home with a central courtyard and steps leading up to a roof made of mud and clay and supported by wooden beams. Such a roof would have to be dug out much like a trench or grave.

On the other hand, Luke envisions a tile roof in which the tile would be lifted up or removed but certainly not dug out. It appears that the Evangelists envision two different types of roofs.

One possible way to reconcile these differences is to deny that the term *exoruxantes* in Mark must be translated "dig up" or "gouge out." This seems difficult. The term clearly means this throughout the literature. Another solution might be to claim that these are two different incidents. But, it was previously pointed out that this is not possible. Perhaps the best way to explain the data is to assume that the house roof is Galilean in construction, as Mark suggests. Luke, in "translating" (not from one language to another but from one environment to another) this incident for the most excellent Theophilus (Luke 1:4), knows that in Theophilus's environment, roofs are constructed of tile. In "translating" this story from Galilee to that environment of Theophilus, how could Luke inform him that the paralytic is lowered through the roof? Digging out a tile roof might not be comprehensible to him. As a result he translated this account by using terms that were meaningful to Theophilus. (One can become sympathetic toward missionary translators of the Scriptures by realizing what Luke might have had to do if Theophilus were an Eskimo!)

Why did Luke recount this story to Theophilus? To explain to him that Jesus saw the faith of the paralytic and his friends because they lowered the paralytic through the roof of the house? Or to explain that Jesus saw their faith because they lowered the paralytic through a roof whose construction materials, unlike that of their own houses, consisted of mud, clay, and wood? If the latter is correct, a conflict exists, because the construction materials do appear to be different in Mark and Luke. On the other hand, if the first view is correct, then there is no conflict. Both Mark and Luke state that Jesus saw the faith of the paralytic and his friends because they lowered him through the roof. Surely this is a better understanding of the purpose and aim of Luke. Luke does not intend to teach Theophilus about construction techniques in Galilee in the first century A.D. Luke is seeking to help Theophilus know the truth of the things he has been taught about Jesus (Luke 1:4), and this involves issues such as Jesus' power to heal and forgive sins. Luke succeeds by telling the story of Jesus and the paralytic who was lowered through the tile.

The Genealogies of Jesus

Matthew 1:1–16	Luke 3:23–38
The book of the genealogy of	Jesus, when he began his

Jesus Christ, the son of David, the son of Abraham. Abraham was the father of Isaac, and Isaac the father of Jacob, and Jacob the father of Judah and his brothers, and Judah the father of Perez and Zerah by Tamar, and Perez the father of Hezron, and Hezron the father of Ram, and Ram the father of Amminadab, and Amminadab the father of Nahshon, and Nahshon the father of Salmon, and Salmon the father of Boaz by Rahab, and Boaz the father of Obed by Ruth, and Obed the father of Jesse, and Jesse the father of David the king. And David was the father of Solomon by the wife of Uriah, and Solomon the father of Rehoboam, and Rehoboam the father of Abijah, and Abijah the father of Asa, and Asa the father of Jehoshaphat, and Jehoshaphat the father of Joram, and Joram the father of Uzziah, and Uzziah the father of Jotham, and Jotham the father of Ahaz, and Ahaz the father of Hezekiah, and Hezekiah the father of Manasseh, and Manasseh the father of Amos, and Amos the father of Josiah, and Josiah the father of Jechoniah and his brothers, at the time of the deportation to Babylon. And after the deportation to Babylon: Jechoniah was the father of Shealtiel, and Shealtiel the father of Zerubbabel, and Zerubbabel the father of Abiud, and Abiud the father of Eliakim, and Eliakim the father of Azor, and Azor the father of Zadok, and Zadok the father of Achim, and Achim the father of Eliud, and Eliud the father of Eleazar, and Eleazar the father of Matthan, and Matthan the father of Jacob, and Jacob the father of Joseph the husband of Mary, of whom Jesus was born, who is called Christ.

ministry, was about thirty years of age, being the son (as was supposed) of Joseph, the son of Heli, the son of Matthat, the son of Levi, the son of Melchi, the son of Jannai, the son of Joseph, the son of Mattathias, the son of Amos, the son of Nahum, the son of Esli, the son of Naggai, the son of Maath, the son of Mattathias, the son of Semein, the son of Josech, the son of Joda, the son of Joanan, the son of Rhesa, the son of Zerubbabel, the son of Shealtiel, the son of Neri, the son of Melchi, the son of Addi, the son of Cosam, the son of Elmadam, the son of Er, the son of Joshua, the son of Eliezer, the son of Jorim, the son of Matthat, the son of Levi, the son of Simeon, the son of Judah, the son of Joseph, the son of Jonam, the son of Eliakim, the son of Melea, the son of Menna, the son of Mattatha, the son of Nathan, the son of David, the son of Jesse, the son of Obed, the son of Boaz, the son of Sala, the son of Nahshon, the son of Amminadab, the son of Admin, the son of Arni, the son of Hezron, the son of Perez, the son of Judah, the son of Jacob, the son of Isaac, the son of Abraham, the son of Terah, the son of Nahor, the son of Serug, the son of Reu, the son of Peleg, the son of Eber, the son of Shelah, the son of Cainan, the son of Arphaxad, the son of Shem, the son of Noah, the son of Lamech, the son of Methuselah, the son of Enoch, the son of Jared, the son of Mahalaleel, the son of Cainan, the son of Enos, the son of Seth, the son of Adam, the son of God.

One difficulty with the Gospels is the conflicting genealogies given in the opening chapters of Matthew and Luke.
One difference between these two genealogies, which has
theological significance, is that Matthew 1:1–17 traces the
genealogy of Jesus back to Abraham through three sets of
fourteen descendants. (This may be due to the fact that the
numerical value of the Hebrew consonants *dvd* in David is
fourteen.) Matthew's desire to trace Jesus' lineage back to
David and Abraham is understandable. He seeks to demonstrate that Jesus is the fulfillment of all the hopes and
promises of Israel: in Jesus the Old Testament is fulfilled.[20]

On the other hand it is understandable why Luke,
(3:23–38) addressing a Gentile, Theophilus, is concerned
about demonstrating that Jesus is the fulfillment of the
hopes of all nations, and so he traces Jesus' lineage back to
Adam.

The ability to trace ancestry was quite common in Jesus'
day. Paul knew that he was a Benjaminite (Phil. 3:5).
Josephus reproduced his own genealogical table and mentions that Jews living outside of Israel sent the names of
their children to Jerusalem to be registered in the official
archives. He also mentions that a priest must marry one of
his own race and thus recommends investigating the
genealogy of a prospective wife in the archives.[21] The
Babylonian Talmud refers to a rabbi who investigates the
genealogy of his prospective daughter-in-law and traces it
back to David.[22] The fact that Matthew and Luke record
Jesus' genealogy is not a problem.

However, when the two genealogies are compared the
major problem is immediately apparent. The two listings
of the descendants between Abraham and David essentially are the same, although Luke adds two additional
names: Arni and Admin. From Jesus to David, however,
there are only three names in common: Shealtiel, Zerubbabel, and Joseph. The first five names in Matthew's
listing before Joseph are: Jacob, Matthan, Eleazar, Eliud,
and Achim. The first five in Luke after Joseph are: Heli,

Matthat, Levi, Melchi, and Jannai. Even if Matthan and Matthat refer to the same individual, the differences are apparent.

Over the centuries numerous attempts have been made to resolve this apparent conflict. Aristides, according to Julius Africanus (ca. A.D. 220), explains the differences as due to the fact that Matthew records Jesus' royal genealogy through the kings of Judah, whereas Luke records Jesus' priestly genealogy. Calvin, and more recently J. Gresham Machen, argue that Matthew records the genealogy of Joseph through David, or, the legal lineage, and Luke records the genealogy of Joseph through his real descendents, or, the actual physical lineage.[23] Julius Africanus suggests that Jacob (Matt. 1:15–16) and Heli (Luke 3:23) were half-brothers. After Heli's death Jacob arranged a Levitical marriage and fathered Joseph. Matthew records Jesus' lineage through Jacob (the actual father) and Luke records it through Heli (the legal father— Deut. 25:5–6). Augustine (ca. A.D. 400) suggests that Joseph had two fathers—his natural one, as recorded by Matthew, and an adopted one, as recorded by Luke.

The best attempted solution, however, is that Matthew records the genealogy of Joseph and Luke records the genealogy of Mary. Luke was especially interested in Mary. This is evident by the space he devotes to her and especially by Luke 2:19 and 51 where he speaks of Mary keeping these things in her heart.

Grammatically it is possible to interpret Luke 3:23 in several ways. The RSV and most modern translations, state that "Jesus, when he began his ministry, was about thirty years of age, being the son (as was supposed) of Joseph, the son of Heli. . . ." Another possibility, in the NASB, is, "And when He began His ministry, Jesus Himself was about thirty years of age, being supposedly the son of Joseph, the son of Eli . . ." This translation means that Jesus was about thirty when he began his ministry. Although it was supposed that he was the son of Joseph, in reality this was not true. He was the virgin-born son of Mary, whose father was Heli. Jesus was the son of Heli by Heli's daughter Mary. Luke, in contrast to Matthew's Gospel, gives a genealogy of Mary. This is the neatest and probably the "least unlikely" solution.

How this apparent conflict can be resolved is uncertain. The last suggestion is possible, but not necessarily probable. Most translations agree in separating the parenthetical statement "as was supposed" from "of Joseph." This indicates that the favored interpretation is that Luke's Gospel is also a genealogy of Joseph rather than Mary. Our inability to obtain a perfectly satisfactory solution to this difficulty is frustrating, but should not disturb us too greatly. An evangelical view of Scripture does not claim that the Scriptures can be understood perfectly or infallibly. According to 1 Corinthians 13:12, we know now only in part. We walk by faith and not by sight (2 Cor. 5:7)! Although the teachings of Scripture are infallible, the believer's understanding and interpretation of them is quite prone to fallibility.

Because of this view of the Scriptures, Christians over the centuries sought to reconcile their understanding with its teachings. This is not always possible. To profess uncertainty does not necessarily denote a weak faith. It means that a partial and fallible understanding cannot reconcile particular biblical passages. To profess this uncertainty occasionally is not a weakness of faith but an agreement with what the Scriptures teach: "Now I know in part; then I shall understand fully, even as I have been fully understood" (1 Cor. 13:12).

The Lord's Supper

Matthew 26:26–29	Mark 14:22–25	Luke 22:15–20
		And he said to them, "I have earnestly desired to eat this passover

Now as they were eating, Jesus took bread and blessed, and broke it, and gave it to the disciples and said, "Take, eat; this is my body."

And he took a cup, and when he had given thanks he gave it to them, saying, "Drink of it, all of you; for this is my blood of the covenant, which is poured out for many for the forgiveness of sins.
    I tell you I shall not drink again of this fruit of the vine until that day when I drink it new with you in my Father's kingdom."

And as they were eating, he took bread, and blessed, and broke it, and gave it to them, and said, "Take; this is my body."

And he took a cup, and when he had given thanks he gave it to them, and they all drank of it. And he said to them, "This is my blood of the covenant, which is poured out for many.

Truly, I say to you, I shall not drink again of the fruit of the vine until that day when I drink it new in the kingdom of God."

with you before I suffer; for I tell you I shall not eat it until it is fulfilled in the kingdom of God." And he took a cup, and when he had given thanks he said, "Take this, and divide it among yourselves; for I tell you that from now on I shall not drink of the fruit of the vine until the kingdom of God comes." And he took bread, and when he had given thanks he broke it and gave it to them, saying, "This is my body which is given for you. Do this in remembrance of me." And likewise the cup after

supper, saying,

"This cup which is poured out for you is the new covenant in my blood."

The parallel accounts of the Lord's Supper contain a number of difficulties. The first is a textual problem surrounding Luke's account. This difficulty is most apparent in a Greek text of the New Testament, such as the Nestle or United Bible Society texts, but is also apparent in some of the newer translations such as the Revised Standard Version, the New English Bible, and the New American Standard Bible. The issue involves whether Luke 22:19b–20 ("which is given for you. Do this in remembrance of me." And likewise the cup after supper, saying, "This cup which is poured out for you is the new covenant in my blood.") were part of Luke's original text or were later added by a scribe. If these verses are not part of the original text, then Luke's account of the Lord's Supper is most unusual. Instead of the normal order—bread and then cup as found in the accounts in Matthew, Mark, and 1 Corinthians—the order would be cup and bread!

The question remains: are verses 19b–20 part of the original text? Arguments can be presented for both views. These arguments are raised in favor of the view that the original autograph (the Gospel which Luke personally penned, not a subsequent copy) omits verses 19b–20:

1. It is a general rule of textual criticism that the shorter reading is preferred to the longer one. The copyists had a greater tendency to add material to the text than to eliminate it.
2. The verses do not appear to be in Luke's style.
3. The verses are similar to Paul's account of the Lord's Supper in 1 Corinthians 11:24b–25 and may have been added to Luke's account by a copyist who sought to make Luke's version of the Lord's Supper look more like Paul's.
4. The omission of verses 19b–20 is a more difficult reading and it is likely that any scribal error or change would tend to remove a difficulty (add verses 19b–20) than to create one (to remove the verses).

These arguments are raised in favor of the view that verses 19b–20 were part of the original autograph:

1. By far the largest number of Greek manuscripts of the New Testament and, more importantly, the better

Greek manuscripts contain verses 19b–20. Only one Greek manuscript omits verses 19b–20.

2. These verses are found in all of the Greek text types. Their omission is only found in part of the "Western" type of text.

3. It is not difficult to understand how a scribe could have omitted these verses. A cup was mentioned in verses 15–18.

4. The atypical style found in verses 19b–20 may be due to Luke faithfully producing an early tradition of the Lord's Supper which he is content to record. Strong textual support in favor of the longer ending argues for its inclusion in the original autograph of the Gospel. It would appear best to conclude that Luke 22:19b–20 is part of the original text. For some unknown reason it was omitted in a small part of the textual tradition. This conclusion eliminates this textual problem surrounding Luke's account of the Lord's Supper.

Another problem is found in Mark 14:12, "And on the first day of Unleavened Bread, when they sacrificed the passover lamb, his disciples said to him, 'Where will you have us go and prepare for you to eat the passover?' " At first glance this looks like a contradiction of the Old Testament description of the Passover. Leviticus 23:5–6 reads, "In the first month, on the fourteenth day of the month in the evening, is the LORD's passover. And on the fifteenth day of the same month is the feast of unleavened bread to the LORD. . . ." It appears that a clear conflict exists in these accounts. Mark dates the slaying of the Passover lamb on the first day of the Feast of Unleavened Bread. The account in Leviticus 23:5–6 states that this event took place one day earlier. Is it possible that Jesus and the disciples followed a different order in the celebration of the Passover than the Old Testament delineated? Some scholars suggest this. (See pp. 62–66.) If so, then Mark's description of the Lord's Supper does not contain any errors. The issue now involves whether Jesus has the authority to rearrange the Passover timing in this manner. There is evidence that Jesus acts as if he has such authority. Matthew 5 and its many "You have heard that it was said . . ." and "but I say to you. . . ," prove that Jesus claims such authority.

However, a simpler explanation exists for this apparent contradiction. A present-day parallel may help. In many family traditions, "Christmas" begins on the evening of December 24, when Christmas presents are opened. On the other hand, in many family traditions "Christmas" always begins on the morning of December 25, when Christmas presents are opened. In practice Christmas begins at different times even though most families agree that the calendar date for Christmas is December 25.

Similarly, the key for understanding Mark 14:12 is not when the Feast of Unleavened Bread actually begins but how the feast was popularly thought of as beginning. Mark's dating portrays nontechnical dating of the Feast of Unleavened Bread. The feast begins when the ritual search of the house for leaven is made and the Passover lamb is slain (December 24). Technically the Feast of Unleavened Bread begins on the next day (December 25)!

The final problem regarding the Lord's Supper is the apparent conflict surrounding its actual date. Was it a Passover meal celebration as Mark 14:12 and Luke 22:15 suggest? Or was a meal eaten before the Passover as John 18:28 suggests? This question is addressed later in this chapter (see pp. 62–66).

The Audience of the Parable of the Lost Sheep

Matthew 18:12–14	Luke 15:1–7
	Now the tax collectors and sinners were all drawing near to hear him. And the Pharisees and the

"What do you think? If a man has a hundred sheep, and one of them has gone astray, does he not leave the ninety-nine on the mountains and go in search of the one that went astray? And if he finds it, truly,

I say to you, he rejoices over it more than over the ninety-nine that never went astray.
So it is not the will of my Father who is in heaven that one of these little ones should perish."

scribes murmured, saying, "This man receives sinners and eats with them." So he told them this parable: "What man of you, having a hundred sheep, if he has lost one of them, does not leave the ninety-nine in the wilderness, and go after the one which is lost, until he finds it? And when he has found it, he lays it on his shoulders, rejoicing. And when he comes home, he calls together his friends and his neighbors, saying to them, 'Rejoice with me, for I have found my sheep which was lost.' Just so, I tell you, there will be more joy in heaven over one sinner who repents than over ninety-nine righteous persons who need no repentance.

The Gospels often contain identical, or very similar, sayings addressed to different audiences. An example would be the parable of the lost sheep. In Luke's setting, the parable is addressed to the Pharisees and scribes who protest Jesus' practice of eating with tax-collectors and sinners. The parable serves as an apology (in the classical sense; a defense or apologetic) for Jesus' actions. The emphasis of this parable (and of all three parables in Luke 15) can be summarized: "Why are you Pharisees and scribes upset that my ministry brings salvation to the outcasts of society? Why do you not rejoice that the lost sheep/coin/son are being found?" (The two main characters in the parable of the prodigal son are the father and the older, not the younger, brother whose attitude is similar to that of the Pharisees and scribes in Jesus' audience.)

The parable in Matthew 18:12–14 appears to be identical to the parable in Luke 15:3–7. Yet, Matthew's account is addressed to the disciples (Matt. 18:1). It can be argued that Jesus told two similar parables on two different occasions to two different audiences. This is frequently done! Yet several factors go against this explanation. One factor involves how the relationship between these two Gospels is understood. If it is argued that Matthew and Luke are independent works with no literary relationship at all, this view can be maintained. But, if there is some literary relationship (such as Luke using Matthew, which was the common view of the early church, or that both use a similar source of sayings, which is the general view today) then such a view becomes much more difficult. Both explanations assume a single source which almost certainly did not have the parable addressed to both audiences at the same time.

Another difficulty with this view is that there are numerous other biblical examples which contain identical, or at least very similar, sayings addressed to a particular audience in one Gospel and then to a different audience in another Gospel. The following are examples:

Mark 9:50a	Luke 14:34
"Salt is good; but if the salt has lost its saltness, how will you season it?"	"Salt is good; but if salt has lost its taste, how shall its saltness be restored?"

Matthew 6:22–23	Luke 11:34–36
"The eye is the lamp of the body. So, if your eye is sound, your whole body will be full of light; but if your eye is not sound, your whole body will be full of darkness. If then the light in you is darkness, how great is the darkness!	"Your eye is the lamp of your body; when your eye is sound, your whole body is full of light; but when it is not sound, your body is full of darkness. Therefore be careful lest the light in you be darkness. If then your whole body is full of light, having no part dark, it will be wholly bright, as when a lamp with its rays gives you light."

Matthew 7:13–14	Luke 13:24
"Enter by the narrow gate; for the gate is wide and the way is easy, that leads to destruction, and those who enter by it are many. For the	"Strive to enter by the narrow door; for many, I tell you, will seek to enter

gate is narrow and the way is hard, and will not be able."
that leads to life, and those who find
it are few."

In the first example Mark's account is addressed to the
disciples in a house (Mark 9:33). The saying in Luke is
addressed to the multitudes (Luke 14:25). In the second
and third examples Matthew's sayings are addressed
primarily to the disciples (Matt. 5:1), but the saying in
Luke 11:34–36 is addressed to the crowds (Luke 11:27, 29)
and in Luke 13:24 to the people in the villages and towns
on the way to Jerusalem (Luke 13:22).

It seems doubtful that in each case Jesus spoke the same
saying twice to two different audiences. A better explanation would be to question the purpose of the Evangelists.
Were they merely copyists of Jesus' words? The Evangelists record that they were inspired of God not only to
record Jesus' words but also to interpret them for the
church. The Holy Spirit caused them to remember not
only what Jesus had said but also what he taught them
(John 14:25–26). This teaching involved not only remembering to whom Jesus spoke his words but also applying
those teachings to new audiences. Were some things that
Jesus said to Pharisees and scribes applicable to Christians? If not, they could not be recorded, because no
Gospel was written to Pharisees and scribes. If they were,
could the Evangelists apply those teachings directly to the
church and group them with other similar material? Also
were some accounts addressed to the disciples also applicable to the church? Were some things said to men also
applicable to women? Were some things said to individuals applicable to the church? Is it only for later readers to
make an application of such sayings to a new situation?
Could the Evangelists guided by the Spirit do so for us?
The easiest explanation of this phenomenon of parallel
sayings addressed to different audiences is to see that the
Evangelists, through the Spirit, applied the sayings of
Jesus to a new situation.

Thus the Spirit led Matthew to take the parable of the lost sheep, originally addressed to Pharisees and scribes (Luke 15:1–2), and to group it with other sayings of Jesus spoken elsewhere in order to form a chapter dealing with life in the church (Matt. 18). This parable is valuable for Christians and not just for Pharisees and scribes. Jesus in his apologetic rebukes any despising of outcasts and demonstrates God's great love for the lost. The church also needs to be reminded of this great love and not to despise her outcasts. As a result, the divine word spoken by Jesus to the Pharisees and scribes becomes a new divine word in Matthew. The Spirit gave to the Evangelist an authoritative and infallible interpretation of this great parable.[24]

Difficult Parallel Passages in the Synoptic Gospels and John

John the Baptist and Elijah

Matthew 17:10–13	Mark 9:11–13	John 1:19–22
And the disciples asked him, "Then why do the scribes say that first Elijah must come?" He replied, "Elijah does come, and he is to restore all things;	And they asked him, "Why do the scribes say that first Elijah must come?" And he said to them, "Elijah does come first to restore all things; and how is it written of the Son of man, that he should suffer many things and be treated with contempt? But I tell you that Elijah has come, and they did to him whatever they pleased, as it is written of him."	And this is the testimony of John, when the Jews sent priests and Levites from Jerusalem to ask him, "Who are you?" He confessed, he did not deny, but confessed, "I am not the Christ." And they asked him, "What then? Are you Elijah?" He said, "I am not." "Are you the prophet?" And he answered, "No."
but I tell you that Elijah has already come, and they did not know him, but did to him whatever they pleased.		
So also the Son of man will suffer at their hands." Then the		

disciples understood
that he was speaking to
them of John the
Baptist.

In the time of Jesus a widespread view existed that the prophet Elijah, who ascended into heaven, would one day return to earth. The primary basis for this expectation was the prophecy in Malachi 4:5–6:

> Behold, I will send you Elijah the prophet before the great and terrible day of the LORD comes. And he will turn the hearts of fathers to their children and the hearts of children to their fathers, lest I come and smite the land with a curse.

This expectation was widespread. There are many references to the return of Elijah in the Gospels (Mark 6:14–15; 8:27–28; 9:11; 15:36) as well as the intertestamental (Sirach 48:10; cf. also Enoch 90:31 in the light of 89:52f.) and rabbinic literature (Shekalim 2.5; Sotah 9.15; Baba Metzia 1.8; Eduyoth 8.7). Within the Gospels an apparent conflict as to the relationship of the coming of John the Baptist and the return of the prophet Elijah is encountered. The problem is immediately apparent when the Synoptic Gospels are compared to the Gospel of John. Matthew 11:14 states, "and if you are willing to accept it, he [John the Baptist] is Elijah who is to come." When asked about the return of Elijah Jesus replies,

> Elijah does come first to restore all things; and how is it written of the Son of man, that he should suffer many things and be treated with contempt? But I tell you that Elijah has come, and they did to him whatever they pleased, as it is written of him (Mark 9:12–13).

Matthew also adds to the account the following editorial comment, "Then the disciples understood that he was speaking to them of John the Baptist" (Matt. 17:13). Yet in

John 1:21 when John the Baptist is asked, ". . . Are you Elijah?", he replies, "I am not." In the Gospels of Matthew and Mark Jesus declares that John the Baptist is Elijah and to this Matthew adds his clear support by his editorial comment. In the Gospel of John, John the Baptist explicitly states that he is not Elijah.

One attempted resolution of this conflict argues that the accounts of Matthew and Mark are correct. John the Baptist is in fact the fulfillment of Malachi's prophecy. He fulfills the role of the returning Elijah. On the other hand, this view argues that the Gospel of John is also correct in that it accurately records John the Baptist's answer to the question addressed him. John the Baptist did say that he is not Elijah, *BUT*, according to this view, he is wrong in this. Such a resolution of the problem claims to be faithful to the Scriptural accounts. Each Gospel accurately records what was said. In the case of John's Gospel, John the Baptist is not correct in what he said. An example of this kind of reasoning is found in the Old Testament where Satan is correctly reported as saying that Eve would not die if she ate of the tree of the knowledge of good and evil (Gen. 3:4). Satan's words are clearly incorrect!

Such a solution, however, is not very helpful nor attractive for at least two reasons. How can it be known when a gospel writer is accurately recording an incorrect statement unless the writer reveals this to us in some way? It is clear that the writer of Genesis 3:4 wants us to understand that Satan's statement is incorrect because in the latter part of the chapter and in the following chapters death plays a prominent part. John, on the other hand, gives no hint that when John the Baptist denies that he is the Christ, Elijah, and Jeremiah, he is correct on two of the answers but is incorrect on the third! Second, it is clear that John the Baptist consciously dresses in a particular manner. He was "clothed with camel's hair, and had a leather girdle around his waist" (Mark 1:6). The Evangelists Matthew and Mark clearly see an allusion to the way

Elijah dressed. Elijah, too, wore camel's hair and a leather girdle (2 Kings 1:8). It is most unlikely that John the Baptist dressed this way by chance. If he intentionally dressed in this manner, it is difficult to deny that he thought that he was in some way fulfilling the role of the one who in the Old Testament dressed in this manner. For these two reasons this attempt to resolve the conflict is not very attractive.

One other attempted resolution, with a long history, involves the differentiation of the "role" of Elijah and the "person" of Elijah. It is clear that the son of Zechariah and Elizabeth (Luke 1:5f.) is not the same person as the prophet Elijah who lived some nine centuries earlier during the days of King Ahab. In essence (ontologically) the "soul" of John the Baptist is not the same "soul" of the prophet Elijah. On the other hand it is clear that the Gospels portray the Baptist as fulfilling the function and role of Elijah. He comes before the great and terrible day of the Lord.[25] That Jesus, himself, interpreted the prophecy of Malachi functionally rather than literally is evident from Matthew 11:14 when he states, "and if you are willing to accept it. . . ." Understood in this manner, there is a sense in which John the Baptist is Elijah and a sense in which he is not.[26]

Perhaps the best way to understand these apparently conflicting passages is to see in John 1:21 a denial on the part of John the Baptist that he is actually the Old Testament Elijah returned from heaven. How else could he have answered the question of whether he was actually the Messiah, Elijah, or Jeremiah? He was in essence none of these. The Gospel of John is correct in recording John the Baptist's answer and John the Baptist is correct in giving this answer. (This also fits the theological emphasis of the Gospel of John which seeks to emphasize the ontological difference between Jesus and John the Baptist and also seeks to maximize the role of the Baptist in bearing witness to the Word becoming flesh.) Despite not being in essence the Elijah who ascended into heaven, the Baptist fulfills the role of Elijah in the prophecy of Malachi 4:5–6 and functions as Elijah by his mission of preparation. Therefore Matthew and Mark are also correct in their portrayal of John the Baptist as the coming Elijah.

Was the Lord's Supper a Passover Meal?

Matthew 26:17–18	Mark 14:12–14	Luke 22:7–11	John 18:28
Now on the first day of Unleavened Bread	And on the first day of Unleavened Bread, when they sacrificed the passover lamb,	Then came the day of Unleavened Bread, on which the passover lamb had to be sacrificed. So Jesus sent Peter and John, saying, "Go and prepare the passover for us, that we may eat it." They said to him, "Where will you have us prepare it?"	
the disciples came to Jesus, saying, "Where will you have us prepare for you to eat the passover?"	his disciples said to him, "Where will you have us go and prepare for you to eat the passover?" And he sent two of his disciples,		
He said, "Go into the city to a certain one,	and said to them, "Go into the city, and a man carrying a jar of water will meet you; follow him, and wherever he enters, say to the householder,	He said to them, "Behold, when you have entered the city, a man carrying a jar of water will meet you; follow him into the house which he enters, and tell the householder,	Then they led Jesus from the house of Caiaphas to the praetorium. It was early. They themselves did not enter the praetorium, so that they might not be defiled, but might eat the passover.
and say to him,			
'The Teacher says, My time is at hand; I will keep	'The Teacher says, Where is my guest room, where I am to	'The Teacher says to you, Where is the guest room, where I am to	

| the passover at your house with my disciples.'" | eat the passover with my disciples?" | eat the passover with my disciples?" |

Earlier, problems involving the various accounts of the Lord's Supper were discussed. (See pp. 42-46.) A final problem with the Lord's Supper is the confusion concerning the actual date. All Gospel accounts agree that Jesus was crucified on a Friday (Matt. 27:62; Mark 15:42; Luke 23:54; John 19:31, 42), but there is confusion as to whether or not the Lord's Supper was a Passover meal. In the Synoptic Gospels the Lord's Supper is clearly portrayed as a Passover meal. Mark 14:14 states that the two disciples sent by Jesus to prepare for the meal which preceded the Lord's Supper are to say, "The Teacher says, Where is my guest room, where I am to eat the Passover with my disciples?"[27] On the other hand, John reports that Jesus' arrest apparently preceded the Passover. John 18:28 states, "Then they led Jesus from the house of Caiaphas to the praetorium. It was early. They themselves did not enter the praetorium, so that they might not be defiled, but might eat the Passover."[28] According to John, the Passover occurs after Jesus' arrest. How could Jesus, according to the Synoptic Gospels, have eaten the Passover with his disciples before his arrest?

Numerous attempts have been made to explain this apparent discrepancy. Many reveal both the seriousness and reverence with which scholars treat the Word of God. These attempts can be divided into three main classifications:

1. The Synoptic Gospels are correct. According to this view the word *Passover* in John 18:28 does not refer to the eating of the Passover lamb but to the celebration of the entire Feast of Unleavened Bread.[29] The first day of the feast is the Passover. In other words, the

term *passover* refers not to the Passover feast that begins the Feast of Unleavened Bread, but it refers to the eating of the other sacrifices during the feast, the *haghigha*. The main problem with this interpretation is that the term used in John 18:28 is *pascha*. This term certainly would have been understood by the readers of John as referring to the Passover itself.

2. John is correct. It is assumed that Jesus knew that he would die and not be able to eat the Passover. He anticipates the Passover and shares the meal with his disciples one day before its normal time. This explanation contains a number of problems; only two will be mentioned. First, in Mark 14:12 Mark dates the Lord's Supper at the normal time of the Passover celebration. Second, it is extremely doubtful that a private celebration of the Passover, which would still involve the sacrificing of the lambs in the temple by the priesthood of Israel, would be possible. The sacrifice of the Passover lambs was determined by the religious calendar of Israel, not by individual preference.

3. Both the Synoptic Gospels and John are correct. There are a number of variations to this explanation:

   a. In this year the Passover fell on the Sabbath and the Pharisees celebrated the Passover a day earlier, whereas the Sadducees celebrated the Passover at the regular time. The Synoptic Gospels follow the reckoning of the Pharisees and the Gospel of John follows the reckoning of the Sadducees.

   b. That year a dispute arose as to when the month of Nisan (the month in which the Passover occurs) actually began. The Pharisees believed that it began one day earlier than the Sadducees. The Synoptic Gospels follow the Pharisaic reckoning and John follows the Sadducaic.

   c. Since so many sacrifices have to be slain for the Passover, the Galileans celebrate the Passover one day earlier than the Judeans. The Synoptic Gospels follow the Galilean practice and John follows the Judean.

d. It is known that two different calendars existed in Israel. One was a solar calendar, which the Qumran community followed. The other, which the rest of the Jews followed, was a lunar one. It is possible that different groups in Israel may have celebrated the Passover on two different days.

e. The Jews employed two different ways of calculating when a day began and ended. One group believed that a day is reckoned from daybreak to daybreak. Another believed that it is reckoned from sunset to sunset. According to this theory, the Synoptic Gospels (and Jesus) reckon a day from daybreak to daybreak, whereas John (and the priests) reckon it from sunset to sunset.

All these explanations represent serious and devout attempts to harmonize the conflict between the Synoptic Gospels and John. It is clear that they cannot all be correct. Some appear to have a rather low probability of being correct. In this particular instance, it is doubtful that any of the explanations has a particularly high degree of certainty. The fact that there are so many different explanations suggests that no one explanation is extremely convincing.

It would appear that the evangelical can take one of two positions with regard to this apparent conflict in the dating of the Lord's Supper. First, choose one of the explanations listed above and accept it as a correct explanation. Second, confess the presence of a difficulty which, at the present time, does not have a good explanation. The latter position may be quite frustrating, but at times such a position may be required due to a lack of sufficient information. The evangelical's confidence in the Bible, however, should enable him to accept the fact that there are instances where a satisfactory explanation is not available. The truthfulness of the Bible remains even if its teachings cannot be understood or explained perfectly.

The Hour of the Crucifixion

Mark 15:25

And it was the third hour, when they crucified him.

John 19:14–15

Now it was the day of Preparation of the Passover; it was about the sixth hour. He said to the Jews, "Behold your King!" They cried out, "Away with him, away with him, crucify him!" Pilate said to them, "Shall I crucify your King?" The chief priests answered, "We have no king but Caesar."

Another difficulty in dating the last events in the life of Jesus involves the hour of his crucifixion. Mark 15:25 states that Jesus was crucified at the third hour. John 19:14, however, records that at about the sixth hour Jesus had not been crucified.

Augustine made an attempt to explain this conflict when he states that the "third hour" in Mark 15:25 is not the actual time when Jesus is physically crucified, but the hour in which the Jews cry out that he should be crucified.[30] According to Augustine, at the third hour the Jews crucify Jesus when they say, "Crucify him" (Mark 15:13–14). Therefore, it would be about the sixth hour when the Roman soldiers actually nail Jesus to the cross. Augustine's solution is interesting but unconvincing. If this was Mark's intention, he would place this temporal designation immediately after Mark 15:13–14 rather than after Mark 15:24. Also, grammatical considerations require that the subject "they" in Mark 15:25 must be the same "they" as the previous verse, unless the Evangelist indicates otherwise. The "they" in Mark 15:24 clearly refers to the Roman soldiers!

Other attempts to explain this problem are based on different meanings for the word *hour (hora)* in Mark and

John. One suggests that the word *hour* in Mark means "watch." Supposedly the third watch began at noon. Closely related to this explanation is the view that Mark refers to the third hour of Hebrew time (time measured from dawn to dark) and John refers to the sixth hour of Roman time (time measured from midnight on). Since the events of John 19:14f. would require several hours, Jesus was probably crucified at 9 A.M., as Mark records.

There are several strong arguments against these explanations. Concerning the first, a separate Greek word exists which means "watch": *phulake*. If Mark intended to say third watch he could have used this word. He knew of this word because he used it in Mark 6:48! Concerning the latter explanation, it seems clear from John 4:6 that, in this instance, John calculates time according to the Hebrew reckoning. According to this verse Jesus, while passing through Samaria, came to the city of Sychar wearied from his journey and sought water around the sixth hour. By Roman reckoning, this would be approximately 6 A.M. which would leave insufficient time for a wearying journey. According to the Hebrew reckoning, this would be around noon. In light of this it seems that the reference to the sixth hour in John 19:14 should be calculated according to the Hebrew reckoning of time.[31]

Another explanation of this problem involves the possibility of a textual corruption. Again, there are several variations of this approach. A small group of manuscripts for both Mark 15:25 and John 19:14 seek to harmonize these passages. A small number of Greek manuscripts in Mark 15:25 read "sixth" instead of "third," and a few in John 19:14 read "third" instead of "sixth"! In these instances scribes sought to harmonize the two accounts by changing one of them. The vast number of Greek manuscripts, and by far the best, witness to "third" in Mark and "sixth" in John. If the earliest original copies of Mark and John were in agreement, it is hard to understand why there would ever have been any reason for a difference to have arisen.

Another suggestion argues that originally Mark and John agree on the hour but that a copyist later made a mistake. At times, numbers were not written out but given letter equivalents: A = 1, B= 2, etc. The letter for three is a capital *gamma* and for "six" is a capital *digamma*. These look like a capital "F" (for the *digamma*) and a capital "F" minus the middle bar (for the *gamma*). Supposedly, one of these letters was misread by a scribe and the resulting "third" and "sixth" hour conflict arose. It must be pointed out, however, that the best Greek manuscripts all have "third" (Mark) and "sixth" (John) and they also have the numbers spelled out rather than in letter equivalents.

Another attempted resolution along these lines argues that Mark 15:25 is a scribal gloss. It was never part of the inspired text but was added by a scribe. There is no textual evidence for this, however, and it is difficult to understand why a scribe would add a temporal designation which clearly conflicted with the Johannine designation. The scribal tendency was to harmonize such differences, not create them!

A better approach to this problem would be to reconsider the general attitude toward time in the first century A.D. It is clear that the twentieth-century precision toward time, prevalent in Western culture, did not and could not exist in the first century A.D. Such exactness was impossible. Furthermore, the day was commonly divided into four periods: 6 to 9 A.M., 9 to 12 P.M., 12 to 3 P.M., and 3 to 6 P.M. In denoting these periods the hours referred to were the third, the sixth, and the ninth hours. Specific references to time in the New Testament are found in the following passages: Matthew 20:3 (3), 5 (6, 9), 9 (11); 27:45 (6, 9), 46 (9); Mark 15:25 (3), 33 (6, 9), 34 (9); Luke 23:44 (6, 9); John 1:39 (10); 4:6 (6), 52 (7); 19:14 (6); Acts 2:15 (3); 3:1 (9); 10:3 (9), 9 (6), 30 (9); 23:23 (3). There are twenty-three specific references to time in the New Testament and only three (Matt. 20:9; John 1:39, 4:52) use a designation other than 3, 6, or 9 to describe the hour. From this it appears that the usual way of expressing time is to refer to the third, sixth, or ninth hour and that time periods between tend to be rounded off to one of these three designations.

It seems clear that something occurring late in the morning could be rounded off and described by one writer as occurring at the third hour, the 9–12 A.M. period, and by another writer as occurring at the sixth hour, near the 12–3 P.M. period. Calvin argues that for Mark the third hour refers to the ending of the 9–12 A.M. period and for John the sixth hour refers to the beginning of this 12–3 P.M. period.[32] John used the expression "about" to indicate the approximate nature of the time and may have sought to round off the time of Jesus' crucifixion as "about" noon because it was at that time that the passover lambs were to be slain.

When understood in this manner the conflict between the Evangelists is greatly minimized. Even if the third hour occurs between 8–10 A.M. and the sixth hour between 11 A.M. and 1 P.M., the latter part of the first period is close to the beginning of the other. If the time references in these passages are understood as approximate designations in a period where exact time was difficult to achieve, the "third" and "sixth" hour difference should not cause any insurmountable problem.

2

Teachings of Jesus

This section investigates some of the more difficult sayings of Jesus. The term *difficult* is not used to denote sayings of Jesus in parallel accounts that appear to contradict each other. These have been investigated in the previous chapter. Nor does this designation mean sayings or teachings of Jesus that are hard to keep. The term *difficult* refers to sayings of Jesus that appear to contradict some of his other teachings or the teachings of the rest of Scripture, or passages which by their literary form appear to be incorrect. Eleven passages will be investigated.

"Do not swear at all" (Matt. 5:34–37)

> But I say to you, Do not swear at all, either by heaven, for it is the throne of God, or by the earth, for it is his footstool, or by Jerusalem, for it is the city of the great King. And do not swear by your head, for you cannot make one hair white or black. Let what you say be simply "Yes" or "No"; anything more than this comes from evil.

In the history of the Christian church this passage has been interpreted in various ways. Some Christians interpret Jesus' words quite literally and refuse to swear an oath. Even in a court of law they will not swear an oath. They believe that they will violate the explicit command of

Jesus found in Matthew's passage. Should all Christians follow this interpretation and refuse to take such oaths?

Interpreting Jesus' words in this manner runs into serious problems. Four reasons will be examined in the reverse order of importance. First, such an interpretation would stand in sharp conflict with the explicit teachings of the Old Testament. In Leviticus 5:1, 19:12; Numbers 30:2–15; Deuteronomy 23:21–23; and Exodus 20:7 the legitimacy of such oaths is assumed. Taking an oath and not keeping it is rebuked! The relationship of the Old Testament Scriptures and covenant to the New Testament Scriptures and covenant comes to the forefront at this point. If the Old Testament is seen as contradicting the New Testament, a denial of all oath-taking is not a major problem. This will also be true if the Old Testament is viewed as a more primitive and crude revelation which is superseded by the New Testament.

If, however, both the Old and the New Testament are seen as witnessing to a common covenant of grace and are equally the Word of God, any interpretation which finds a contradiction between the Old Testament commands concerning oaths and the New Testament command to refrain from all oaths presents a serious problem! Regardless of whether a continuity is seen between the two Testaments (an emphasis found in "covenantal theology") or a discontinuity (an emphasis found in "dispensational theology"), the Christian should be most sensitive to rejecting any explicit Old Testament command too easily. The Old Testament is still part of the canon of Scripture. The least that can be said concerning a literal interpretation is that this passage's apparent conflict with explicit Old Testament teachings allows the believer to question whether this is a correct interpretation.

Second, a more serious objection to a literal interpretation of this passage is the fact that various oaths in the New Testament were made that are viewed positively. In Acts 2:30 and Hebrews 6:16–18, 7:20–22 positive mention is made of God's having sworn to emphasize the certainty of the promises He made. The apostle Paul also calls "God to witness" (2 Cor. 1:23), states "before God, I do not lie" (Gal. 1:20), and mentions that "God is my witness" (Phil. 1:8). Was Paul wrong to swear? It would appear that Paul did not interpret Jesus' teaching in this area literally. It might be argued that Paul was not aware of Jesus' teaching on this subject, but this is an assumption that cannot be proven, and does not solve the problem for the evangelical. It creates a greater one. A sharp conflict now exists between the New Testament teachings and Matthew 5:34–37; not just between the Old Testament and this passage. If any sort of doctrine of biblical infallibility is believed, it would seem reasonable to assume that Jesus' words in Matthew 5:34–37 should not be interpreted as an absolute and universal condemnation of all oath-taking.

The third reason why a literal interpretation of this passage should be rejected is because Matthew never interpreted these words in this manner. Before various antitheses in Matthew 5 ("You have heard that it was said . . . but I say. . . .") are interpreted as a rejection of the Old Testament teachings, it should be noted how they are introduced! Matthew 5:17 introduces these antitheses (of which this passage is one), by stating, "Think not that I have come to abolish the law and the prophets; I have come not to abolish them but to fulfil them." Matthew does not interpret these antitheses as contradicting the Old Testament teachings but as fulfilling them! A literal interpretation of this passage would appear to be destroying the law and the prophets rather than fulfilling them. Also, Matthew, as shall be seen shortly, records an instance where Jesus accepts being placed under an oath.

The fourth, and most important, reason why a universal and literal interpretation of Jesus' words cannot be accepted is that Jesus, himself, did not. At the trial of Jesus, during the questioning of the high priest, ". . . Jesus was silent" (Matt. 26:63). However, his silence ends when he is placed under an oath by the high priest who says, "I adjure you by the living God, tell us if you are the Christ, the Son of God" (Matt. 26:63). In accordance with Leviticus 5:1, Jesus realizes that he could not remain silent. To do so would be to violate the Old Testament command and to be judged guilty. (There was no possibility of "pleading the fifth amendment" in Israel.) Jesus accepts the validity of this oath and responds (Matt. 26:64).

It would appear that Jesus is reacting against the abuse of oaths common among certain elements in Jewish society. This seems clear from the context of this passage.[1] As a result he teaches by use of overstatement that the Christian's character is to be of such a quality that his word possesses absolute veracity. A simple yes or no is all that is needed. Those who follow "the way, and the truth, and the life" (John 14:6) only speak the truth! To ask such people to swear is unnecessary. Perhaps this teaching of Jesus means that when called upon in a court of law to "swear to tell the truth, the whole truth, and nothing but the truth, so help you God," the Christian can respond, "That is unnecessary, for Jesus has taught me to tell only the truth, but if it makes the court happy, 'I do!' "

"And forgive us our debts, As we also have forgiven our debtors" (Matt. 6:12)

In the Lord's Prayer (Matt. 6:9–13) the interpreter encounters a number of exegetical and theological problems. The exegetical issues include questions such as what is referred to by the expression "On earth as it is in heaven"? Does it refer to the last "Thou Petition" ("Thy will be done") or does it belong with all three "Thou Petitions" concerning the name, the kingdom, and the will of God? Another exegetical problem is the meaning of the term *daily*. Since this Greek term, *epiousion*, is found in only two places in Greek literature (in Matthew's and Luke's accounts of the Lord's Prayer), it is almost impossible to know exactly how this term should be translated.

Although these exegetical questions are troublesome, the theological issues in the Lord's Prayer pose greater problems. There are two main problems. The first problem involves the second "We Petition": "And forgive us our debts, As we also have forgiven our debtors." A minor issue involves the meaning of the term *debts*. This term was a common metaphor in Jesus' day for sins. This is most apparent in Luke's version of the Lord's Prayer. Luke 11:4 states, "and forgive us our sins, for we ourselves forgive every one who is indebted to us." It is clear by the interchange of these two terms that debts means sins. This is also evident from Matthew 18:32–35 and Luke 7:41–49.[2]

The major theological problem in this passage, however, is the issue of how God's forgiveness of the Christian is related to the Christian's forgiveness of others. It is clear that this is an important issue. Its importance is heightened by the fact that this petition is the only part of the Lord's Prayer in which the activity of the believer is involved! Only here is the person who prays the Lord's Prayer required to do anything.

Yet exactly how are Christian forgiveness and God's forgiveness related? The "as" in the petition should not be interpreted to mean "to the same degree" or "in the exact same manner." No believer wants his imperfect forgiving to limit the perfect forgiveness of God. And clearly no believer wants the extent of his forgiving to limit God's boundless forgiveness. No Christian praying this prayer is sinned against by his neighbor as greatly as he sins against God. The Christian clearly needs to be forgiven more by God than he needs to forgive others! Therefore, the term *as* cannot refer to a simple comparison of God's and the Christian's forgiveness.

Another issue that this petition raises involves the time frame of God's forgiveness. Some scholars suggest that the scene envisioned is the Great Day of Judgment and that the believer is seeking God's forgiveness in that day. It seems more reasonable, however, to see here a request for daily cleansing from sin and to interpret this along the lines of 1 John 1:9, "If we confess our sins, he is faithful and just, and will forgive our sins and cleanse us from all unrighteousness." This seems reasonable for at least two reasons. First, the person praying this prayer is a believer. He is redeemed. He is already justified and is a child and heir of God, because he addresses God as "Father."[3] He thus is assured of salvation in that day (Rom. 5:9).

Second, the Lord's Prayer was meant not only to be a pattern for prayer but also to be a prayer uttered continually by the followers of Jesus. The fact that this prayer would identify them as the disciples of Jesus, even as John the Baptist's disciples had such an identifying prayer, indicates that God is not being repeatedly asked to forgive in the Judgment Day, or in a sense to resave sinners.[4] Rather, Christians should seek continual restoration and cleansing in order to maintain a close Father-child relationship. An adopted son who offends his father needs to apologize and seek forgiveness not in order to remain adopted but to maintain a good relationship with his father. Similarly believers pray "forgive us our debts" in order to maintain a good relationship with their heavenly Father and not in order to be readopted, rejustified, or reforgiven.

The most significant issue in this petition involves the question of time. Which comes first: Christians forgiving others and as a result God forgiving them, or God forgiving believers and as a result Christians forgiving others? If the former is correct, does this imply a "works" type of righteousness? Is not faith the only necessity for divine forgiveness? The theological issue involved here is important and perplexing. In the Lord's Prayer it seems that God's forgiveness follows and is contingent on Christian forgiveness of others. The Christian can ask God to forgive because he has forgiven. Matthew 5:23–24 also implies this. It is necessary for a Christian to be reconciled to his neighbor before coming to God. Likewise, Luke 6:37 states, ". . . forgive, and you will be forgiven." Mark 11:25 teaches the same view. More important, Matthew 6:14, states, "For if you forgive men their trespasses, your heavenly Father also will forgive you."[5] It seems clear that Jesus teaches that divine forgiveness is dependent on and follows the believer forgiving others.

Yet, other biblical passages seem to teach that Christian forgiveness is simultaneous with or follows God's forgiveness. With regard to the former, the parallel account of the Lord's Prayer, Luke 11:4, reads, ". . . forgive us our sins, for we ourselves forgive every one who is indebted to us." Here Christian forgiveness is contemporaneous with God's forgiveness. On the other hand, Luke 7:47b states that God's forgiveness is followed by love and that love is a response to God's forgiveness. It is also clear from Luke 7:42–43 that one who is forgiven much, as a result, loves much. The idea that it is in response to God's grace of forgiveness that the Christian in turn forgives (or loves) is also found in Paul. Ephesians 4:32 and Colossians 3:13 both state that believers should forgive one another just as God in Christ forgave (note tense!) us.

At times it is necessary to forgive in order to be forgiven, to forgive because we are forgiven, to forgive as we are being forgiven! In the search for a proper and exact chronology, however, the central truth all these verses are shouting out must be kept in sight. That truth is the fact that being forgiven and forgiving are interdependent; they cannot be separated. At times the focus may be on one side and at other times on the other, but forgiving and being forgiven cannot be separated. Unforgiving means unforgiven (Matt. 6:15)!

At times the focus of Jesus may be directed to the initial experience of repentance and faith, where in humility the Christian seeks God's forgiveness and shows the necessary attitude for coming to God by forgiving debtors first. (To see in such humility and contrition, however, a works righteousness is absurd. A works righteousness does not seek mercy and grace, it demands it!) At other times the focus of Jesus or the biblical writer may not be on the initial act of repentance but on the outworking of that repentance and faith. Having tasted God's forgiveness, the believer now is both willing and able to forgive others.

Jesus and the writers of the New Testament appear to be less concerned with constructing a time scheme in this area than on proclaiming the necessary and integral tie between the experience of divine forgiveness and the practice of forgiving. Divine forgiveness results in and requires a willingness, on the believer's part, to forgive. To emphasize the former implies that the willingness to forgive others must follow being forgiven. To emphasize the latter implies that divine forgiveness follows the believer's forgiving. The parable of the unforgiving servant (Matt. 18:23–35) clearly teaches this interrelatedness. What appears like forgiveness which precedes forgiving (Matt. 18:27) disappears when forgiving does not follow (Matt. 18:32–35). These cannot be separated. Whether forgiveness occurs before, is simultaneous, or occurs after being forgiven is of little real consequence. The crucial concern is to realize there cannot be forgiveness without forgiving!

"And lead us not into temptation" (Matt. 6:13a)

The second theological problem in the Lord's Prayer is found in Matthew 6:13a: "And lead us not into temptation. . . ." Before dealing with the main difficulty found here, it may help to clarify a couple of minor issues. Some scholars define the term *temptation* as the eschatological "Temptation": "lead us not into the Great Temptation which is coming upon the earth." However, in Matthew 6:13a "temptation" lacks the article "the." (Even though an article is not necessary in a prepositional phrase to make the noun definite, its omission here is significant.) This indicates that the term *temptation* is used in a more general sense to refer to inward seductions. A good example of this is found in Matthew 26:41, Mark 14:38, and Luke 22:40. The same term is used, but it refers to the immediate temptation facing Peter and the disciples when Jesus is about to be betrayed.

The term *temptation* is used nine times in the Gospels, but it is never used to refer to the Temptation coming at the end of history. In fact, the expression is found twenty-one times in the New Testament and in only one instance it clearly refers to the Temptation (Rev. 3:10), although it may on two other instances as well (1 Peter 4:12; 2 Peter 2:9). Therefore it seems certain that in the Lord's Prayer Matthew is not referring to the eschatological Temptation that is coming at the end of history but to the daily temptation to sin that Christians face.

A second minor issue involves whether the term *temptation* is to be understood in an active ("lead me not into tempting God")[6] or in a passive sense ("let me not be tempted"). The active sense is unlikely since the parallel expression in the latter part of the verse is concerned with "being delivered." It is passive in meaning.

The main problem in this text is clear. Does God lead His children into temptation? Does He seek to cause us to sin? James 1:13, in sharp opposition to such a view, states, "Let no one say when he is tempted, 'I am tempted by God'; for God cannot be tempted with evil and he himself tempts no one." It furthermore is suggested that James 1:13 specifically was written in reaction to a misunderstanding of this petition in the Lord's Prayer. This cannot be demonstrated, but James 1:13 does highlight the problem with Matthew 6:13.

In the Lord's Prayer does the Christian plead with God in this petition not to bring temptation that can cause him to fall? If so, how is the believer to interpret all the great promises of divine deliverance and help during times of temptation? ". . . The Lord knows how to rescue the godly from trial . . ." (2 Peter 2:9). "No temptation has overtaken you that is not common to man. God is faithful, and he will not let you be tempted beyond your strength, but with the temptation will also provide the way of escape, that you may be able to endure it" (1 Cor. 10:13).[7] This interpretation of the text by which the Christian prays that God will not bring him into temptation stands in sharp contrast with the teachings of the rest of Scripture which emphasizes that God is the One who brings the believer through and out of temptation, not into it. (It is hypothetically possible that Jesus in this petition of the Lord's Prayer teaches something that stands in sharp conflict with the rest of the Bible, but before such a judgment is made it would be wise to see if such an interpretation is really demanded by this text.)

It should be noted that the term *temptation* can be understood both in a positive as well as in a negative sense. In James 1:13 "temptation" is clearly a negative reality, for it stems from lust and leads to sin (James 1:14–15). Yet in James 1:2, 12 and 1 Peter 1:6 "temptation" is seen as positive and as a means of growth and maturation of faith. To seek not to be tempted, in the negative sense of being enticed to sin, makes good sense. Temptation which seeks to mislead us into sin should be avoided. Yet temptation, in the sense of trial which leads to spiritual growth, should not be avoided but welcomed. "Count it all joy, my brethren, when you meet various trials [same Greek term!], for you know that the testing of your faith produces steadfastness" (James 1:2–3). If God leads the believer into temptation in the negative sense, a clear conflict with James 1:13 exists. According to this verse, God does not lead his children into this sort of temptation. As a result, to ask God not to lead and entice us into sin would be a very strange request, since God never does this! That kind of temptation fits the behavior of a god of

Greek mythology better than the God of our Bible. But should the believer, on the other hand, ask God not to permit him to experience those trials which produce steadfastness and patience? On the contrary, the believer should pray for perseverence in such trials, not preservation from them.

To resolve this petition's difficulty it seems necessary to define what "lead us not" actually means. It is probable that behind these words lies an Aramaic expression which, rather than asking God not to lead the Christian into temptation, is asking Him not to allow him to succumb to temptation. A helpful parallel to this is found in the Babylonian Talmud:

> Lead me not into the power of transgression,
> And bring me not into the power of sin,
> And not into the power of iniquity,
> And not into the power of temptation,
> And not into the power of anything shameful.[8]

In this example the pious Jew is not pleading with God not to lead him or bring him into these evils. He is asking God to keep him from succumbing to or committing them. In a similar way in the Lord's Prayer the Christian asks God to aid him so he will not succumb to temptation rather than asking God not to force him into experiencing such temptation. This petition is best understood as an idiomatic expression which can be translated, "Let us not succumb to temptation."

This understanding of this petition is supported not only by parallels in Jewish literature but also by the parallelism of the succeeding phrase. The phrase "but deliver us from evil," which formally is an example of antithetical parallelism, is, in meaning, an example of synonymous parallelism. This means that another way of expressing the meaning of "lead us not into temptation" is "deliver us from evil." In both petitions the believer is seeking God's aid in times of trial and the request is made for divine deliverance from trial or evil. If it is understood as a request that God not permit the believer to succumb to temptation, this petition in the Lord's Prayer no longer poses any major difficulty.

"If you forgive the sins of any" (John 20:23)

Another passage in the Gospels that raises numerous questions is John 20:23. Jesus tells the disciples after his resurrection, "If you forgive the sins of any, they are forgiven; if you retain the sins of any, they are retained." Two related passages are Matthew 16:19 and 18:18. Matthew 16:19 is addressed to Peter after his confession that Jesus is the Christ. It states, "I will give you the keys of the kingdom of heaven, and whatever you bind on earth shall be bound in heaven, and whatever you loose on earth shall be loosed in heaven." Matthew 18:18 appears to be addressed to the disciples (18:1), but it is evident that this entire chapter consists of teachings of Jesus addressed to the entire church. (See especially Matt. 18:2–4, 5–6, 7–9, etc.)

In Matthew 18:18 the church is given the same commission and responsibility that Peter receives in Matthew 16:19, "Truly, I say to you, whatever you bind on earth shall be bound in heaven, and whatever you loose on earth shall be loosed in heaven." In Matthew 18:18 it seems clear that this "binding" and "loosing" are associated with the forgiveness of sins. The verses preceding (vv. 15–17) and following (vv. 21–22) deal with the forgiveness of sins. Also, the concluding part of this chapter contains the parable of the unforgiving servant (vv. 23–35). It would seem, at least to Matthew, that the "binding" and "loosing" mentioned in Matthew 18:18 (and probably 16:19) are associated with the forgiveness of sins.

The primary problem that this passage raises is how the disciples and the church can "forgive" or "retain" the sins of others. Is this forgiveness effective or declaratory? Does the church have the authority to forgive the sins of others ("I, by the authority given me, forgive you of all your sins"), or is this the authority to declare and pronounce God's forgiveness of sins ("I, due to the promises of God's Word, declare that because you sincerely repent and confess your sins, God forgives all your sins")?

The latter is a better interpretation of this passage for at least three reasons. First, the Gospels make it clear that only God can forgive sins (Mark 2:5–7; Luke 7:48–49). Although the statement, "Who can forgive sins but God alone?" (Mark 2:7) comes from the lips of Jesus' opponents, it is evident that Jesus and the gospel writers all assume the truth of the statement and associate Jesus' authority to forgive sins with their understanding of Jesus' divine nature. God alone can forgive the sins of his people.[9]

Second, it is important to note how the early church fulfilled this commission. No examples of the early church effectively forgiving the sins of others can be found in Acts, but frequent examples of the proclamation of the forgiveness of sins are discovered in the preaching.[10] Acts reveals that the early church members understood this responsibility to mean that they were to proclaim the gospel of Jesus Christ. By doing this, they had the ability to bring about the forgiveness of sins when listeners responded in repentance and faith.

Finally, it should be observed that this passage speaks not only of the forgiveness of sins but of the "retaining" of sins as well! It is difficult to assume that God gives to his erring church, which is itself in continual need of repentance and renewal, the authority to effectively forgive or not forgive the sins of mankind for eternity. Surely, such authority lies only with God. Only God can know the true condition of the heart.

The means by which the church is to fulfill this commission is exemplified in 1 John 1:8–10. The writer declares how the forgiveness of sins can be received. To claim to have no sin (v. 8) means that the believer remains in sin; to confess sin (v. 9) results in God's faithful forgiveness of sins. The author of these words, by the proclamation of this truth, helps to bring about the forgiveness of sins to the repentant and the withholding of forgiveness to the unrepentant. It is also important to observe how the other gospel writers end their Gospels. Luke concludes with Jesus commanding his disciples that after the receiving of the Holy Spirit ". . . repentance and forgiveness of sins should be preached in his name to all nations, beginning from Jerusalem" (Luke 24:47). Matthew concludes with the commission to "Go therefore and make disciples of all nations, baptizing them in the name of the Father and of the Son and of the Holy Spirit" (Matt. 28:19).

Perhaps John 20:23, Luke 24:47, and Matthew 28:19 should be understood as different ways of expressing the same truth. With the coming of the Spirit, the disciples' proclamation of the gospel message would ". . . convince the world concerning sin and righteousness and judgment" (John 16:8). Through the preaching of the early church (and the preaching of today) others would believe (John 17:20) and receive the forgiveness of sins, or would not believe and be condemned (John 3:18). Baptism was frequently involved in this experience (Matt. 28:19–20). As the Book of Acts clearly reveals, baptism was intimately associated with the conversion experience in the early church. It generally occurred on the same day and often was seen as its culminating expression.

William Barclay seems to be on the right track when he states, "This sentence [John 20:23] does not mean that the power to forgive sins was ever entrusted to any man or to any men; it means that the power to proclaim that forgiveness was so entrusted; and it means that the power to warn that that forgiveness is not open to the impenitent was also entrusted to them."[11] The awesomeness of this commission should not be minimized. Each Christian has the opportunity to "forgive" or "retain" the sins of others! In the faithful proclamation of the gospel message the believer is a vital instrument in God's program of forgiveness and redemption!

Jesus' Teachings on Prayer (Mark 11:22–24; Matthew 7:7–8)

The Gospels contain numerous sayings of Jesus concerning prayer that are troublesome.

> And Jesus answered them, "Have faith in God. Truly, I say to you, whoever says to this mountain, 'Be taken up and cast into the sea,' and does not doubt in his heart, but believes that what he says will come to pass, it will be done for him. Therefore I tell you, whatever you ask in prayer, believe that you have received it, and it will be yours" (Mark 11:22–24).

> "Ask, and it will be given you; seek, and you will find; knock, and it will be opened to you. For every one who asks receives, and he who seeks finds, and to him who knocks it will be opened" (Matt. 7:7–8).

Matthew 18:19; Luke 11:5–13; John 14:13; 15:7, 16; 16:23–24, also are problematic. What makes these passages even more difficult is that some of them are not qualified or made conditional in any way. It is true that some of these promises do have qualifications: Mark 11:22–24 requires faith and not doubting but believing, as does its parallel, Matthew 21:21–22; Matthew 18:19 requires agreement in prayer between at least two people; John 15:7 requires abiding in Christ; John 14:13, 15:16, and 16:23–24 require asking in Jesus' name; but Matthew 7:7–8 and its parallel, Luke 11:5–13, are not conditional.

The problem created by these verses is evident. Christians through the centuries have at times asked and not received, sought and not found, knocked and not found it open. Furthermore, Christians have prayed in great unity numbering not just two or three (Matt. 18:19) but in the thousands, and have not been heard. Christians often have prayed with much faith, doubting nothing (Mark 11:22–24; Matt. 21:21–22), believing that they were indeed abiding in Christ (John 15:7), and praying in Jesus' name (John 14:13; 15:16; 16:23–24) and still have not had their prayers answered. How can this be explained?

The author quite vividly remembers being part of a prayer group and praying that a young man, who was listed as missing in action and presumed dead, would soon return home. We knew he was alive; we prayed persistently month after month in faith believing; and we prayed in Jesus' name. The young man never returned home. It might be argued that he is still alive and a prisoner of war. But these prayer sessions took place during the Korean War! Undoubtedly there have been similar prayers for the missing in action in World War II, World War I, and the Civil War.

One explanation for this apparent lack of answers to prayer is to raise additional qualifications. James 4:3 states, "You ask and do not receive, because you ask wrongly, to spend it on your passions." Are we to assume that Jesus' hearers would have known James 4:3 and added this and all the other biblical qualifications to the teachings of Jesus on prayer? Another rationalization for unanswered prayer is to say that all prayers are answered; God answers them with a "yes," a "no," or a "wait." This explanation appears to play with words and does not explain the serious problem of Christians who ask and do not receive. Furthermore Matthew 7:7–8 does not appear to allow "no" as an answer to prayer.

Another explanation is to say that the purpose of prayer

is not to receive things from God but to change; to become a different kind of person. There is an element of truth in this argument. Prayer is not synonymous with request or petition. Prayer does involve adoration, worship, and confession! The prayer Jesus taught, the Lord's Prayer, teaches this clearly. The problem lies in the fact that Jesus bids us to ask in order to receive. Prayer is not simply petition, but it does include it! Prayer does change the person praying, but it also, according to Jesus, changes "things." The fact cannot be evaded that Jesus encourages his followers to pray to the Father in his name in order to have their prayers and petitions answered.

Perhaps a more satisfying explanation of these verses is to be found in one of the methods Jesus uses in his teaching. This is a method every teacher uses: exaggeration or overstatement. When the use of qualifiers weakens the point being made or makes it more confusing, or when seeking to emphasize a point, exaggeration often is used. A parent utilizes overstatement when he tells his child, "Tell Daddy what you want for Christmas, and he will get whatever you want." Daddy will not get just anything for his child. There are things that could hurt him physically or impair his mental-moral-emotional-spiritual growth. The statement can be qualified: "Of course, Daddy must be able to afford it; he must believe that it will not be dangerous to your health; he must believe that it will not harm your developing sense of values, etc." But, this would only confuse the child and weaken the point. The point, that Daddy loves to give good things to his child, is brought home forceably by means of the exaggeration.

Jesus uses exaggeration or overstatement in his teaching, although the degree to which he uses these techniques may be debated. Luke 14:26; Matthew 5:23–24, 29–30; 7:1; and 10:34 demonstrate that Jesus frequently uses overstatement to drive home forcefully his point. Jesus' statements on prayer should be understood in this vein. Jesus wants his followers to know that the Father delights in answering the requests of his children. He, in effect, says, "Tell *Abba* (literally "Daddy") what you want and he will grant it that your joy might overflow." Although Jesus did not expect his listeners to know James 4:3, or similar verses in the New Testament, he did expect them to assume that such qualifiers would be understood.

In conclusion, Jesus' promises on prayer should be interpreted as broad general statements meant to emphasize God's readiness and desire to hear and answer the prayers of his people. Built into these statements is the understanding that believers should pray only for those things that will be good for their well-being, or, what will be in accord with God's will. At times believers may not even know for what or how they should actually pray (Rom. 8:26). In so praying they know that when they ask, they shall receive.

The Parable of the Unjust Steward (Luke 16:1–8)

He also said to the disciples, "There was a rich man who had a steward, and charges were brought to him that this man was wasting his goods. And he called him and said to him, 'What is this that I hear about you? Turn in the account of your stewardship, for you can no longer be steward.' And the steward said to himself, 'What shall I do, since my master is taking the stewardship away from me? I am not strong enough to dig, and I am ashamed to beg. I have decided what to do, so that people may receive me into their houses when I am put out of the stewardship.' So, summoning his master's debtors one by one, he said to the first, 'How much do you owe my master?' He said, 'A hundred measures of oil.' And he said to him, 'Take your bill, and sit down quickly and write fifty.' Then he said to another, 'And how much do you owe?' He said, 'A hundred measures of wheat.' He said to him, 'Take your bill, and write eighty.' The master commended the dishonest steward for his shrewdness; for the sons of this world are more shrewd in dealing with their own generation than the sons of light."

Perhaps the one parable of Jesus that causes the greatest difficulty is the parable of the unjust steward in Luke 16:1–8. Undoubtedly the original hearers, and believers today, are surprised by the conclusion: "The master commended the dishonest steward for his shrewdness . . ." (Luke 16:8). The reader expects the master to rebuke, judge, condemn, punish, or damn the steward for his dishonesty. But the parable takes an unexpected twist, and he not only does not condemn him but commends the scoundrel. How can Jesus in this parable commend such a person? Does this not reward and encourage dishonesty?

This is not the only parable in which people of questionable character and morality are commended. In the parable of the hidden treasure (Matt. 13:44) the man, whose behavior serves as an example, obtains the treasure by less than exemplary means. He may not have swindled or defrauded to obtain the land with its treasure, but it is impossible to hold him up as an example of one who practices the Golden Rule (Matt. 7:12). Furthermore, in the parable of the wise and foolish maidens (Matt. 25:1–13) the Christian is taught to emulate the wise maidens who did not share their oil with those who had need. Are Christians to follow this kind of an example or are they to "Give to him who begs from you, and do not refuse him who would borrow from you" (Matt. 5:42)?

The problem these parables raise is due to a misunderstanding of the purpose and function of parables. In the history of the church parables have frequently been understood as allegories in which each detail has meaning and significance. An example would be the parable of the good Samaritan (Luke 10:30–35). The following analogies are drawn:

Man	=	Adam
Jerusalem	=	Paradise
Jericho	=	This world
Robbers	=	The Devil and his angels
Wounds	=	Disobedience or sins
Priest	=	Law
Levite	=	Prophets
Good Samaritan	=	Christ
Beast	=	The body of Christ
Inn	=	Church
Two Denarii	=	Two commandments of love
Innkeeper	=	Angels in charge of church
Return of Good Samaritan	=	Second coming of Christ

Since the turn of this century it is clear that parables are not allegories. Details are important in allegories. However, a parable usually contains one basic point of comparison. The details are generally unimportant and should not be pressed for meaning. As a result, in the parable of the good Samaritan, if the man were going up from Jericho or if it were three denarii rather than two, the point of the parable would not change at all. A parable then is a basic metaphor in which an analogy is presented. "A" (for example, the kingdom of God) is likened to "B" (for example, a grain of mustard seed). The very nature of any analogy guarantees that the analogy will eventually break down if pressed beyond the basic point of comparison. The reason for this is that "A" can only be identical in all areas of comparison with itself. In other words, the kingdom of God is identical in all points only with the kingdom of God, or with itself. It is similar to something else (a grain of mustard seed, leaven which a woman took, or a merchant in search of pearls) only in its basic point of comparison.

Another example is to say that "God is like. . . ." No analogy can be used for God if the analogy must correspond to God in all its details, for no one or nothing is Infinite, Omniscient, Omnipresent, or Omnipotent but God. Yet it can be said that God is like a father, who . . . , if the one basic comparison that the analogy is seeking to make can be accepted.

In interpreting any analogy, the interpreter should content himself with the basic point of comparison being made. If the details are not pressed in the parable of the unjust steward, the problem that the parable causes will disappear. What is the point of comparison Jesus is making in the parable? What does he commend? It is not the dishonesty of the steward but his shrewdness: his cleverness and skill for self-preservation. He is commended for preparing himself for judgment coming on him from his master. After being fired, he still has "friends" who owe him favors and will receive him into their houses when he is put out of his stewardship.

This point of comparison was surely applicable to Jesus' audience. Jesus' message to "Repent, for the kingdom of God is at hand" encouraged believers to be prudent and prepare themselves. Also, knowing that ". . . it is appointed for men to die once, and after that comes judgment" (Heb. 9:27), should not Christians today be prudent and prepare for this accounting of stewardship? How to prepare for this is suggested, in part, by Luke 16:9. It is by the judicious use of possessions ("unrighteous mammon"). The parable therefore does not exhort believers to be cunning thieves but to be at least as shrewd or prudent as the scoundrel in the parable and make ready for that great day in which an account must be rendered to God.[12]

"Let him who has no sword . . . buy one" (Luke 22:36)

Luke 22:36 contains a saying of Jesus which seems to be out of character with the tenor of Jesus' teachings elsewhere. Jesus says, "But now, let him who has a purse take it, and likewise a bag. And let him who has no sword sell his mantle and buy one." This passage can be translated a couple of ways: (1) Let the person who has a purse and wallet take them and buy a sword, and let the person who does not have them sell his cloak and buy a sword; or (2) Let the person who has a sword take his purse or wallet; and let the person who does not have a sword sell his cloak and buy one. With each interpretation, however, the difficulty remains.

There have been numerous attempts to interpret this saying and others such as Matthew 10:34: "Do not think that I have come to bring peace on earth; I have not come to bring peace, but a sword." to indicate that Jesus was a political revolutionary: a zealot or at least a zealot sympathizer.[13]

Such an interpretation is clearly impossible for several reasons. First, there are many other passages in which Jesus' words are clearly not non-revolutionary but are anti-revolutionary.[14] Second, Jesus' frequent association with publicans (tax collectors) would be impossible for anyone holding zealot sympathies. The zealots hated tax collectors and considered them traitors because they collected taxes for the Roman oppressors. Furthermore, to have a disciple who was a tax collector would be inconceivable for a zealot sympathizer.

In Matthew 10:34 the "sword" Jesus comes to bring has nothing to do in the context with politics but speaks of the family division and strife that he frequently brings.

For I have come to set a man against his father, and a daughter against her mother, and a daughter-in-law against her mother-in-law; and a man's foes will be those of his own household (Matt. 10:35–36).

Finally, if two swords are "enough" (Luke 22:38), Jesus did not intend to establish a military revolution. Two swords are clearly not "enough" against the legions of Rome!

Since Luke 22:36 does not promote a revolutionary outlook, a reasonable interpretation of this passage must be found. It is clear that any literal interpretation of the passage is incorrect. When the disciples think literally of swords and respond, "Look, Lord, here are two swords," Jesus rebukes them with "It is enough." Perhaps the best interpretation is to see these words as an idiomatic way of stopping a conversation that is on the wrong track by saying, "That is enough [of such foolish talk]." An example of this can be found in Deuteronomy 3:26 where, in the LXX, the Lord puts a stop to Moses' conversation by stating, "Let it suffice you; speak no more to me of this matter." In the context of Luke 22:36, the disciples have completely misunderstood Jesus' words by taking them literally. Jesus simply ends the conversation.

What then is Jesus seeking to teach by this saying on buying a sword? If the context is noted, it can be seen that in the preceding verse Jesus reminds his disciples that earlier in his ministry when he sent them out to preach they had no need for purse or bag or sandals. They were completely taken care of by the cordial reception of their audience. This took place during the height of Jesus' popularity and they experienced great hospitality from the people.[15] But now the situation has changed. Jesus will soon be crucified. Instead of hospitality, the disciples can expect hostility and persecution. They need to prepare for this new situation by providing themselves with a purse and a bag. The need for a sword can be understood as a metaphorical way of describing the hardship and struggle

of the "war" they are to fight for the cause of Christ. This
"war" will at times involve persecution and perhaps
martyrdom.[16] At times the struggle will involve a "war"
against sin and temptation. Jesus' use of the sword metaphor is to prepare the disciples to enter this battle with
dedication, fully armed. The use of other related metaphors of war may lend support to this interpretation.[17]

Rather than interpreting this saying literally, which is
impossible in the light of Jesus' life and teachings elsewhere, perhaps it is best to interpret it as a metaphor
describing the war his followers are now involved in.[18]

> The saying can be regarded only grimly ironical, express-
> ing the intensity of the opposition which Jesus and the
> disciples will experience, endangering their very lives.
> They are summoned to a faith and courage which is
> prepared to go to the limit.[19]

"You are Peter, and on this rock
I will build my church"(Matt. 16:18)

Matthew 16:18 has been a continual battlefield for
commentators. It states "And I tell you, you are Peter, and
on this rock I will build my church, and the powers of
death shall not prevail against it." The importance of this
verse is evident. It serves as the theological cornerstone
for the establishment of the papacy in Roman Catholic
theology. The traditional Catholic interpretation of this
verse is that the rock upon which Christ will build the
church is Peter, who will serve as Christ's vicar on the
earth. This role subsequently passed to succeeding bishops who serve as Christ's vicar or pope.

The Protestant interpretation argues that the rock Jesus
refers to is not Peter but rather Peter's confession: that
Jesus is the Christ. According to this view, Christ is the
foundation of the church. No other foundation exists
(1 Cor. 3:11). He alone possesses the keys of death and

Hades (Rev. 1:18). For the Roman Catholic exegete, the issue is clear. The rock on which Jesus will build the church must be the same rock Jesus refers to earlier in the verse: Peter.

Without discussing immediately the correctness or incorrectness of these interpretations, it may be profitable to consider the danger of approaching the Scriptures with preconceived ideas on what a text can or cannot say. Regardless of which interpretation is correct, it is frightening that the meaning of the text no longer serves as a final authority. On the contrary, it is the present theology that predetermines what the text means and that serves as a final authority! Hopefully, theology is derived from the Scriptures. But the believer continually must be aware of which determines which and never allow any theological formulations to supersede the Scriptures. The final authority in all religious matters is the Scriptures. Theology is "final" only to the degree that it accurately understands and interprets the meaning of the Scriptures. For a Protestant or a Roman Catholic to predetermine what Matthew 16:18 can or cannot mean is to place a particular theology above the Scriptures.

This passage, in the Greek translation, contains a pun: a play on the words *Peter (petros* in Greek) and *rock (petra* in Greek). Some commentators seek to minimize the importance of the pun by pointing out that these words are not identical. "Peter" is a masculine noun whereas "rock" is a feminine noun. Two considerations argue against this. First, the difference between the two is due to the fact that the word *rock* is always feminine in Greek, whereas Peter's name must be masculine. Second, in Aramaic, which Jesus spoke, there would be no difference in the two words. The word used by Jesus for *Peter* and for *rock* would be the same: *Cephas.*

Without claiming that the following interpretation is inerrant, perhaps the best interpretation of the word *rock* is that it refers to Peter. This interpretation alone does justice to the play on words found in the verse. Yet what did Jesus mean by this? How does the New Testament portray Peter's fulfillment of this role? The New Testament does not present an infallible Peter.[20] Peter is used by God to preach to the Jews at Pentecost (Acts 2) and to Cornelius at the "Gentile Pentecost" (Acts 10), and he provided the leadership for the early church. It is in his role as apostle and in his proclamation of the gospel that Peter serves as a foundation for the church. It is in a similar manner that all the early apostles serve as a "foundation" on which the church is built, although Jesus Christ is the cornerstone (Eph. 2:20). Peter is the "rock" of Matthew 16:18 in the sense that without the apostles (and Peter was the leader at the beginning) there would be no church.

According to this understanding both traditional interpretations of this passage are right in one sense and wrong in another. The Roman Catholic view is correct in that the pun demands that the rock refer to Peter, but is incorrect in building a papal edifice based on this verse. The traditional Protestant interpretation is incorrect in ignoring the pun and saying that the rock refers to Peter's confession, but it is certainly correct in realizing that the only ultimate foundation on which the church can be built is Jesus Christ. There is no need for Protestants to minimize the important role our Lord gave to the apostle Peter as leader of the apostles. This man was one of the great gifts God gave for the establishment of His church (Eph. 2:20). Protestants and Roman Catholics alike can give God thanks for his leadership.

The Parable of the Rich Man and Lazarus (Luke 16:19–31)

There was a rich man, who was clothed in purple and fine linen and who feasted sumptuously every day. And at his gate lay a poor man named Lazarus, full of sores, who desired to be fed with what fell from the rich man's table;

moreover the dogs came and licked his sores. The poor man died and was carried by the angels to Abraham's bosom. The rich man also died and was buried; and in Hades, being in torment, he lifted up his eyes, and saw Abraham far off and Lazarus in his bosom. And he called out, "Father Abraham, have mercy upon me, and send Lazarus to dip the end of his finger in water and cool my tongue; for I am in anguish in this flame." But Abraham said, "Son, remember that you in your lifetime received your good things, and Lazarus in like manner evil things; but now he is comforted here, and you are in anguish. And besides all this, between us and you a great chasm has been fixed, in order that those who would pass from here to you may not be able, and none may cross from there to us." And he said, "Then I beg you, father, to send him to my father's house, for I have five brothers, so that he may warn them, lest they also come into this place of torment." But Abraham said, "They have Moses and the prophets; let them hear them." And he said, "No, father Abraham; but if someone goes to them from the dead, they will repent." He said to him, "If they do not hear Moses and the prophets, neither will they be convinced if some one should rise from the dead."

The account of Lazarus and the rich man, Luke 16:19–31, is prone to serious misinterpretation. There is considerable debate whether this passage is to be interpreted as a true story or as a parable. There are two arguments in favor of it being a true story of an actual rich man and a poor man named Lazarus. First, the story is not called a parable nor is it introduced like many parables ("the kingdom of God is like"; or "the kingdom of God can be compared to"). This is not a weighty argument. Many of the most famous parables also are not explicitly called parables nor introduced by a phrase such as "the kingdom of heaven is like. . . ."[21] But the strongest argument in favor of the non-parabolic nature of this passage is the fact that the poor man is explicitly given a name: Lazarus. No other parable gives a character a specific name!

There are at least two strong reasons in favor of interpreting this passage as a parable. First, there are details in
the account which do not seem to conform with other
Scriptural teachings concerning life after death. This
would not be a problem in the context of a parable. It
would be if this were an historical account. The strongest
and most conclusive argument in favor of a parable is the
way in which the story is introduced. "There was a
[certain—*tis* in Greek] rich man, who. . . ." The Gospel of
Luke uses this introduction only to introduce various
parables.[22] It would seem best to interpret Luke 16:19–31
as a parable rather than as an historical story; most
scholars do.

The parable is unusual in that, in Luke, it is a two-part
parable similar to the parable of the gracious father (or the
prodigal son) in Luke 15:11–32. Interpreters frequently
place the emphasis on the first half of both parables. The
point of the parable of the rich man and Lazarus would be
the reversal of fortune in the hereafter. Luke 15:11–32
would teach about the love of God toward the outcasts of
society.

Yet the emphasis in a parable comes at the end! In
parabolic interpretation this technique is termed "the rule
of end stress": at the end of a parable the main stress or
emphasis should be sought. The main two characters in
the parable of the gracious father therefore are not the
father (God) and the prodigal (the publicans and sinners),
but the father (God) and the older brother (the Pharisees
and scribes). This parable is directed to older brothers. Luke
15:2–3 states, "And the Pharisees and the scribes murmured, saying, 'This man receives sinners and eats with
them.' So he told them this parable. . . ." The parable of
the lost sheep, the parable of the lost coin, and the parable
of the gracious father follow. Jesus addresses these three
parables to the Pharisees and scribes who protest his offer
of divine forgiveness to the publicans and sinners, to
"prodigals." The emphasis of the parable comes at the end

where the Pharisaic attitude of the older brother toward the prodigal (the publicans and sinners) is rebuked by Jesus.

Similarly, the emphasis of the parable in Luke 16:19–31 comes at the end. It is true that there will be a reversal of roles in the hereafter: "So the last will be first, and the first last" (Matt. 20:16). But the emphasis in Luke's parable falls on the rejection by Jesus of a sign! Jesus says, "This generation is an evil generation; it seeks a sign, but no sign shall be given to it except the sign of Jonah" (11:29). Although the sign of one coming back from the dead would not force people to believe, if their hearts were open Moses and the prophets (and the life and teachings of Jesus) would suffice. On the other hand, if their hearts were closed, nothing would persuade them to believe. The resurrection of Jesus did not bring about a mass conversion to him. It is helpful to note the account of the resurrection of Lazarus (note the name!) in John 11–12 and the response of those whose hearts were closed.

> When the great crowd of the Jews learned that he was there, they came, not only on account of Jesus but also to see Lazarus, whom he had raised from the dead. So the chief priests planned to put Lazarus also to death, because on account of him many of the Jews were going away and believing in Jesus (John 12:9–11).

The greatest hindrance to faith in Jesus lies not in the mind's lack of knowledge, but in the heart's unwillingness to repent!

Another rule for interpreting parables is to realize that parables are not allegories. Parables teach one main point and the details should not be pressed for meaning. This does not mean that in some parables the details are not important. Clearly some parables such as the parable of the soils (Mark 4:3–9) and the parable of the evil tenants (Mark 12:1–11) contain details that are significant and that must be interpreted. In general, most parables, like any metaphor or simile, contain one main point of comparison. If their details are pressed, the analogy sooner or later breaks down. In the parable under discussion it is especially important not to press some of the details. If this is done an incorrect picture of the hereafter will be gained. Jesus was not seeking to teach his audience that heaven can be seen from hell (Luke 16:23). Nor was he teaching that the damned in hell can speak to Abraham in heaven (v. 24). It is not certain if being thirsty and in flames (v. 24) are literal in Jesus' understanding of life after death or are simply metaphors to describe the horrors of judgment and the final state for the unrighteous.

If the specific details in this parable are not pressed and its main point is studied, can our Lord's beliefs concerning life after death be understood? It would appear that this is possible. Jesus must have believed in certain realities pictured in this parable or the entire parable would be meaningless. In his parables he uses real-life, down-to-earth examples and analogies to make his points. It is true that the parables often include exaggeration (not all fathers are like the gracious father of the prodigal son), but Jesus' parables are not fables! They always portray real-life situations even when they contain unusual features.

Although certain aspects in the portrayal of the life to come may be exaggerated, the general portrayal of that life must generally agree with what Jesus believes. Jesus believes in life after death as evidenced in this parable and his teachings elsewhere.[23] Jesus clearly agrees with the Pharisees, not the Sadducees in this instance. The Pharisees believe in life after death; in particular in the resurrection of the body. The Sadducees did not believe in either.[24] The apostle Paul also gives clear evidence of the same belief of a conscious individual existence after death;[25] as does Peter (1 Peter 1:3–5; 4:6); the writer of Revelation (7:9–17; 19:1–21:27; 22:1–5); John (5:25–29); and the writer of Hebrews (12:22–23).

Additional aspects of Jesus' belief in the hereafter also can be obtained from the parable. He believes that both righteous and unrighteous exist in a conscious state of awareness after death and that for the former this is a state of great bliss (Luke 16:22, 25) and for the latter a place of great torment (vv. 24–25, 28). The state of the righteous (Lazarus) and the unrighteous (the rich man) as unchangeable seems to be suggested by Jesus (v. 26). Any other attempts to ascertain more of Jesus' (and Luke's) beliefs concerning life after death from this parable would probably be unwarranted.

In summarizing Jesus' teaching in this parable it must again be stressed that pressing the various details of the parable should be avoided. The main emphasis should be placed on the particular point Jesus makes. That point involves Jesus' rejection of the demand for a sign by his opponents. No amount of signs can produce faith if the heart is hard toward God. Even his own resurrection, and that of a different Lazarus in John 11, could not produce faith in the hearts of his opponents. When there is present a desire to know and a willingness to obey (John 7:17), then the Scriptures are sufficient for faith. Through the ministry of the Spirit, the truth of Scriptures is impressed in the minds of those whose hearts are open to the Gospel and faith results. Luke hoped this would result from Theophilus' reading of his Gospel (Luke 1:1–4) just as it did through the written Word and its interpretation to the Ethiopian eunuch (Acts 8:26-39) and through the proclamation and interpretation of the Word to the two disciples on the way to Emmaus (Luke 24:13–35).

"No one has ascended into heaven but he who descended" (John 3:13)

One passage in the Gospel of John that causes numerous interpretation problems is John 3:13. Jesus says to

Nicodemus "No one has ascended into heaven but he who descended from heaven, the Son of man." One major question frequently raised is: Does not the statement "No one has ascended into heaven but . . . the Son of man" conflict with the well-known fact that both Enoch (Gen. 5:24) and Elijah (2 Kings 2:1–12) ascended into heaven? Did Jesus or John err here? Another question that causes difficulty is: How could Jesus say "No one has ascended into heaven but he who descended [note tense!] . . ." since he had not yet ascended into heaven?

It should be noted that the first question tends to lose sight of the context of this verse. In John 3:12 Jesus states, "If I have told you earthly things and you do not believe, how can you believe if I tell you heavenly things?" The immediate context deals with the subject of divine revelation and the source of such revelation. If Nicodemus cannot understand and believe the more basic spiritual truths portrayed in the earthly analogies of birth and wind (the "earthly things") how can Jesus teach him more advanced spiritual truths (the "heavenly things")?[26] Where does such truth come from? Where does one learn of such heavenly things?

The human inability to ascertain divine truth, or the need for divine revelation, is not only a basic evangelical belief but was and is a basic belief of Judaism as well. The inability to bring down revelation from heaven is strongly attested to in the Old Testament as well as in the other Jewish literature.

> For this commandment which I command you this day is not too hard for you, neither is it far off. It is not in heaven, that you should say, "Who will go up for us to heaven, and bring it to us, that we may hear it and do it?" Neither is it beyond the sea, that you should say, "Who will go over the sea for us, and bring it to us, that we may hear it and do it?" But the word is very near you; it is in your mouth and in your heart, so that you can do it (Deut. 30:11–14).[27]

Your understanding has utterly failed regarding this world, and do you think you can comprehend the way of the Most High? (2 Esdras/4 Ezra 4:2)

We can hardly guess at what is on earth, and what is at hand we find with labor; but who has traced out what is in the heavens? (Wisdom of Solomon 9:16)

The Emperor also said to Rabban Gamaliel: "I know what your God is doing, and where He is seated." Rabban Gamaliel became overcome and sighed, and on being asked the reason, answered, "I have a son in one of the cities of the sea, and I yearn for him. Pray tell me about him." "Do I then know where he is," he [the Emperor] replied. "You do not know what is on earth, and yet (claim to) know what is in heaven!" he retorted (Sanhedrin 39a).

For the Judeo-Christian tradition, revelation, like salvation, is not a human achievement from below but a gift of God's grace from above!

This inability to attain the knowledge of God and his will by human effort is expressed idiomatically by the inability to ascend to heaven to acquire such truth. Whatever the original source for the expression (and it may be Deuteronomy 30:12), its frequent occurrence in Jewish literature reveals that it was a common idiom in Judaism.

Who has ascended to heaven and come down? (Prov. 30:4a)

. . . perhaps you would have said to me, "I never went down into the deep, not as yet into hell, neither did I ever ascend into heaven" (2 Esdras/4 Ezra 4:8).

Who has gone up into heaven, and taken her [wisdom], and brought her down from the clouds? (Baruch 3:29)

It is apparent that the thought in John 3:13 is a common expression: that no one has ascended into heaven in order to bring down the truth of God's nature and will. Enoch and Elijah were not exceptions. Their ascensions were of a totally different nature. They ascended but did not descend and the idiom always refers to, or at least implies, descending or returning to bring back knowledge of God. Enoch's and Elijah's ascension clearly had nothing to do with bringing divine revelation to mankind. (It should be assumed that both Jesus and John knew the Old Testament too well to make a simple historical blunder of this sort and that it is probable that they did not see Enoch or Elijah as exceptions to their statement.)

The only exception to the idiom that no one has ascended into heaven is, of course, Jesus, the Son of man, who descended from heaven. This then brings us to our second major difficulty with this passage. How can Jesus state that the Son of man ascended into heaven since his ascension had not yet taken place. His descension is not a problem. When he said these words he had already descended. The Word became flesh! But the ascension was in the future.

There have been numerous attempts to explain this difficulty:

1. Some scholars suggest that this reference speaks of Jesus' future ascension by way of anticipation. In other words, the passage uses a futuristic or dramatic aorist in which the past tense is used because of the certainty of the event which is about to take place. This is a possible use of the aorist tense, but is not a likely explanation.

2. One writer suggests that the term *ascended* should be understood metaphorically as referring to Jesus' experience at his baptism when he directly communed ("ascended") with God. This explanation presents two problems. First, it conflicts with the fact that the term *descended* in this passage is not to be understood

metaphorically. Second, no reader of John would have interpreted the term *ascended* in this way. For the early readers the natural reading of ascended would have been perfectly acceptable since Jesus indeed ascended into heaven.

3. Another possibility is that John 3:13 is not spoken by Jesus but is an interpretive comment by the Evangelist. The statement was true when he wrote. By then Jesus had ascended into heaven. In support of this interpretation is the well-known fact that it is impossible to know exactly where Jesus' words in John 3 end and the words of the Evangelist begin. If a red-letter edition of John were composed and red letters were used to indicate the words of Jesus, where would the red end? Would it end at verse 21, or 13? This question is impossible to answer. Furthermore, even if some of the verses after verse 13 should be red, this does not mean that verse 13 should not be interpreted as a parenthetical comment by the Evangelist and should therefore be in black!

4. A final possibility is that John 3:13 is an actual saying of Jesus (it should be colored in red) and that Jesus uses the future tense "shall ascend" because he had not yet ascended. John changed the tense "shall ascend" to "ascended" because when he wrote his Gospel Jesus had ascended into heaven. In other words, John changed the future tense of Jesus' saying to the past tense because the passage had been future for Jesus and is now past for John's readers. One of the last two explanations is probably correct.

"But of that day . . . no one knows . . . [not even] the Son" (Mark 13:32)

One of the most important christological passages in the Gospels is Mark 13:32. This passage also presents problems for many Christians. At the end of the Olivet discourse Jesus states: "But of that day or that hour no one knows, not even the angels in heaven, nor the Son, but only the Father." The importance of this verse is evident for two reasons. First, Jesus clearly distinguishes between himself as the Son and others. He makes a clear distinction between "no one" (mankind), the angels, and himself. He is the Son! Jesus states that he understood his Sonship as distinct and unique from his disciples and us. Others might become "sons of God" through faith and the receiving of the Spirit (Rom. 8:14; Gal. 3:26), but he was the Son of God by his very nature.[28] This passage is important because it demonstrates Jesus' self-understanding as the unique Son of God. Second, the passage is important because of its strong claim to authenticity. Even for skeptics who question whether the words found in the Gospels actually came from the lips of Jesus, this passage's authenticity is hard to deny. Who in the early church would create a saying in which the Son of God claims to be ignorant, and then place it on the lips of Jesus? The Apocryphal Gospels written in the second, third, and fourth centuries A.D. heighten the divine nature and miraculous ministry of Jesus to an absurd degree. (In these works the child Jesus commands trees to bend down, makes sparrows out of clay, stretches wood for Joseph, strikes people dead because they bump into him, etc.) To create a saying in which Jesus is ignorant of anything goes against this tendency to emphasize the divine nature of the Son of God at the expense of his humanity. Mark 13:32 must be an authentic saying of Jesus.

Another problem with this verse, which should assure its authenticity, is the question of how the Son of God, who was "very God of very God" according to the creeds and possessed unique knowledge,[29] could not have known the "day or that hour." One type of reasoning that raises this question is deductive logic:

Jesus was (and is) God.

As God, he must have possessed the attributes of God.

One of the attributes of God is omniscience.

Therefore Jesus, as God, possessed omniscience; he knew all things. This reasoning makes the passage difficult. The difficulty does not lie in the grammar of the passage and is not exegetical. On the contrary, the text can be interpreted only as a statement that the Son knows neither the day nor the hour of his return. The problem is clearly a theological one. How can this passage be interpreted to fit a particular theological understanding of the nature of Jesus' deity?

One solution is to say that Jesus may not know the exact day or hour but that he certainly knows the year or the month. This solution must be rejected. Any ignorance, whether the day or the hour or the minute or second, cannot be accepted if Jesus as the Son of God possessed divine omniscience during his ministry. Another attempted explanation is that in his human nature Jesus of Nazareth did not know the exact day or hour but that in his divine nature as the Son of God he does. Jesus is speaking with regard to his human nature in this passage. The problem with this solution is that Jesus is speaking of himself as the Son. It is as the unique Son of God, distinct from all others, that he does not know!

In this instance, rather than trying to make the passage fit a theological understanding of the divine nature of Jesus, a theological understanding of the divine nature of Jesus should fit the text! The text is clear. Jesus as the Son did not know the exact time of the end. No theological formulation of the natures of the Son of God possesses the authority that our text of Scripture possesses! Such formulations are not infallible but must always be judged by the Scripture. We need to make theological formulations fit Mark 13:32; not the reverse. Furthermore, no theological formulation about the natures of the Son of God is as simple to understand or as clear as this passage. The more complicated passages should be interpreted in the light of the clear and simple. In other words, more complicated theological summaries about the natures of the Son of God should be formulated in the light of clear and simple biblical statements.

In conclusion it may not be possible to know how Jesus could be "very God of very God" and not know the exact time of his return. It may not be possible to formulate exactly how both could be true, but the clear meaning of Mark 13:32 cannot be sacrificed to fit any formulation. Perhaps a clue for an understanding may be found in Philippians 2:6–11 which speaks of the emptying (kenosis) of the Son of God at the incarnation. However, the Son of God does not know when he will return, because he said so in Mark. Concerning the question of when the Lord will return, it does not require a great deal of humility for a Christian to say, "Just like Jesus I do not know exactly when the end will be." On the other hand, Jesus' words in this passage serve as a powerful rebuke of all who make such claims!

3

Actions of Jesus

Various actions of Jesus in the Gospels occasionally cause problems for the reader. In certain instances Jesus' actions seem inconsistent both with his actions and with his teachings elsewhere. Throughout the Gospels Jesus is portrayed as gently, loving, and kind. He is especially a friend to the poor and to the needy. However, several actions of Jesus, at first glance, appear cruel, harsh, and unkind.

Jesus' Cursing of the Fig Tree (Mark 11:12–14)

> On the following day, when they came from Bethany, he was hungry. And seeing in the distance a fig tree in leaf, he went to see if he could find anything on it. When he came to it, he found nothing but leaves, for it was not the season for figs. And he said to it, "May no one ever eat fruit from you again." And his disciples heard it.

The Gospels contain several instances in which Jesus appears to act in a way that seems out of character with his gracious and loving demeanor. Examples of this would be:

1. His destruction of the property of others in the case of the two thousand swine (Mark 5:11–13).

2. His apparent reluctance to heal the daughter of a Canaanite, or Gentile, woman (Mark 7:24–30).
3. His apparent unwillingness to permit a young man to honor his father by seeing that he receive a decent burial (Luke 9:59–60) or for another to bid farewell to his family (Luke 9:61–62).
4. His destruction or cursing of a fruitless fig tree (Mark 11:12–14, 20–25).

In the latter instance, this action of Jesus is particularly distasteful and a stumbling-block for many. One commentator remarks that this is the least attractive narrative about Jesus in the Gospels. It seems unworthy of him. Others deny its historicity because they cannot conceive of Jesus blasting a fruit tree simply because it did not have fruit for him. Some see this as a tale of miraculous power wasted in the service of an ill-tempered Jesus.

As a result, many commentaries deny this incident and claim that it is a fictitious miracle story which arose out of the parable of the unfruitful fig tree in Luke 13:6–9. Mark 11:12–14 becomes more difficult still with the explanatory comment, "for it was not the season for figs" (Mark 11:13). Such clauses are a favorite way for Mark to explain certain things to his readers.[1] Why would Jesus curse a fig tree if the fig tree could not bear figs at this time of year? Mark's explanatory comment, at first glance, not only does not help to understand Jesus' behavior; on the contrary, it makes it more difficult to understand.

The first thing that can be said in regard to Jesus' behavior is that to condemn the cursing of a single fig tree seems like a drastic measure for a society that consumes millions of trees for the production of pornographic materials. Can any person eating meat or fish, which demands the destruction of much higher forms of life, condemn the destruction of a single fig tree? Nevertheless, if Jesus in anger or rage cursed the fig tree for no good reason, then this action seems to stand in conflict with the general portrayal of Jesus in the New Testament. How can Jesus' behavior be explained?

No answer can be satisfactory if it does not take into consideration Mark's explanatory comment in verse 13 and the arrangement of the materials in Mark 11, 12, and 13. Mark's arrangement of this incident is different than Matthew's. Mark splits this story and places the cleansing of the temple between the two parts. This is a frequent stylistic feature of Mark, evidenced by Mark 3:19–21 and 31–35; 5:21–24 and 35–43; 6:6–13 and 30f.; 14:1–2 and 10–11.

In this instance Mark causes the cursing of the fig tree to "rub off" on the account of the cleansing of the temple. Jesus' cleansing of the temple is understood by Mark not as a reformation of the temple worship but as an act of judgment. The cursing of the fig tree is not an act of Jesus performed in rage against an innocent tree but a symbolic act. It is an acted-out parable, meant to teach his disciples the true meaning of the cleansing of the temple. Both are acts of judgment! The Messiah comes to his temple and instead of the fruit of righteousness he finds nothing but the dry leaves of sterile formalism and hypocrisy, and he judges it. The cursing of the fig tree serves as a symbolic act by which the disciples are to interpret what Jesus is about to do in the temple.

Support for this interpretation comes from observing the arrangement of materials in Mark 11:1–13:32. After the account of the cleansing of the temple (Mark 11:15–19), Mark 11:27–33 contains an account in which Jesus' authority to do this is questioned. The other two Gospels which contain accounts of the cleansing, Matthew and John, are followed by a similar account in which Jesus' authority to do this is questioned. Next, the parable of the wicked tenants (Mark 12:1–11) treats God's judgment on Israel. Mark places this account at this point to reinforce the point he seeks to make in Mark 11:12f. God is about to judge Israel. Immediately following this parable is a fourfold account of Jesus' controversies with his opponents, followed by the story of the widow's mites. Chapter thirteen contains the prophecies of Jesus concerning the destruction of Jerusalem (Mark 13:1–4). In chapters twelve and thirteen Mark gathers various materials to support his interpretation of the cursing of the fig tree and the cleansing of the temple. God is about to bring judgment on Israel.

Interpreting the cursing of the fig tree as an acted parable of the coming judgment also explains the difficult explanatory comment in Mark 11:13. Mark tells us that the cursing of the fig tree is not due to it being fruitless. It was not the time for figs! It must be due to another reason which he points out to his readers. Jesus acts out a parable of judgment for his disciples. The cursing reveals that the cleansing of the temple was an act of judgment! Judgment is coming on Israel. This judgment is further foretold and described in Mark 12:1–11 and 13:1–37.

The cursing of the fig tree ceases to be a problem with this interpretation. It is not an angry act of destruction but a parabolic act of Jesus. There is little difference between Jesus' use of the wood of this tree to symbolize a spiritual truth and in the use of wood to build a manger scene or the use of a cross to decorate the church. The cursing of the fig tree was not a senseless act of rage on the part of Jesus, but the use of a single tree to reveal the truth that judgment was coming. A tree used to teach the truth of God, whether that truth involves the portrayal of the grace of God or the coming judgment, need not be a stumbling block for the believer.

Jesus and the Syrophoenician Woman (Mark 7:24–30)

And from there he arose and went away to the region of Tyre and Sidon. And he entered a house, and would not have any one know it; yet he could not be hid. But immediately a woman, whose little daughter was possessed by an unclean spirit, heard of him, and came and fell down at his feet. Now the woman was a Greek, a Syrophoenician by birth. And she begged him to cast the demon out of her daughter. And he said to her, "Let the children first be fed, for it is not right to take the children's bread and throw it to the dogs." But she answered him, "Yes, Lord; yet even the dogs under the table eat the children's crumbs." And he said to her, "For this saying you may go your way; the demon has left your daughter." And she went home, and found the child lying in bed, and the demon gone.

Mark 7:24–30 and Matthew 15:21–28 contain accounts in which Jesus speaks to a Syrophoenician, or Canaanite, woman. The woman comes to Jesus and begs him to heal her daughter. To this request Jesus replies, "Let the children first be fed, for it is not right to take the children's bread and throw it to the dogs" (Mark 7:27).

The problem is obvious. Jesus' words appear harsh, austere, and insensitive. They seem atypical of Jesus. In the Gospels he is portrayed as kind, loving, and compassionate.[2] The words of Mark 7:27 would cause little difficulty coming from a mean, harsh, and unloving individual. The Jesus of the Gospels, however, is a loving and kind Jesus with special compassion for the outcasts of society and this Gentile woman is an outcast in the Jewish mind![3] The problem in the text is this apparent inconsistency of Jesus' words and behavior with his known character and teachings found throughout the Gospels. This inconsistency should alert us to the possibility that a superficial reading of this text may be incorrect.

A closer examination provides several reasons for not interpreting this text as harsh and unloving. First, neither Mark nor Matthew interpreted it that way. If they were convinced that this passage conflicted with the love of God manifested in Jesus Christ which they had written about in their Gospels, they would not have included this account. If they interpreted this passage as conflicting with the general picture of Jesus they describe in their works, they would have excluded it from their Gospels. After all, not everything which Jesus said and did is recorded in our Gospels (John 20:30–31; 21:25).

Second, the woman in this story is not deterred. She does not think that Jesus' reply is so negative that no response is possible. She senses that a response is possible, perhaps even expected, and she continues with the conversation. It is as if she sees in Jesus' reply a kind of riddle which challenges her to respond.

Third, Jesus' reply presents two terms which soften the apparent harshness of his words. The first is not apparent in the English translation. It involves the term *dogs*. In Greek the term is *kunaria*. If Jesus wanted to refer to wild stray dogs, scavengers, he would have used a different term, *kunes*. His use of the former term means that he is talking about pet household dogs or puppies, not curs. (The use of *kunaria* rather than *kunes* also reveals that the idea that for Jews all Gentiles were "dogs" should not be brought into this analogy. Gentiles were "dogs" in the sense of *kunes* not *kunaria!*) If the expression "dogs" is replaced with the expression "puppies," a great deal of the apparent harshness is removed.

The second term found in Mark's text is *first*. This implies that "puppies" can be fed after all. Jesus did not say, "Let the children *only* be fed. . . ." He said, "Let the children *first* be fed. . . ." This term also removes a great deal of the apparent harshness. Undoubtedly these terms provided encouragement for the Syrophoenician woman, and she continued to engage Jesus in conversation.

Finally, it should be noted that Jesus spoke with the woman prior to this point. The text states, "And he said to her" (Mark 7:27). The Greek verb used is *elegen*. This is the imperfect tense in Greek and indicates there is a running conversation between Jesus and the woman ("and Jesus was saying to her").[4]

The parallel account, Matt. 15:22–25, also indicates that this is part of a continuing dialogue between Jesus and the Syrophoenician woman. Jesus' words are not a one-line rejection of the woman's request. Mark 7:27 contains words spoken in the middle of a dialogue. The woman's response indicates that she, in light of this conversation, assumes that the dialogue is not over. The text seems to suggest that the woman senses that she is expected to respond to these words.

One of the unfortunate liabilities of written speech is the fact that the tone of voice cannot be recorded. In conversation a change in tone, a wink, a pause, or a smile suggest how the words are to be interpreted. This text uttered with a frown would mean something quite different than if it were uttered with a wink or a smile. The former would mean, "Be off! Don't bother me, for it is not right to take the children's bread and throw it to the dogs!" In the latter instance it would mean, "It is not right to take the children's bread and throw it to the dogs, is it? What do you think?"

In the absence of voice tone, these words of Jesus must be interpreted with any verbal hints the verse contains and in the context of Jesus' life and teachings. In light of the verbal hints mentioned above (the terms *puppies, first,* and *elegen*—"he was saying"), the response of the woman, and the character of Jesus found in this Gospel and all the Gospels, it seems best to interpret the text as a match of wits in which Jesus seeks to lead the Syrophoenician woman to a more persistent and deeper faith. This he accomplishes. Her reply, "Yes, Lord; yet even the dogs under the table eat the children's crumbs" (Mark 7:28) brings the following response, "For this saying you may go your way; the demon has left your daughter" (Mark 7:29).[5]

Jesus and Mary Magdalene After the Resurrection (John 20:17)

A final example of difficult actions of Jesus takes place on Easter morning. After Mary Magdalene recognizes Jesus, he says to her in John 20:17, "Do not hold me, for I have not yet ascended to the Father; but go to my brethren and say to them, I am ascending to my Father and your Father, to my God and your God." The difficulty lies in the fact that later Jesus bids Thomas, "Put your finger here, and see my hands; and put out your hand, and place it in my side; do not be faithless, but believing" (John 20:27).[6]

Why is Mary forbidden to "touch" Jesus (KJV) whereas Thomas, one week later, is not only permitted to touch Jesus but is invited to touch his wounds? The difficulty with this verse is compounded by the fact that Mary is not to touch or hold Jesus because he has not yet ascended to the Father. Thomas is invited to do so even though Jesus still has not ascended.

Numerous suggestions have been made on how to interpret this verse:

1. Mary is not to touch Jesus because his wounds have not yet healed.
2. Mary is not to touch Jesus in order that she not be ceremonially defiled by touching a "dead" body.
3. Mary holds on to Jesus in order to have him give her holy communion. She did not participate in the Last Supper along with the disciples.
4. Mary is not to touch Jesus because he left his grave clothes behind and is naked.
5. Mary is not showing sufficient respect to Jesus' glorified body.
6. The Greek text of John 20:17 has been amended or changed. Instead of reading "touch not" (*me haptou*), it is made to read "fear not" (*me ptoou*). According to this view an error was made by the Evangelist, or

someone before him, and Jesus' actual words were mistranslated in John 20:17.

7. Mary is not to hold on to Jesus because Jesus is not ascending to the Father immediately.

It often is easier to see incorrect interpretations of the passage than to discover the correct one!

First, it should be observed that the translation "Touch me not," (kjv) is not found in newer translations. The Revised Standard Version states, "Do not hold me"; the New International Version, "Do not hold on to me"; the New English Bible, the Jerusalem Bible, and the New King James Version, "Do not cling to me"; and the New American Standard Bible, "Stop clinging to me." The newer translations are clearly correct. The negative particle in the Greek text (me) used with a present imperative indicates a prohibition to stop doing something Mary is already doing. Mary is told by Jesus to "Stop clinging/holding me," not "Do not begin to touch me."

This command can be understood in one of two ways. First, the prohibition is tied closely with the command to go and tell the disciples. "Time is wasting away. Stop holding me, but go tell the disciples. . . ." This interpretation does not deal with the phrase, "for I have not yet ascended to the Father." This latter phrase is difficult. Does it imply that holding on to Jesus after his ascension would be acceptable? It would appear that after the ascension, holding the exalted Lord would be even more inappropriate.

Perhaps the best interpretation is: Mary has been clinging on to Jesus due to the joy that Jesus is indeed alive, that he has "revived." She sought to resume the former relationship that she had with the rabbi, Jesus of Nazareth. (Note Mary's address to Jesus in John 20:16 of "Rab-boni," or teacher.) But, Jesus has not simply been resuscitated; he has been raised from the dead and is now Lord![7] C. K. Barrett states, "Both by her address to Jesus as teacher, and physical contact, she is trying to recapture the past."[8]

The prohibition of Jesus is due to the mistaken understanding of Mary. With Thomas this was not a problem. John 20:28 reveals that he recognizes Jesus not as Rab-boni but as "My Lord and my God." The clause, "for I have not yet ascended to the Father," serves to reveal to Mary that the old relationship must give way to a new one. Jesus is now the risen Lord and must ascend into the presence of the Father. This passage can be paraphrased: "Mary, stop clinging to me. The situation has changed. I have been raised from the dead as Lord, and I am about to go to be with the Father. But go and tell the disciples. . . ."

4

Predictions of Jesus

The final chapter deals with three sayings of Jesus. These sayings were not discussed in chapter two, which deals with difficult sayings of Jesus, because they form a specific and unique category. These three sayings are predictions of Jesus which do not appear to have come to pass! All three predictions appear to refer to events that were to be fulfilled in Jesus' lifetime or at his resurrection. At first glance, at least, they were not.

Jesus' Being Three Days and Three Nights in the Heart of the Earth (Matt. 12:38–40)

> Then some of the scribes and Pharisees said to him, "Teacher, we wish to see a sign from you." But he answered them, "An evil and adulterous generation seeks for a sign; but no sign shall be given to it except the sign of the prophet Jonah. For as Jonah was three days and three nights in the belly of the whale, so will the Son of man be three days and three nights in the heart of the earth."

It is clear that Jesus rejects the call to perform various signs before the Jewish religious leadership in order to justify his claims and actions.[1] Jesus would not give them signs, however, for he did not come to be a wonder-worker but a Savior. Jesus performed many miracles in private and with a warning not to tell others about them.[2] Yet, one great miracle would be given as a sign. This would be the "sign of Jonah," his resurrection from the "heart of the earth."

The main problem encountered in Matthew 12:38–40 involves the temporal designation "three days and three nights." Interpreting this designation literally, some argue that Jesus was crucified on Thursday rather than Friday. A Friday crucifixion and a Sunday resurrection do not provide sufficient time for three days and three nights.

There are numerous ways of figuring out the day-night scheme for this period of time, but it is clear that three separate days and nights cannot be obtained by a Friday crucifixion and Sunday resurrection scheme. Yet, it is clear from the Gospels that Jesus was crucified on Friday, the ". . . day of Preparation, that is, the day before the sabbath" (Mark 15:42) and raised on Sunday, the ". . . first day of the week . . ." (Mark 16:2). If the temporal designation of Matthew 12:40 is taken literally, a conflict does exist between the time indicated in this verse and the time indicated in the accounts of the passion story.

But should the expression "three days and three nights" be interpreted literally? Three arguments indicate that it should not. First, it appears that this expression is another way of stating "on the third day" or "in three days." This can be illustrated from 1 Samuel 30:12–13. The same Greek expression is found in 1 Samuel 30:12 in the Greek translation of the Old Testament (the LXX) as in Matthew 12:40. Verse 13 refers to this three-day and three-night period as "three days ago" or, as the LXX literally states, "the third day today." If "three days and three nights" can mean "on the third day," there is no major problem in our passage. By Jewish reckoning Jesus could have been crucified on Friday and raised on Sunday, the third day. Friday afternoon = day one; Friday 6

P.M. to Saturday 6 P.M. = day two; Saturday 6 P.M. to Sunday 6 P.M. = day three.[3]

A second argument against a literal temporal interpretation is the fact that Matthew did not see any conflict between this expression and either a third-day resurrection (Matt. 16:21; 17:23; 20:19) or a Friday crucifixion and Sunday resurrection scheme (Matt. 27:62; 28:1). For him, as well as for the other Evangelists, expressions such as "three days and three nights," "after three days," and "on the third day" could be used interchangeably.

Finally, it should be pointed out that the main point of Jesus' analogy in Matthew 12:40 does not involve the temporal designation but the sign of the resurrection. Only one miracle or sign will be given to this evil and adulterous generation. That sign will be Jesus' resurrection from the dead. The temporal designation is much less significant. Perhaps Jesus refers to three days and three nights because this expression is found in the Old Testament passage which he wants to quote (Jonah 1:17).

Understood in the context of biblical Judaism, the designation "three days and three nights" poses no problem with the Friday crucifixion and Sunday resurrection scheme described in the passion narratives. It is only if a twentieth-century reckoning of time is imposed or if the idiomatic nature of this temporal designation is not understood that a problem appears.

Seeing the Angels Ascending and Descending Upon the Son of Man (John 1:51)

Another passage with a prediction of Jesus which does not appear to have taken place is John 1:51. "And he [Jesus] said to him, 'Truly, truly, I say to you, you will see heaven opened, and the angels of God ascending and descending upon the Son of man.'"

The problem in this verse is self-evident. Where, in the life of Jesus, is it recorded that angels literally ascend and

descend on him? Attempts to resolve this difficulty fall
into one of two classifications: (1) attempts to interpret this
passage literally; and (2) attempts to interpret this passage
metaphorically.

Several attempts have been made to establish a literal
interpretation of this verse. Some commentators see a
reference to the angels who ministered to Jesus during his
Temptation. However, there is no account of the Temptation in John. If this passage refers to the Temptation, it
would be expected the Evangelist would refer to such an
account. Furthermore, this verse refers to a future event
("you will see"). At this point in Jesus' ministry the
incident of the Temptation, which is only recorded in the
Synoptic Gospels, would be a past event.

Another "literal" interpretation has been to see a reference to the resurrection of Jesus. All four Gospels refer to
angels present at the empty tomb. Yet their presence does
not appear to fulfil the reference to the "angels of God
ascending and descending upon the Son of man." John
gives no hint that this verse refers to the resurrection.

A final literal interpretation is to see a reference to the
parousia, or second coming. Jesus' return is frequently
associated with accompanying angels.[4] The wording of the
text concerning angels "ascending and descending upon
the Son of man" seems strange if the *parousia* is meant and
John does not specifically refer to angels being present at
the *parousia*.

In the absence of any event in John, or in the Synoptic
Gospels, which resembles the fulfillment of a literal interpretation of this verse, it is not surprising that many
interpreters seek a non-literal or metaphorical meaning. It
is evident that John (and Jesus) were inclined to use
metaphorical language. The many "I am" sayings found
in his Gospel point this out.[5] It would not be surprising to
see that John interprets this passage in a metaphorical
way. This possibility is enhanced by the fact that this text
is a clear reference to Genesis 28:12, "And he [Jacob]

dreamed that there was a ladder set up on the earth, and the top of it reached to heaven; and behold, the angels of God were ascending and descending on it!" Apparently Augustine first made reference to this Genesis passage in which the same order of "ascending and descending" is found.

In the Genesis account this vision of Jacob is connected to a revelatory event. The God of Abraham and Isaac appears to Jacob and reveals that he will renew with him the covenant he made with Abraham and Isaac. This incident and vision of the angels ascending and descending upon Jacob is associated with revelatory matters. The Midrash Rabbah (an ancient Jewish commentary on Genesis) associates this passage with Sinai and with Moses and Aaron ("the angels of God") ascending ("Moses went up to God") and descending ("Moses went down from the mount").[6] It is not surprising that John 1:51 is frequently interpreted as a reference to the revelation of God in or to Christ.

There are other metaphorical interpretations of this verse. Some suggest that this verse refers to Jesus' baptism where heaven opens to Jesus and Jesus has direct access to the revelation of God. There are two strong objections to this interpretation. First, the Gospel of John contains no specific reference to Jesus' baptism. Again, such a reference would be expected if John interpreted the text in this manner. Second, the baptism of Jesus is a past event when these words are spoken and Jesus uses a future tense ("will see").

Another suggestion is that Jesus is the "gate of heaven,"[7] the place of God's grace upon earth, or the tent of God among men (John 1:14). Similarly, others interpret this text to mean that Jesus is the link between heaven and earth.[8] In a more general way this verse is interpreted as teaching that the Son of man is the "place" of the full revelation of God. It is in Jesus Christ that God fully manifests his glory and revelation. This latter interpretation seems attractive. It is clear that for John the glory of God is manifested in Jesus (John 2:11; 11:40). To behold Jesus in faith is to have an open door to heaven and to the revelation of God (John 14:8–31), even as Jacob in Genesis 28:12 had an open door to heaven and the revelation of God. It is not primarily in Jacob and the covenant God made with him that the greater revelation of God is now found. It is in Jesus, the Son of man, that such revelation is found.

This interpretation fits well the next account found in the Gospel of John. In John 2:1–11 Jesus performs his first miracle. John states, "This, the first of his signs, Jesus did at Cana in Galilee, and manifested his glory; and his disciples believed in him" (John 2:11). Metaphorically understood, the angels of God ascend and descend upon the Son of man as he manifests here (and on other occasions) his glory as the only begotten Son of God.

The Son of Man Coming During the Lifetime of the Disciples (Matt. 10:23)

The final passage causes numerous problems in its interpretation. In Matthew 10:23b Jesus states, "for truly, I say to you, you will not have gone through all the towns of Israel, before the Son of man comes." On this passage Albert Schweitzer based his view that Jesus expected the kingdom of God to come during his ministry. When it did not come he was greatly disappointed. As a result he sought to force God's hand and make him bring the kingdom only to be even more bitterly disappointed and cry out in despair on the cross, "My God, my God, why hast thou forsaken me!" (Matt. 27:46).

The problem that this text raises is clear. If Jesus is referring to his second coming and if this is said to his disciples as they are going out on a preaching mission (Matt. 10:1 and 5 give that impression), then the evangelical Christian encounters a real problem. The second coming obviously did not take place during the mission of the disciples!

Numerous attempts have been made to resolve this problem. It has been suggested that the "coming of the Son of man" could refer to: the spread of the gospel throughout the world; the gradual recognition of Jesus as King and the establishment of his reign on the earth; the fall of Jerusalem as a sign of Jesus' judgment upon unbelieving Israel; or the coming of the Spirit on the disciples during this mission. Calvin favored the latter explanation.[9]

All these attempts to alleviate this problem seek to do so at the expense of the clear meaning of the text. In light of the other references to the coming of the Son of man in Matthew, it is clear that this passage refers to the second coming of Christ.[10]

It is especially important to judge carefully the context in which this verse is found. Although Matthew 10:5–42 looks like a simple mission charge of Jesus to his disciples it is clearly more than this. Why would Matthew devote so much space to a mission charge to the disciples unless it had relevance for the church of his own day as well? Matthew understood that Jesus' instructions to the disciples were a pattern for his own day, and he took those instructions and added other teachings of Jesus spoken on other occasions. As a result Matthew 10:5 ("Go nowhere among the Gentiles, and enter no town of the Samaritans, but go rather to the lost sheep of the house of Israel.") is clearly a specific reference to this mission of the disciples during Jesus' ministry. After the resurrection the Christian mission is to all the world (Matt. 28:18–20).

Other relevant teachings that Jesus spoke elsewhere were included by Matthew in this mission charge. These include a section on persecution for the sake of Christ (10:16–25) and the conditions of discipleship (10:26–42). It is evident that the section in which the passage under consideration is found looks beyond the immediate situation of the disciples because: (1) the reference to appearing before governors and kings, for the disciples' mission was only to the lost sheep of Israel and not the regions of the Gentiles or Samaritans (10:5–6); and (2) the language of 10:17–18;[11] 10:19;[12] and 10:21–22[13] which portray not merely times of persecution but the time of the Great Persecution. Matthew therefore uses the mission of the disciples in Jesus' day as an opportunity to teach about future missions and persecutions that Christians will encounter for the cause of Christ.

This understanding of the arrangement of this chapter by Matthew is supported by the overall arrangement found in the Gospel of Matthew. Matthew arranged his Gospel carefully and quite artistically. He arranged the teachings (T) of Jesus into five blocks and surrounded them with six narrative (N) sections: N (1–4); T (5–7); N (8–9); T (10); N (11–12); T (13); N (14–17); T (18); N (19–23); T (24–25); N(26–28). From this arrangement it seems reasonable to conclude that the teachings found in these five blocks (one of which is Matthew 10) are collections of Jesus' teachings which Matthew arranged according to theme rather than chronology.

It appears reasonable to assume that Matthew 10:23b need not have been said to the disciples as they went out on their mission. It is a saying of Jesus that could have been said on a different occasion and brought into the present context of chapter ten by Matthew. In the immediate context of this verse, the theme involves persecution for the sake of Jesus. Interspersed with the warnings of such persecution are three words of encouragement and hope. The first involves the fact that the followers of Jesus need not be concerned at such times with the response they should give to their persecutors because the Holy Spirit will give them the words to say (10:19–20). (It should be noted that this is advice given to prospective martyrs and not to pastors for Sunday morning worship services!) The second word of encouragement is the passage under consideration (10:23b). The third word is the realization that in so suffering they will be following in the footsteps of Jesus (10:24–25).

Therefore, Matthew 10:23b should be interpreted not as a prediction that the Son of man will return before the disciples finish their mission to Israel, but as a word of encouragement in the context of future persecutions or especially in the context of the Future Persecution. It is clear that this is the way that Matthew understood this. He wrote his Gospel after the mission of the disciples and after Jesus' lifetime, and the Son of man had not yet come. It is unlikely that he interpreted this passage as a reference to the second coming during the ministry of Jesus.

Furthermore, how could the coming of the Son of man from heaven take place during the ministry of Jesus? Matthew believed that Jesus was the Son of man and the saying in the text refers to the coming of the Son of man while Jesus was still alive. Matthew clearly did not believe that Jesus told the disciples that before they finished their mission, the second coming would take place. Jesus had not yet ascended into heaven when he spoke these words.

It is true that certain critical scholars suggest that Jesus did not teach that he was the Son of man but that the Son of man was someone else. Therefore Jesus refers to that other Son of man's coming during his ministry. Such a reconstruction is a rejection of the present context of Matthew in favor of a hypothetically reconstructed one that can never be proven. It must assume that Jesus speaks of someone else as being the Son of man. The latter assumption is confronted with the fact that nowhere in the New Testament is there any indication that any writer understands that the Son of man is anyone other than Jesus.

It appears that Jesus' words (". . . for truly, I say to you, you will not have gone through all the towns of Israel, before the Son of man comes") are not a reference to the coming of the Son of man during the mission of the lifetime. The context suggests that another interpretation is preferable. This text can be interpreted as a word of promise and reassurance that during the Tribulation, as the believer flees from place to place, he will not run out of places to flee to. Before this takes place the Son of man will return![14]

Conclusion

In these four chapters various kinds of problems found in the Gospels are discussed. Certainly not all the problems or difficulties found in these four works are treated; and undoubtedly many readers would desire that a specific passage that troubles them would be discussed. This book attempts to treat a representative number of passages in the hope that they will typify the kind of problems encountered in reading the Gospels.

Many problems that arise in reading the Gospels are due to some basic misconception on the part of the modern-day reader. One major difficulty is that the reader often misunderstands the form of Jesus' teachings. He tries to interpret literally what to Jesus was a nonliteral literary form. An example of this is not recognizing the use of hyperbole or overstatement on the part of Jesus. The problems some readers have with regard to various teachings of Jesus such as his teaching on swearing (p. 71) or prayer (p. 85) is primarily due to interpreting literally what Jesus intends as an exaggeration for effect. Not recognizing Jesus' use of metaphor, as in the "sword" saying (p. 92), or the idiomatic nature of some of his teachings, as in the case of his reference to "three days and three nights" (p. 119), the "angels ascending and descending" (p. 121), or the phrase "lead us not into temptation" (p. 78) can also cause problems. Again, the difficulty does not lie in the saying but in the ability to understand what Jesus meant by the saying. The use of a symbolic action, as in the case of his cursing of the fig tree (p. 109), and the use of parables also creates problems for the reader. A tendency to allegorize the parables and press the details for meaning causes great confusion when parables such as the parable of the unjust steward (p. 88) or the rich man and Lazarus (p. 96) are interpreted. These troubles disappear when the parables are treated as teaching by way of analogy one main point.

Perhaps the greatest problem that the reader today faces when reading the Gospels is that he usually brings a preconceived notion of what the Evangelists should or must have done in writing these inspired works. Sometimes by reasoning backwards from a doctrine of Biblical inspiration it is easy to predetermine how the Evangelists must have written their works. For some Christians the doctrines of biblical infallibility and inerrancy require that all the material in the Gospels must be arranged in strictly chronological order with twentieth-century scientific goals. Yet is it possible to impose on the inspired Evangelists a modern sense of how they should have written? If it is believed that the Evangelists were inspired by God and are thus infallible and inerrant in all they wrote, should it not be possible to learn from them and by the way they wrote?

Great defenders of the faith, such as Augustine and John Calvin, understood that at times the material in the Gospels is arranged topically. The Evangelists often arranged their material according to subject matter rather than according to chronology. This is especially true of various teachings of Jesus which originally circulated as independent units. For them the truth of Jesus' beatitudes, metaphors, or parables, is not dependent on knowing exactly when they were uttered. As a result they were able to accept the topical arrangement of many of Jesus' teachings. If the believer accepts this truth, many of the difficulties encountered in the Gospels can be resolved. This is even more important if it is realized that the Evangelists arranged certain similar stories of Jesus, such as his miracles, in topical rather than chronological order. If this is accepted Christians need not postulate that Jesus raised Jairus's daughter from the dead on two separate occasions. We can simply acknowledge that the Evangelists placed this miracle of Jesus at different places in their Gospels.

Of all the kinds of problems encountered in the Gospels, the most evident and the most difficult are those in which parallel passages in various Gospels appear slightly different. It is not surprising that these difficulties have been dealt with the most in the history of the church and in this book. In fact the term *harmonize* is primarily used with this kind of problem where the difficulties in parallel passages are "harmonized."

If the Christian can accept that the Evangelists were permitted to be inspired interpreters of Jesus' teachings, and were not simply stenographers, numerous difficulties disappear. Thus the minor variations in wording—such as in the first beatitude (p. 28), or the change in audience of the parable of the lost sheep (p. 54)—no longer pose problems but are assets in seeking to understand the significance for today of such teachings of Jesus. Also, if the believer is aware that the Evangelists did not come out of a similar scientific training but sought to convey the infallible truth of God in a way that their readers could understand, then additional problems also disappear. As a result the mention or lack of mention of various messengers in the healing of the centurion's servant (p. 34), the telescoping of conversation in the raising of Jairus's daughter (p. 38), or the apparent difference in roof construction materials in the healing of the paralytic (p. 42) no longer pose major problems. It is satisfying to learn that great defenders of the evangelical faith such as Augustine and John Calvin came to similar conclusions.

No attempt has been made in this work to claim that the various explanations and interpretations given are infallible. God is infallible; scholars are not! A teacher or writer is infallible only to the degree that his teaching is in accord with the infallible teachings of God's Word. It is hoped that some of the solutions to difficult passages in the Gospels will help the reader. Even more than this, it is hoped that the method for treating such difficulties will be useful to the reader.

If some of the solutions suggested in this work do not seem to be honoring or truthful to the inspired Scriptures, then it is prayed that the reader will seek—like Augustine, Calvin, and other defenders of the faith—to devise a better solution that will be true to the Word of God.

However, remember two things. First, be true to the meaning of the text. Seek to understand the conscious meaning of the biblical author as it is expressed in the words of the text. Second, be open to the possibility that it may not be possible to understand or to explain a text. Such a confession is not necessarily the result of a weak doctrine of inspiration. It is a confession of human creatureliness.

The Scriptures are infallible because the writers were inspired by an infallible God as they wrote them. But understanding and attempted resolutions may not be inerrant because they come from fallible and fallen creatures. Humility at times forces Christians to confess that they do not have a completely satisfactory solution. Such a confession also believes that if sufficient information were available, this apparent difficulty could also be explained.

Part 2

Difficult Sayings in the Gospels

Introduction to Part 2

The age in which we live is properly described as a scientific one. Precision and exactness unknown in all the preceding millennia are our common everyday experience. Only a little over a decade ago the writer was given a very expensive Swiss watch with the usual twenty-one-jewel movement. It is a beautiful piece of machinery and engineering with finely adjusted parts. It possesses a great sentimental value and it keeps good time. In a week it loses (or gains) only a few minutes of time. Today he wears a quartz watch that cost less and has among its features electronic circuitry, an alarm which can be set not only for the time of day but for a specific day (or days) of the week, a stopwatch which can record two separate events to within a hundredth of a second, and an accuracy to within two minutes a year. The precision is impressive. Yet the atomic clock which is the modern-day standard for time is more impressive still. Using as its basis the vibration of the cesium atom (9,192,631,770 times a second), it is accurate to within one second every one thousand years! In medicine today surgery performed by lasers is so exact and so minute that the finest surgical knives of a few years ago appear as clumsy broadswords in comparison. Measurements are now so exact that they are no longer described in fractions of an inch or millimeter. The present standard is the wavelength of krypton 86 (1,650,763.73 per meter), and with the use of the laser we can now measure to a precision of a ten-millionth of an inch. No longer do we depend on the pendulum, gears, springs, or the yardstick for measurement, but we now depend instead on wavelengths and vibrations of atoms!

As a result of scientific advance, our culture is permeated with the desire and demand for accuracy and precision. This demand seeks to discover even more exact and finer yardsticks. The biblical world, by contrast, was a prescientific one. It had not the ability, the need, nor the desire for such accuracy. It was not concerned with distinguishing between fine shades of blue or various hues of red but with distinguishing between black and white. Its timepiece was the sun; its measuring device a cubit rod or a day's journey. In light of all this it is sometimes difficult for present-day believers to identify with the Bible because the Bible is prescientific. This does not mean that it is antiscientific, but simply that it is ascientific. It was written by people who were inspired but who were nonetheless unacquainted with the scientific values and abilities of our day and age. It was written by people who loved picturesque language, riddles, and analogies. They were a people who loved to exaggerate and tell stories.[1] What T. E. Lawrence said about the Arabs he worked with in the second decade of our century could probably be said also of the people of the Bible:

> In the very outset, at the first meeting with them, was found a universal clearness or hardness of belief, almost mathematical in its limitation, and repellent in its unsympathetic form. Semites had no half-tones in their register of vision. They were a people of primary colours, or rather of black and white, who saw the world always in contour. They were a dogmatic people, despising doubt, our modern crown of thorns. They did not understand our metaphysical difficulties, our introspective questionings. They knew only truth and untruth, belief and unbelief, without our hesitating retinue of finer shades.
>
> This people was black and white, not only in vision, but by inmost furnishing: black and white not merely in clarity, but in apposition. Their thoughts were at ease only in extremes. They inhabited superlatives by choice.[2]

The canonical writers clearly used exaggeration more than

did their contemporaries; in fact, "no Greek or Roman writer of antiquity equals the writers of the Old and the New Testaments in the use of exaggeration."[3] (Using the language of structuralism we might say that the biblical writers were especially fond of binary relations or binary sets.)

Yet exaggeration is not merely a prescientific phenomenon. It is present in our own culture as well. When a young man writes his sweetheart that in her presence his heart skips a beat and the stars sparkle more brightly, he is clearly exaggerating. Even if he is a cardiologist or an astronomer, in this context he eschews scientific precision for the hyperbolic language of lovers. The size of a fish is most likely to be exaggerated, even when it is reported by an engineer in the Bureau of Measurements; in describing his grandchildren a child psychiatrist is less likely to offer a precise psychiatric analysis than an exaggerated comment of a proud grandfather! In baseball we speak of a batter's having hit the ball a mile (or, to mix metaphors, having hit it a ton). In football we speak of pinpoint passing or kicking the ball out of the stadium. To unexpected guests who drop by we say that putting them up for the night is absolutely no trouble at all, even though we must run around the house to make arrangements. For the good student, flunking or "bombing" an exam may mean that he will receive only a B. The concert pianist who has given a poor performance may claim that he made a million mistakes. And when it comes to advertisements, who today does not believe that what is said is grossly exaggerated at best!

In communication of any kind one must be aware of the genre. Exaggeration is permissible and probably expected in fish stories, but not in automobile-repair manuals. The fish can be described as at least three feet long, but the sparkplug gap must be exactly 0.016 of an inch. Instantly and perhaps unconsciously we recognize that the fish story and the repair manual are two different genres, and we adjust our thinking accordingly. To further illustrate this point, we present here two separate pieces of correspondence.

Both are written by the same individual. Note how unconsciously and intuitively we adjust our approach to each of
them.

July 21, 1985

My dearest Joan,
   These last few days that we have been apart have been
the loneliest days of my life. I have not slept a wink since
you returned home. I cannot eat; my studies are meaningless; I cannot get any work done; and I cannot think
about anything but you. I feel that life has become meaningless when we are apart, and without you I would rather
be dead. I cannot wait until we are together again, for only
then will my heart begin to beat once more. I shall hold my
breath until I see you this weekend.

With all my love,
Bob

July 21, 1985

Dear Dr. Anderson:
   I have examined Mr. Smith, whom you referred to me
for cardiac evaluation because of his complaint of palpitations. On clinical exam he has a mid-systolic murmur
preceded by an early to mid-systolic click. Occasional
dropped beats occurred also. Electrocardiogram revealed no
abnormalities other than occasional atrial tachycardia. An
echocardiogram was also performed. Definite evidence of
a prolapsing or "floppy" mitral valve leaflet was found.
With this evidence I believe that Mr. Smith's palpitations
are due to paroxysmal atrial tachycardia related to his prolapsing mitral valve.

Sincerely yours,
Dr. Robert H. Stone

Here we have two examples of correspondence by Dr.
Robert H. Stone, an intern in cardiology. The first is a love
letter to his sweetheart. The same day he wrote a note to
another physician concerning the diagnosis of a patient. It
is evident that we have in these two writings two different
genres which require different methods of interpretation,
that is, different hermeneutics; for if we were to read both

writings in the same way, one of them would of necessity be misunderstood. The medical report is to be read literally. There is no exaggeration present; each line is to be read and interpreted as an exact scientific description of the physical condition of the patient. The purpose is to reveal precise cognitive information about the patient and his heart condition. The first letter, however, does not contain a single sentence that can be interpreted literally. Dr. Stone's heart has not skipped a single beat since he bade farewell to his beloved (literally, he does not have paroxysmal atrial tachycardia). He has, of course, been breathing regularly. Whatever may be his sleeping, eating, study, and work habits, it is certain that he has continued in all these activities. The medical analysis reveals that he is still very much involved in his work. Yet the recipient of Dr. Stone's love letter knows this, for she is aware that in love letters all sorts of exaggeration are not only permitted but expected. She realizes intuitively that the purpose of such a letter is not merely to reveal certain information but also to affect her emotions, and that this can be done far more effectively by the use of exaggerated and picturesque language. The second letter, on the other hand, purposely seeks to avoid all emotions and feelings in order to convey certain information with regard to Mr. Smith's heart.

In our discussion of exaggeration in the teachings of Jesus, we shall seek to do three things. In chapter 1 we will seek to establish that exaggeration is indeed present in the teachings of Jesus. We shall not seek in this work, however, to determine whether the various sayings of Jesus which are discussed are authentic. Rather we shall seek only to establish that certain sayings attributed to Jesus in the Gospels contain exaggeration. We shall leave to the reader the task of determining to what *Sitz im Leben* the individual sayings actually belong. Note, furthermore, that we have not entitled this work *Exaggeration in the Gospels,* because we shall not deal with exaggeration in the narratives in which these sayings of Jesus are found, nor with the overstatements of John the Baptist and others. In chapter 2 we shall seek to establish certain principles or guidelines for recognizing the presence of exaggeration in the teachings of Jesus (and in other literature as well). Finally, in chapter 3 we shall discuss the various purposes of exaggeration. With this knowledge we shall be better able to determine how Jesus' original audience would have reacted and how we today should understand and respond to such sayings.

It should be pointed out that recognizing literary devices in the biblical materials is not the same as treating the Bible purely as literature. Our aim lies far beyond reading the Bible purely as literature, far beyond the pursuit of literary insight and enjoyment, for it is not possible to respond to the message and challenge of Jesus simply by understanding its literary form. The proper response to MARK 8:35 (''For whoever would save his life will lose it; and whoever loses his life for my sake and the gospel's will save it'') is not recognition that the form of this saying is antithetical parallelism. Nor is the proper response to LUKE 14:26 (''If any one comes to me and does not hate his own father and mother and wife and children and brothers and sisters, yes, and even his own life, he cannot be my disciple'') that we have here an example of overstatement. Surely a confrontation with the message of Jesus demands obedience rather than scholarly description, submission rather than mere literary definition! For those who see in the Bible the Word of God, it is impossible to treat the Bible with antiseptic objectivity as mere literature. For the Christian ''it is almost fantastic to suppose that one might read [the Bible] without recognizing that it was written not out of joy in the sonorousness of its own language, out of pleasure in its own literary quality, but because it wanted to say something about God and his works, God and his dealings with man.''[4] Therefore, our discussion of the exaggerated nature of certain sayings of Jesus should not be construed as suggesting that recognition of various passages as overstatement or hyperbole is an end in itself. Rather, this is only one step in the entire hermeneutical process. Our purpose in developing an ability to recognize and understand exaggeration is to hear the message of Jesus (and the Evangelists) more clearly. Our goal is to understand more plainly what

Jesus meant by these words and what their significance is for us today. Unless we come to this point in our investigation of the teachings of Jesus, all our efforts and research will be a mere exercise in literary criticism and will profit us little, for we shall not have heard the Word of God.

5

Exaggeration in the Teachings of Jesus

Within the four canonical Gospels we find numerous occasions of exaggeration on the lips of Jesus. At times the exaggeration is hyperbolic in that what is commanded or portrayed is literally impossible or inconceivable. At other times the exaggeration is more of an overstatement in that what is commanded or portrayed is possible or conceivable, but a literal fulfilment or enactment would be contrary to the intention of Jesus. For our purpose this distinction between hyperbole and overstatement is of no major importance since both are forms of exaggeration in the teachings of Jesus.

Perhaps the clearest way in which we can see Jesus' use of exaggeration is to place side by side, to the degree that this is possible, examples of exaggeration and literal statements which are related in theme.

Why do you see the speck that is in your brother's eye, but do not notice the log that is in your own eye? Or how can you say to your brother, "Let me take the speck out of your eye," when there is the log in your own eye? You hypocrite, first take the	If your brother sins against you, go and tell him his fault, between you and him alone. If he listens to you, you have gained your brother. But if he does not listen, take one or two others along with you, that every word may be confirmed by

log out of your own eye, and then you will see clearly to take the speck out of your brother's eye. [MATT. 7:3–5]	the evidence of two or three witnesses. If he refuses to listen to them, tell it to the church; and if he refuses to listen even to the church, let him be to you as a Gentile and a tax collector. [Matt. 18:15–17]

The saying found in Matthew 18:15–17 has frequently been seen as being nonauthentic due to its proleptic reference to the church. This assumption can be debated. But even if this were a saying that came to the Evangelist not so much from the historical Jesus as from the risen Christ, it nevertheless demonstrates by its more literal character the exaggerated nature of MATTHEW 7:3–5. The saying in Matthew 18:15–17 is not meant to be understood as an exaggeration. On the contrary, there is provided here a clear step-by-step procedure that the individual is to follow in the community of faith. Far from being impossible (hyperbolic), the procedure by which a wronged believer is to seek reconciliation with his fellow believer ("brother") seemed quite obvious to the leaders of the early church, for in their commentaries on this passage we find little or no allegorical interpretation. The words were understood and applied quite literally.[1] On the other hand, the impossibility of carrying out MATTHEW 7:3–5 and the existence here of hyperbolic language are immediately evident. Logs simply cannot fit in human eyes! The image is indeed powerful and impressive, but it is not at all literal. Its very exaggeration forcefully confronts the hearer with the demand of Jesus.

With regard to the need of repentance as a requirement for entering the kingdom of God we can compare the following statements:

If your right eye causes you to sin, pluck it out and throw it away; it is better that you lose one of your members than that your whole body	There were some present at that very time who told him of the Galileans whose blood Pilate had mingled with their sacrifices. And [Jesus] an-

be thrown into hell. And if your right hand causes you to sin, cut it off and throw it away; it is better that you lose one of your members than that your whole body go into hell. [MATT. 5:29–30]

swered them, "Do you think that these Galileans were worse sinners than all the other Galileans, because they suffered thus? I tell you, No; but unless you repent you will all likewise perish. Or those eighteen upon whom the tower in Siloam fell and killed them, do you think that they were worse offenders than all the others who dwelt in Jerusalem? I tell you, No; but unless you repent you will all likewise perish." [Luke 13:1–5]

In MATTHEW 5:29–30 the act of turning away from sin is portrayed as the plucking out of one's right eye or the cutting off of one's right hand. That the saying is an example of overstatement (exaggeration which is literally possible) rather than hyperbole (exaggeration which is literally impossible) is evident from the tragic fact that in the history of the church these words have on occasion been literally carried out! Yet certainly Jesus did not intend a literal observance of his words, for the removal of the right eye does not prohibit the left eye from continuing to look lustfully. Even the removal of both eyes cannot prohibit lust! Such self-mutilation was not practiced by those who heard Jesus, for they knew that the language he used was meant to effect change and impress upon them the need to repent rather than to describe literally how repentance is to be carried out. On the other hand, the commands to repent in Luke 13:3 and 5 were and are to be understood as literal commands, for Jesus continually preached, "Repent, for the kingdom of heaven is at hand" (MATT. 4:17).

In the Sermon on the Mount we find placed next to each other sayings on prayer that are in one instance exaggerated and in the other quite literal:

And when you pray, you must not be like the hypocrites; for they love to stand and pray in the synagogues and at the street corners, that they may be seen by men. Truly, I say to you, they have their reward. But when you pray, go into your room and shut the door and pray to your Father who is in secret; and your Father who sees in secret will reward you. [Matt. 6:5-6]

And in praying do not heap up empty phrases as the Gentiles do; for they think that they will be heard for their many words. Do not be like them, for your Father knows what you need before you ask him. Pray then like this:

Our Father who art in
   heaven,
Hallowed be thy name.
Thy kingdom come,
Thy will be done,
   On earth as it is in
     heaven.
Give us this day our daily
   bread;
And forgive us our debts,
   As we also have
     forgiven our debtors;
And lead us not into
   temptation,
   But deliver us from evil.
[MATT. 6:7-13]

In reacting to the practice of certain hypocrites who prayed both in church (literally, the synagogue) as well as in public places in order to appear as devout and pious men, Jesus tells his followers that true prayer is not a performance for others to see. He remarks ironically that those who pray in this manner have already received their due. The only thing their prayer achieves is recognition by others that they are praying and that they are, supposedly, devout men. God, however, ignores such prayer! Jesus' followers are to pray not in order to be seen by others, but in order to be heard by God. They are therefore to pray in their inner room (probably the storeroom of their home) with the door shut. Then, although unnoticed by men, their prayers will be heard by God. Every Jew who heard Jesus say these words would have known immediately that this statement is an exaggeration. They knew that at both the synagogue and temple there were times of corporate prayer in which they were to take part, and they also knew that they could pray to God anywhere at any time. They had, furthermore, seen Jesus pray—both privately (MATT. 14:23) and publicly (MATT. 19:13)—on occasions when he was not in an inner room.

The teachings on prayer in MATTHEW 6:7-13, on the other hand, are quite literal in character, and, indeed, the church from its inception used the Lord's Prayer corporately in worship. Note the first-person plurals in this prayer: they reveal clearly that the prayer is not to be uttered privately in one's room but corporately with other believers. These plurals are also found in the Lukan version of the prayer (cf. LUKE 11:2-4). It is quite clear, therefore, that Jesus' words about praying in private in one's inner room, given as they were in reaction to the hypocritical practice of some religious leaders, were intended to be an impressionistic portrayal of the kind of prayer that is acceptable before God; they were not meant to be taken as a literal command that his followers should pray only behind closed doors. No, the point Jesus was making was that personal prayer is not to be a stage performance for the sake of an audience and their adulation, but rather is to be a private communion with the Father.

Two declaratory statements regarding the future likewise exemplify the difference between a literal and an exaggerated remark:

And Jesus said to him, "Do you see these great buildings? There will not be left here one stone upon another, that will not be thrown down." [MARK 13:2]

Nothing is covered up that will not be revealed, or hidden that will not be known. [LUKE 12:2]

In Jesus' statement that one day all things will be made manifest, nothing remaining secret, we have a confession of a general Jewish belief and principle, for Jesus' audience readily agreed that the day will come when God, who knows the secrets in the hearts of all people (Ps. 139; Dan. 2:20–23, 27–30), will judge the world. This both Jesus and his audience believed would literally take place. As for the saying concerning the great buildings of Jerusalem, doubtless most would agree that the horrors of A.D. 70 when the Roman armies under Titus destroyed Jerusalem fulfilled these words. The destruction was so massive and extensive that the Tyropoeon Valley simply disappeared as it was filled in with the rubble of the city, the temple, and the temple mount. Yet even today one can see in Jerusalem at the Wailing Wall of the temple mount some of the very courses of Herodian foundation stones to which Jesus referred. Not all of the stones were separated from each other. Some stones even today remain upon each other! MARK 13:2 has not, then, been literally fulfilled. Yet surely no one would deny that the meaning of the words of Jesus was indeed fulfilled in a most horrible way in A.D. 70. MARK 13:2 is an impressionistic saying which uses exaggeration in order to depict in a vivid manner the temporalness of all human monuments and the horror of the destruction that Jerusalem would soon experience. (If an individual were to state that on January 15, ten years from now, an earthquake will destroy the Empire State Building, so that not a single brick will remain attached to another, and if on that very day an earthquake does occur and the Empire State Building collapses into a huge heap of rubble, certainly no one would claim that the prediction has not actually been fulfilled simply because two bricks still cemented together might be found lying in the rubble!)

Within the Sermon on the Mount there are a number of sayings which deal with the subject of forgiveness. Two of them illustrate once again the difference between a statement which is to be interpreted literally and one which is to be understood as using exaggeration:

So if you are offering your gift at the altar, and there remember that your brother

For if you forgive men their trespasses, your heavenly Father also will forgive you;

has something against you, leave your gift there before the altar and go; first be reconciled to your brother, and then come and offer your gift. [Matt. 5:23–24]

but if you do not forgive men their trespasses, neither will your Father forgive your trespasses. [Matt. 6:14–15]

In the first of the six antitheses of the Sermon on the Mount ("You have heard that it was said . . . but I say to you . . .") Jesus deals with the subject of murder and anger. In light of Matthew 5:17–20 it is clear that Jesus here does not reject but intensifies the Old Testament commandment concerning killing (Exod. 20:13): he includes in this commandment prohibition of anger and hatred as well as murder. The believer is always to seek reconciliation with his fellow believer (literally, brother). If in offering a sacrifice in the temple he remembers that a fellow believer has been offended by or is angry with him, he is to leave his gift at the altar, search out and be reconciled to his brother, and then return to offer the gift. But how many of Jesus' audience actually lived close enough to the temple in Jerusalem to fulfil this command literally? The Galileans who heard these words immediately realized that Jesus did not expect them, in such an event, to leave their gift at the altar (what if it were a lamb or goat?), go home to Galilee, seek reconciliation, return to Jerusalem in the hope that the gift would still be before the altar, and then offer it. Furthermore, a literal fulfilment of these words would be even more impossible for Jews from the Diaspora. The listeners therefore understood that the intent of Jesus' words did not lie in their literal meaning but rather in the general principle that one should not come into the presence of God without a willingness to seek reconciliation with one's brother.

On the other hand, the statement in Matthew 6:14–15 is to be taken literally. Whoever would seek the forgiveness of God must be willing to forgive others. Even as the experience of God's love causes the believer to love (1 John 4:19), so the contrition and repentance necessary for forgiveness cause us to forgive others who may be indebted to us (Matt.

18:23–35; Mark 11:26, LUKE 6:37). One cannot reach out with open hands to God for forgiveness and at the same time have a closed fist toward one's brother or neighbor. The words of Jesus in Matthew 6:14–15 are not an exaggeration. This teaching is literally true, and those who claim to take the teachings of Jesus seriously had best take these words at face value. Jesus intended that they be interpreted literally!

Within the Gospels are found numerous proverbial sayings of Jesus. In the next chapter we shall discuss various literary forms which are prone toward exaggeration, and we shall find that proverbs are clearly one of these forms. Because of the absolute manner in which they are usually stated, many proverbs which teach religious principles or truths are actually overstatements. Of the proverbs given below some require a rather literal interpretation and others demand that we recognize the presence of exaggeration.

Then Jesus said to him, "Put your sword back into its place; for all who take the sword will perish by the sword." [Matt. 26:52]

And Jesus said to them, "A prophet is not without honor, except in his own country, and among his own kin, and in his own house." [MARK 6:4]

And he said to them, "Take heed, and beware of all covetousness; for a man's life does not consist in the abundance of his possessions." [Luke 12:15]

You are the light of the world. A city set on a hill cannot be hid. [Matt. 5:14]

In comparing these four proverbs it appears that Luke 12:15 and Matthew 5:14 permit a rather straightforward, literal interpretation. Life does involve more than accumulation of possessions. Almost everyone would recognize that, to varying degrees, other factors are important: family, fame, power, influence, food, health. Very few in Jesus' audience would have claimed that all that matters in life is the possession of material goods. As for Matthew 5:14, it is simply a fact that cities built on the tops of hills cannot be hid. Jesus' audience would readily have acknowledged this. (Bear in mind that the people of that day were not acquainted with modern techniques of camouflage.)

On the other hand, it is also clear that while the proverb in Matthew 26:52 is generally true, not all who take the sword do indeed perish by it. On the contrary, some have found the sword quite profitable. Through service in war or as mercenaries, some people have obtained great wealth or power (perhaps even both). It is also the case that some great religious leaders during their lifetimes have been recognized and honored by their neighbors and relatives. This may indeed be rare, but it nevertheless does happen. The very fact that with regard to Matthew 26:52 and MARK 6:4 people can say, "Yes, that's true, but what about _____?" indicates that these proverbs are overstatements of general truths.

Although not closely related in theme, the two following examples show again the contrast between exaggerated and literal speech:

Again you have heard that it was said to the men of old, "You shall not swear falsely, but shall perform to the Lord what you have sworn." But I say to you, Do not swear at all, either by heaven, for it is the throne of God, or by the earth, for it is his footstool, or by Jerusalem, for it is the city of the great King. And do not swear by your head, for you cannot make one hair white or black. Let what you say be simply "Yes" or "No"; anything more than this comes from evil. [Matt. 5:33–37]

Whatever house you enter, first say, "Peace be to this house!" And if a son of peace is there, your peace shall rest upon him; but if not, it shall return to you. And remain in the same house, eating and drinking what they provide, for the laborer deserves his wages; do not go from house to house. . . . But whenever you enter a town and they do not receive you, go into its streets and say, "Even the dust of your town that clings to our feet, we wipe off against you." [LUKE 10:5–7, 10–11]

Even though there have been those who have interpreted

both of these passages quite literally, the early church fathers understood that these passages are not to be treated in the same manner. They recognized correctly that Matthew 5:33–37 is not to be understood as a literal prohibition against ever taking an oath. On the contrary, Augustine suggested, in light of the example of Paul in Romans 1:9 and Galatians 1:20, that Jesus was teaching that it is better not to swear and to tell the truth than to swear and to commit perjury. There is no sin in swearing to what is true, but due to our weak hearts we will best preserve ourselves from perjury by not swearing at all.[2] (For a number of additional indications that Jesus' teaching on oaths is an overstatement, see pp. 166–68, 169–70.)

On the other hand, the early church fathers interpreted quite literally Jesus' instructions on how itinerant preachers should conduct themselves in an unresponsive city. Hilary, for instance, explained that by wiping off the dust from their feet, missionaries would leave behind everything that belonged to the houses which they had entered.[3] Today, of course, the customs, dress, and general situation have changed considerably, so that a literal wiping off the dust from one's feet would be meaningless and impractical, but the audience of Luke (and Matthew—see the parallel account in MATT. 10:11–15) interpreted these words quite literally, even as Jesus' original hearers did.

There are times when even within a single pericope we find side by side examples of exaggeration and literal language. One such passage speaks of the danger that riches may cause to the individual:

Children, how hard it is to enter the kingdom of God! It is easier for a camel to go through the eye of a needle than for a rich man to enter the kingdom of God. [MARK 10:24b–25]

How hard it will be for those who have riches to enter the kingdom of God! [MARK 10:23]

There has been little difficulty in the past in interpreting verse 23 literally, since most scholars have agreed that riches do indeed pose a grave barrier to serving God. The biblical writer can even say that "the love of money is the root of all evils; it is through this craving that some have wandered away from the faith and pierced their hearts with many pangs" (1 Tim. 6:10). The hyperbolic nature of MARK 10:25, however, has resulted in a number of attempts to soften the force of this statement. Some have suggested that the Greek term *kamēlos* ("camel") should actually read *kamilos*, that is, "cable." The most common attempt to explain away the hyperbolic nature of this verse has been to claim that "the eye of a needle" refers to a small gate in the walls of Jerusalem through which a camel could barely pass. Such attempts are intended to rescue the saying from error, for whereas a camel cannot go through the eye of a (sewing) needle, some rich people do indeed enter the kingdom of God (see MATT. 27:57; MARK 15:42–46; Luke 8:1–3; 19:1–10 [esp. v. 2]). Such attempts to rescue this saying, however, are neither necessary nor helpful. There are several indications that the saying refers to a literal camel and a literal needle. First, the reaction of the disciples in MARK 10:26 indicates that they understood the saying as meaning that it is not merely difficult, but impossible for a rich person to enter the kingdom of God. Second, according to the textual evidence for Mark, and especially for Matthew and Luke, the best reading is "an eye of a needle," not "the eye of the needle." This indicates that we have here a general reference to sewing needles and camels rather than a specific reference to a particular gate in the walls of Jerusalem—"The Eye of the Needle." Finally, it should be noted that there exist several rabbinic sayings about an elephant's going through the eye of a needle.[4] What we have in our text, then, is a well-known idiom for great difficulty. Once we understand that Jesus' words are idiomatic and hyperbolic in nature, the attempts to explain them away become unnecessary.[5]

Finally, we will compare two of the ethical teachings of Jesus. At first glance it appears that Jesus is contradicting himself in his teachings here, but this, as we shall see later, is itself a clue that one of these sayings is an exaggeration.

If any one comes to me and does not hate his own father and mother and wife and children and brothers and sisters, yes, and even his own life, he cannot be my disciple. [LUKE 14:26]

And one of the scribes came up and heard them disputing with one another, and seeing that he answered them well, asked him, ''Which commandment is the first of all?'' Jesus answered, ''The first is, 'Hear, O Israel: The Lord our God, the Lord is one; and you shall love the Lord your God with all your heart, and with all your soul, and with all your mind, and with all your strength.' The second is this, 'You shall love your neighbor as yourself.' There is no other commandment greater than these.'' And the scribe said to him, ''You are right, Teacher; you have truly said that he is one, and there is no other but he; and to love him with all the heart, and with all the understanding, and with all the strength, and to love one's neighbor as oneself, is much more than all whole burnt offerings and sacrifices.'' And when Jesus saw that he answered wisely, he said to him, ''You are not far from the kingdom of God.'' And after that no one dared to ask him any question. [MARK 12:28–34]

Although in our own day there are certain religious sects that have interpreted LUKE 14:26 quite literally and taught their converts to hate their parents, it is clear that this verse cannot be taken at face value. Exactly what Jesus meant by this saying may, at first glance, be somewhat unclear, but it is inconceivable that he intended for these words to be taken as meaning that his followers should literally hate their parents, wives, children, brothers, and sisters. Intuitively we know that this saying is not to be taken literally. Its very oddness constrains us to take a second look.[6] In the next chapter we shall discuss how and why the mind intuitively comes to this conclusion; for the present we need point out only that LUKE 14:26 is not a literal statement but an exaggerated one. On the other hand, the summary of the law given by Jesus in MARK 12:28-34 has universally been understood as being a literal and definitive statement of the essence of the Old Testament commandments. It was so understood not only by the apostles Paul (Rom. 13:8-10; Gal. 5:14) and James (2:8), but by the early church as well (Didache 1:2; 2:7; Barnabas 19:5; Gospel of Thomas 25).

The purpose of this chapter has been to call attention to the existence of exaggeration in the teachings of Jesus found in the canonical Gospels. Other examples could have been given, but after a certain point this becomes unnecessary, for our purpose in this chapter has not been to list all the examples of Jesus' use of exaggeration, but rather to demonstrate that such exaggeration truly exists.[7] While there may be debate as to the extent of exaggeration in the teachings of Jesus and as to the presence of exaggeration in a particular saying, the conclusion that Jesus did in fact use exaggeration in his teaching is inescapable.

6

Recognizing Exaggerated Language

There exist a number of helpful principles or canons by which one can detect if exaggeration is present in the teachings of Jesus. Most of these canons are also applicable in detecting the presence of exaggeration in other literature as well. Not all of them are, of course, equally valuable and not all are applicable in every instance. We shall also have to accept the fact that whereas it may be clear in certain instances that Jesus is using exaggeration, we may at other times not be certain whether Jesus is in fact using exaggeration or whether the magnitude of his actual demand only makes it look like exaggeration. We must be continually on our guard lest by carelessly labeling Jesus' calls to decision as examples of exaggeration, we water down their absolute nature. With this needed caution in view, we will find the following canons useful in detecting exaggeration in the sayings of Jesus.

CANON 1. A statement which is literally impossible may contain exaggeration

We have already divided Jesus' use of exaggeration into the two classifications of hyperbole and overstatement, and we have explained that whereas in overstatement the saying can be literally understood or literally carried out, in the

157

case of hyperbole it cannot. Teachings can be impossible or hyperbolic in at least two ways: they can be physically impossible or they can be logically impossible. The particular teachings of Jesus which are physically impossible are simply inconceivable in light of our understanding of physical reality. Even in a world-view that accepts the supernatural, certain teachings of Jesus are clearly impossible; their impossibility was just as obvious to the original audience as it is to a present-day audience. In the case of logical impossibilities, we are dealing with intellectual or theological assertions that contradict logic or our basic understanding of God.

We can best demonstrate the difference between physical and logical impossibility by means of examples. Two examples of the former are:

> Why do you see the speck that is in your brother's eye, but do not notice the log that is in your own eye? Or how can you say to your brother, "Let me take the speck out of your eye," when there is the log in your own eye? You hypocrite, first take the log out of your own eye, and then you will see clearly to take the speck out of your brother's eye. [MATT. 7:3–5]

> Woe to you, scribes and Pharisees, hypocrites! for you tithe mint and dill and cummin, and have neglected the weightier matters of the law, justice and mercy and faith; these you ought to have done, without neglecting the others. You blind guides, straining out a gnat and swallowing a camel! [Matt. 23:23–24]

The impossibility of there being a log in a person's eye or of swallowing a camel is self-evident. Logs are simply too big to fit into a human eye and camels likewise too big to swallow. The hyperbole in these two passages serves to make Jesus' warnings against critically judging others and against religious hypocrisy most forceful and memorable.

Another example of a statement which is physically impossible to carry out is Matthew 6:2–4:

> Thus, when you give alms, sound no trumpet before you,

as the hypocrites do in the synagogues and in the streets, that they may be praised by men. Truly, I say to you, they have their reward. But when you give alms, do not let your left hand know what your right hand is doing, so that your alms may be in secret; and your Father who sees in secret will reward you.

How can one keep one's left hand from knowing what the right hand is doing? What can a hand know anyway? It is with the mind that a person knows. The hand has no means of knowing. Actually the saying is paradoxical in that Jesus tells us to make a conscious effort ("do not let") not to know what we are consciously doing (giving alms)!

One cannot help but think here of the similar use of hyperbolic language in the Old Testament. When God promised Abraham, "I will multiply your descendants as the stars of heaven and as the sand which is on the seashore" (Gen. 22:17), Abraham understood the exaggerated nature of the promise, for although he may not have known the total number of the stars in the heavens, he did have some idea of how much sand was on the seashore. Another example of a physical impossibility can be found in Isaiah 66:24, where the Lord says in judgment:

And they shall go forth and look on the dead bodies of the men that have rebelled against me; for their worm shall not die, their fire shall not be quenched, and they shall be an abhorrence to all flesh.

To have the worm present in a description of the judgment of the unrighteous is understandable; to have unquenchable fire present is likewise understandable; but to have both present together is not, for the fire would kill the worm. To claim that Isaiah conceived of a new kind of worm, an asbestos worm as it were, is to miss the point. The worm and the unquenchable fire are two well-known metaphorical portraits of judgment.[1] Placing them side by side simply reinforces Isaiah's proclamation of the certainty of the judgment. Additional Old Testament examples of physical impossibilities can be found in 2 Samuel 1:23; Job 38:7;

Psalm 19:1–4; Lamentations 2:11; and Amos 9:2–3.
Hyperbole can also be detected in instances of logical
impossibility:

> All things are possible to him who believes. [Mark 9:23]

> Think not that I have come to abolish the law and the proph-
> ets; I have come not to abolish them but to fulfil them. For
> truly, I say to you, till heaven and earth pass away, not an
> iota, not a dot, will pass from the law until all is accom-
> plished. [Matt. 5:17–18]

> You, therefore, must be perfect, as your heavenly Father
> is perfect. [MATT. 5:48]

The first example is clearly hyperbolic in that all things are
simply not possible for the believer. He cannot become God!
He cannot do away with the law of contradiction! He cannot cause God to cease existing! All things are therefore not
logically possible for the believer. As for the second example, it is clear that it is logically impossible for iotas or dots
to be fulfilled. Statements, promises, and hopes can be
fulfilled, but letters (of the alphabet) and parts thereof cannot. And who can be as perfect as God? Who can be like
the heavenly Father in any area of life? The hyperbole in
this last example impresses upon us in a most powerful way
the need to be gracious and merciful towards all even as
God has been gracious and merciful towards us.[2]

CANON 2. A statement which conflicts with what Jesus says elsewhere may contain exaggeration

We assume that a reasonably intelligent person is logically
consistent, and therefore we seek to interpret what he says
in one place in the light of what he says elsewhere. It is
a basic rule of hermeneutics that a particular teaching should
be interpreted in the light of general teaching, that is, in
light of its context.[3] Every teacher expects that his pupils
will not take his words out of context. That context is the

totality of what he has said or written elsewhere.[4] The term *harmonize* has fallen into disfavor due in part to past attempts to unify into a harmonious whole teachings that are clearly dissimilar. Nevertheless, any reasonably intelligent person hopes that whoever hears or reads his words will seek to harmonize his teachings, that is, to understand each teaching in the light of his other teachings.

Apart from any christological considerations, the least we can say of Jesus is that he was a reasonably intelligent person; we should therefore seek to understand his individual teachings in the light of the total context of his teachings. It may be that at times he does contradict in one place what he has said elsewhere, but courtesy requires that before we assume contradiction, we attempt to see if what appears to be contradictory may in fact not be contradictory at all. This courtesy should be extended to every speaker and writer unless there is sufficient evidence that the individual is in fact inconsistent.

As we look at various teachings of Jesus we do find statements that appear to conflict with one another; this conflict is often due to his use of exaggeration. Compare the following examples:

If any one comes to me and does not hate his own father and mother and wife and children and brothers and sisters, yes, and even his own life, he cannot be my disciple. [LUKE 14:26]	And he said to them, ''You have a fine way of rejecting the commandment of God, in order to keep your tradition! For Moses said, 'Honor your father and your mother'; and, 'He who speaks evil of father or mother, let him surely die'; but you say, 'If a man tells his father or his mother, What you would have gained from me is Corban' (that is, given to God)—then you no longer permit him to do anything for his father or mother, thus making void

the word of God through your tradition which you hand on. And many such things you do." [MARK 7:9–13]

But when you pray, go into your room and shut the door and pray to your Father who is in secret; and your Father who sees in secret will reward you. [Matt. 6:6]

Pray then like this:
   Our Father who art in
     heaven,
   Hallowed be thy name.
   Thy kingdom done,
   Thy will be done,
     On earth as it is in
      heaven.
   Give us this day our daily
     bread;
   And forgive us our debts,
     As we also have
      forgiven our debtors;
   And lead us not into
     temptation,
     But deliver us from evil.
     [MATT. 6:9–13]

The scribes and the Pharisees sit on Moses' seat; so practice and observe whatever they tell you, but not what they do; for they preach, but do not practice. [Matt. 23:2–3]

Jesus said to them, "Take heed and beware of the leaven of the Pharisees and Sadducees. . . . How is it that you fail to perceive that I did not speak about bread? Beware of the leaven of the Pharisees and Sadducees." Then they understood that he did not tell them to beware of the leaven of bread, but of the teaching of the Pharisees and Sadducees. [MATT. 16:6; Matt. 16:11–12]

In isolation, LUKE 14:26 could be misunderstood as teaching hatred of one's family, but the minute one seeks to interpret this saying in the light of Jesus' teachings elsewhere (as in MARK 7:9–13; cf. also MARK 10:19), it becomes clear that we cannot take these words literally. Jesus is exaggerating for effect. He who taught his followers to love their enemies (LUKE 6:27) surely could not literally mean that they were to hate their own families. To do so would be to treat their families as enemies, which would in turn require the love for enemies which is commanded in LUKE 6:27! No, Jesus must be exaggerating in LUKE 14:26. (For a discussion of the idiomatic nature of ''love-hate'' language in the Bible see pp. 200–2.)

Jesus' command to pray only in one's closet (Matt. 6:6) conflicts with the corporate nature of the Lord's Prayer (MATT. 6:9–13), which, as we have already noted in the previous chapter, uses the first-person plural. Clearly the Evangelist who placed the Lord's Prayer immediately after the command to pray in secret did not think that Matthew 6:6 should be interpreted literally so as to contradict MAT-THEW 6:9–13. No doubt he, like most Christians since, interpreted Jesus as teaching in 6:6 that personal prayer is not for show or for the applause of people but rather is a private matter between the believer and God.

With regard to the last example above, Jesus is in the one case condemning the Pharisees in certain particulars (MATT. 16:6; Matt. 16:11–12), and in the other case agreeing with them in general (Matt. 23:3). Only if we seek to find in both these passages an absolute reference to every single teaching of the Pharisees do we have an unresolvable problem. In general Jesus' teaching was similar to that of the Pharisees. The oral traditions which they observed he vigorously re-jected (MARK 7:1–13), but doctrinally he was quite close to them in contrast to a group like the Sadducees (Acts 23:8). Could not a teacher or preacher today give similar advice concerning some well-known religious leaders? Rather than seeing in these two passages two contradictory statements of Jesus concerning the Pharisees, it is more reasonable to see in them two exaggerated, unqualified teachings concern-ing certain aspects of the Pharisees' doctrines and practices. The disciples were to be aware of the hypocritical nature of the Pharisees and the danger of the oral traditions; but inasmuch as the Pharisees sat on Moses' seat (i.e., in their role as teachers of the Old Testament), the disciples could for the most part practice what the Pharisees said the Old Testament taught. Surely this is a better way of understanding these two passages than to assume that Jesus was so dimwitted as to utter (and Matthew so dimwitted as to record) totally contradictory sayings about the Pharisees.[5]

We find a similar example of conflict within the Old Testament as well. In the Book of Isaiah two passages clearly conflict with each other. In describing the bliss of the coming period the prophet declares:

> The wolf shall dwell with the lamb, and the leopard shall lie down with the kid, and the calf and the lion and the fatling together, and a little child shall lead them. The cow and the bear shall feed; their young shall lie down together; and the lion shall eat straw like the ox. The sucking child shall play over the hole of the asp, and the weaned child shall put his hand on the adder's den. They shall not hurt or destroy in all my holy mountain; for the earth shall be full of the knowledge of the LORD as the waters cover the sea. [Isa. 11:6–9]

Yet later on we read a differing description:

> And a highway shall be there, and it shall be called the Holy Way; the unclean shall not pass over it, and fools shall not err therein. No lion shall be there, nor shall any ravenous beast come up on it; they shall not be found there, but the redeemed shall walk there. And the ransomed of the LORD shall return, and come to Zion with singing; everlasting joy shall be upon their heads; they shall obtain joy and gladness, and sorrow and sighing shall flee away. [Isa. 35:8–10]

Without entering into the issue of authorship, it is clear that Isaiah (or the last editor) placed these ostensibly contradictory passages within the text. Rather than attributing ineptitude to the author or editor, however, it is better to seek an interpretation which makes sense of the fact that both statements appear in the same work. Rather than understanding Isaiah 11:6–9 as teaching that in the coming period carnivorous animals will be transformed into herbivorous animals, it is better to see this passage as an exaggerated picture of the bliss and peace of the coming messianic age. Isaiah 35:8–10, with its statement that all nonpeaceful animals will be excluded, is, from a different angle, another idyllic picture of future bliss and peace. Both pictures, though literally contradictory, are in fact simply portraying via different analogies the very same reality—peace in the coming messianic age. The surface contradiction is an indication that at least one (perhaps both!) of the passages should not be interpreted literally but is an exaggerated description.

CANON 3. A statement which conflicts with the behavior and actions of Jesus elsewhere may contain exaggeration

Another signal that exaggeration may be present is a particular saying of Jesus which stands in sharp contrast to his behavior and actions. It is true that some religious teachers do not act in accordance with their teachings. Jesus knew this (Matt. 23:2–36, esp. vv. 2–3). Yet there are few people who would claim that Jesus did not practice what he preached. On the contrary, most scholars acknowledge that Jesus' life and actions are a perfect commentary on his teaching. If therefore a statement of Jesus conflicts with his behavior or actions elsewhere, we should consider the possibility that we have in this particular teaching an example of exaggeration. A clear instance of this is found in LUKE 14:26, which supposedly endorses hatred of one's parents and family. Surely this statement conflicts with the specific behavior of Jesus on the cross when he entrusted his mother into the care of the beloved disciple (John 19:26–27) as well as with the general nature of Jesus' entire ministry. It also conflicts with Luke's specific comment that Jesus "went down with [his parents] and came to Nazareth, and was obedient to them; and his mother kept all these things in her heart" (Luke 2:51).

A second example which we can note is MATTHEW 10:34, where Jesus states, "Do not think that I have come to bring peace on earth; I have not come to bring peace, but a sword." Not only do these words, if interpreted literally, conflict with what Jesus states elsewhere (cf. Matt. 5:9; 10:12-13; MARK 5:34; Luke 19:42), they conflict with his nonresistance when arrested at Gethsemane (MARK 14:43-50) and his forgiveness of his enemies from the cross (Luke 23:34). The context in which MATTHEW 10:34 is found also indicates that the Evangelist understood that the sword Jesus had in view had nothing to do with politics or military activity, but was a metaphorical description of the division that faith in Christ can and sometimes does bring within the family unit when one member becomes a follower of Jesus and the others do not (MATT. 10:35-39).

Another example that can be mentioned in this regard is the conflict between Jesus' own practice of prayer and his teaching on the subject. In Matthew 6:6 Jesus states that prayer should be offered in one's own room with the door shut; nevertheless, even though Jesus himself did at times seek privacy in order to pray, he did not always pray in his closet (MARK 6:46; 14:32; Luke 6:12; LUKE 9:28). At times, furthermore, Jesus prayed publicly as well (MATT. 19:13— Mark and Luke in the parallel accounts simply mention Jesus' touching of the children, but he no doubt also prayed a blessing upon them as Matthew states; cf. Gen. 48:17-20).

A final example that can be mentioned is Jesus' teaching on swearing in Matthew 5:33-37:

> Again you have heard that it was said to the men of old, "You shall not swear falsely, but shall perform to the Lord what you have sworn." But I say to you, Do not swear at all, either by heaven, for it is the throne of God, or by the earth, for it is his footstool, or by Jerusalem, for it is the city of the great King. And do not swear by your head, for you cannot make one hair white or black. Let what you say be simply "Yes" or "No"; anything more than this comes from evil.

At first glance this passage might be interpreted as an absolute prohibition against swearing in any form. Jesus' teaching in Matthew 23:16–22 should, however, make us cautious of such an interpretation. In this passage Jesus condemns the view of the Pharisees that swearing by the temple or the altar amounts to nothing (since no one could hold a lien on the temple or the altar against the one who made the oath), whereas swearing by the gold of the temple or the gift that one is to offer on the altar makes the oath binding (in that a lien could be placed on them). Here Jesus is not totally prohibiting swearing but is rebuking the way in which certain Pharisees made oaths. What is decisive, however, with regard to Matthew 5:33–37 is the fact that Jesus himself was willing to be placed under oath. We read that Jesus was silent at his trial (MATT. 26:63a); but when the high priest said, "I adjure you by the living God, tell us if you are the Christ, the Son of God" (Matt. 26:63b), Jesus no longer remained silent but responded. According to the law (Lev. 5:1; see also 1 Kings 22:16 and Prov. 29:24), when placed under an oath ("a public adjuration") one could not remain silent. There was no pleading of the fifth amendment here! To remain silent was to admit one's guilt. Jesus by his response to the high priest revealed that he accepted the validity of oaths. It seems clear by his action here that Jesus did not interpret his teaching in Matthew 5:33–37 as prohibiting his swearing under oath in this instance.

Canon 4. A statement which conflicts with the teachings of the Old Testament may contain exaggeration

Another factor that should alert the reader to the possible presence of exaggeration is conflict between a particular teaching of Jesus and the teachings of the Old Testament. Much has been written concerning Jesus' view of the Old Testament and of the law, and widely opposing positions have been advanced. Some see the New Testament faith as standing in opposition to the Old Testament religion. Frequently the Matthean antitheses ("You have heard that it was said . . ."—Matt. 5:21, 27, 33, 38, 43) are offered as support for this view. The New Testament faith is furthermore often portrayed as pure gospel and grace whereas the Old Testament is supposedly sheer law and works, and we of course "are not under law but under grace" (Rom. 6:14). This view, which misunderstands Paul at this point, was held by Marcion and various Gnostic groups early in the history of the church, but was rightly seen to be heretical. Others see in both Old and New Testament a single covenant of grace with very little difference between them. This was the view held by many of the early church fathers in opposition to Marcion. The truth, however, lies in neither of these two extremes, for the new covenant (i.e., the New Testament) is not a religion which originated in A.D. 30 but the same faith held by Abraham, Isaac, and Jacob (Gal. 3:6–9), and yet it is a *new* covenant as well (Heb. 8). We should therefore not be surprised to see elements of both continuity and newness in Jesus' teaching.

What, then, was Jesus' view toward the Old Testament? Jesus did not see himself as usurping the law and the prophets, but rather as fulfilling them (Matt. 5:17–19).[6] In the Old Testament commandments, *correctly understood,* there was life (MARK 10:17–19), and Jesus' own summary of his ethical teachings consisted of two Old Testament commands (Deut. 6:5 and Lev. 19:18) which in turn summarized all the Old Testament commandments (MARK 12:28–34). His strong antagonism towards the oral traditions of the Pharisees was due to the fact that these traditions countered the Old Testament commandments (MARK 7:8–13). At a few points Jesus did suggest that the Old Testament commandments were outdated because of the coming of the kingdom of God (Matt. 5:38–39; MARK 7:14–23; 10:2–12), but these instances are few in number. It would appear, then, that unless Jesus taught explicitly to the contrary, he regarded the ethical teachings of the Old Testament to be the revealed will of God and still binding. So if we find a teaching of Jesus which conflicts with the Old Testament, it is quite possibly an example of exaggeration.

Once again we raise the example of LUKE 14:26. In light of the commandment to honor one's father and mother

(Exod. 20:12; Deut. 5:16) and in light of the frequent Old Testament emphasis in this area (Lev. 19:3; Prov. 10:1; 15:20; 23:22), it would be strange indeed to think that Jesus was actually commanding his followers to hate their parents.

Another example can be found in Matthew 5:33–37. The apparent prohibition of swearing raises the issue of what to do with all the Old Testament references in which swearing is seen as perfectly acceptable (Lev. 5:1; 19:12 [cf. Exod. 20:7]; Num. 30:2–15; Deut. 23:21–23). To these can be added the many instances in the Old Testament in which God himself is described as having sworn (Deut. 1:8; Ps. 110:4; 132:11; Isa. 14:24; Ezek. 20:5). These many references make it doubtful whether Jesus was actually forbidding in Matthew 5:33–37 all instances of swearing, for knowing full well of the many times when God had sworn an oath, Jesus would certainly never have issued a command which might seem to imply that God himself was wrong in so doing.

CANON 5. A statement which conflicts with other teachings in the New Testament may contain exaggeration

Conflict between a particular teaching of Jesus and other New Testament passages may also be a clue to the presence of exaggeration in Jesus' words. We must be aware, however, that this canon does not serve as an infallible guide. It is certainly possible that the writers of the New Testament misunderstood various teachings of Jesus. Indeed, there have been many extravagant claims to the effect that they did in fact greatly misunderstand his words and that we are now just beginning to understand what he truly meant. C. S. Lewis has warned, however, against scholarly presumption of this nature: ''The idea that any man or writer should be opaque to those who lived in the same culture, spoke the same language, shared the same habitual imagery and unconscious assumptions, and yet be transparent to those who have none of these advantages, is in my opinion preposterous.''[7] Without denying the possibility of misunderstanding on the part of the New Testament writers, it nevertheless appears reasonable to assume that if they did not interpret a particular teaching of Jesus literally, apparently regarding it instead as exaggerative in nature, they were probably correct in so doing.

A good example is Jesus' teaching on swearing in Matthew 5:33–37. In both Acts 2:30 and Hebrews 6:16–17; 7:20–22 we read of God's swearing in order to emphasize the absolute certainty of his promises. Moreover, we know that Paul did not believe that Jesus taught an absolute prohibition of swearing, for the apostle voluntarily "call[s] God to witness" (2 Cor. 1:23), declares that "before God, I do not lie" (Gal. 1:20), and proclaims that "God is my witness" (Rom. 1:9; Phil. 1:8). It is true that James 5:12 reiterates Jesus' prohibition in Matthew 5:33–37, but it would seem best to conclude that James, like Jesus, was by the use of exaggeration emphasizing the danger of a routine swearing of oaths in daily speech, a practice which was prevalent in his day. One's character should be such that a simple yes or no will suffice.

Another example is found in the same chapter of the Sermon on the Mount. In MATTHEW 5:42 Jesus states, "Give to him who begs from you, and do not refuse him who would borrow from you." Yet within the New Testament there is at least one clear example in which the church is told not to grant the requests of those who beg. In seeking to remedy the problem of those at Thessalonica who, because of their belief in the nearness of the parousia, were no longer working but living off their Christian friends, the apostle Paul states, "For even when we were with you, we gave you this command: If any one will not work, let him not eat" (2 Thess. 3:10). Rather than seeing a contradiction between Jesus and the apostle, it is more reasonable to conclude that Jesus, in teaching of the need to be generous, was exaggerating in MATTHEW 5:42 simply because he did not want to list various exceptions to the general rule. To have listed exceptions would have changed the meaning, for the focus would then have shifted to the exceptions. Surely it is not unreasonable to think that Jesus would have agreed with Paul's injunction not to give to those who were begging if giving to them what they asked would perpetuate their deficiencies (laziness).

Another saying of Jesus which other passages in the New Testament do not interpret literally is MATTHEW 7:1: "Judge not, that you be not judged." Similar teaching is found in Romans 14:10 and 1 Corinthians 4:5. Yet how can one obey MATTHEW 7:1 literally and practice the kind of discipline taught in the rest of the New Testament? How can one rebuke (1 Tim. 5:20; 2 Tim. 4:2) or pronounce judgment (1 Cor. 5:3)? Paul even rebukes the Corinthian Christians because they failed to judge when they should have (1 Cor. 6:1–6). August Tholuck's advice concerning such sayings of Jesus can still be quoted with profit: "we must never forget that they are to be interpreted according to the analogia fidei, according to the whole scope of the Christian doctrine, according to the spirit of Christ."[8]

CANON 6. **A statement which is interpreted by another Evangelist in a nonliteral way may contain exaggeration**

Anyone who has ever used a harmony of the Gospels has noticed that the sayings of Jesus occasionally occur in slightly different forms in the different Gospels. Frequently such differences are due to grammatical considerations, but there are times when the differences have theological significance. In seeking to determine if a particular saying of Jesus is an example of exaggeration, we can at times be assisted by comparing the saying under investigation with its parallel in another Gospel. If the parallel qualifies the suspected exaggeration, it is reasonable to assume that this Evangelist sought to clarify Jesus' original saying (his *ipsissima verba*) by expressing the meaning of Jesus' exaggerated statement in a form less likely to be misunderstood. It may, of course, be the case that the exaggeration is due to the Evangelist's attempt to heighten Jesus' original teaching, but usually we find that the exaggeration was part of the original.

A good example is found in LUKE 14:26 and its parallel in MATTHEW 10:37:

If any one comes to me and does not hate his own father and mother and wife and children and brothers and sisters, yes, and even his own life, he cannot be my disciple. [LUKE 14:26]

He who loves father or mother more than me is not worthy of me; and he who loves son or daughter more than me is not worthy of me. [MATT. 10:37]

It is reasonably certain that in this particular instance Luke's account is closer to the actual words of Jesus. Matthew, however, is nevertheless true to the teaching of Jesus at this point; although Matthew uses a different wording, he does not change the meaning or sense of Jesus' saying. Through the form of the saying in Matthew, we are able to see that Jesus' original command to hate one's family was not meant to be taken literally but was an exaggeration used for effect. "Hate" is simply an idiomatic way of saying "love less." In this instance the exaggerated nature of LUKE 14:26 is evident not only from the fact that it conflicts with what Jesus says elsewhere (canon 2), with Jesus' behavior (canon 3), with the teachings of the Old Testament (canon 4), and with other passages in the New Testament (canon 5), but also from the fact that the Evangelist Matthew obviously understood Jesus' actual words as an overstatement.

A second example is the "exception clause" in Jesus' teaching on divorce. We find the teaching in its absolute form in three instances and with the exception clause in two:

And he said to them, "Whoever divorces his wife and marries another, commits adultery against her." [MARK 10:11]

And I say to you: whoever divorces his wife, except for unchastity, and marries another, commits adultery. [MATT. 19:9]

Every one who divorces his wife and marries another commits adultery, and he who marries a woman divorced from her husband commits adultery. [LUKE 16:18]

But I say to you that every one who divorces his wife, except on the ground of unchastity, makes her an adulteress; and whoever marries a divorced woman commits adultery. [MATT. 5:32]

> To the married I give charge,
> not I but the Lord, that the
> wife should not separate
> from her husband (but if she
> does, let her remain single or
> else be reconciled to her hus-
> band)—and that the hus-
> band should not divorce his
> wife. [1 Cor. 7:10–11]

Although some would argue the reverse, most scholars believe that the unqualified form of the saying in Mark, Luke, and 1 Corinthians is closer to Jesus' actual words than are the Matthean versions with the exception clause. In the three non-Matthean versions we have a more authentic teaching of Jesus on divorce.[9] Some have suggested that Matthew by including the exception clause has in fact rejected the absoluteness of Jesus' teaching on this matter. According to this view, Matthew realized that the teaching of Jesus would be quite unpalatable to his Jewish-Christian audience and therefore perverted it. But is such a harsh judgment upon the writer of the first Gospel necessary or even warranted?

We have already established that Jesus made frequent use of exaggeration. Is it possible that his saying on divorce is an exaggeration, and that Matthew introduces the exception clause to bring out its true meaning? Let us for a moment suggest the following scenario as a possible context for Jesus' teaching on the subject. Jesus walks into the midst of a rabbinic debate on divorce. The debate among the Pharisees on this issue is a lively one, and the views range from the conservative position of Shammai, who argues via a narrow interpretation of Deuteronomy 24:1 that the only cause for divorce is unchastity, to that of the liberal Hillel, who interprets Deuteronomy 24:1 broadly and concludes that a burned supper or even finding a more attractive woman is a just cause for divorce. Jesus, being asked his view on divorce (MARK 10:2), realizes that the whole debate is focusing upon speculations about when the divine plan for marriage can be ignored. Out of concern for the basic plan and purpose of God in marriage he replies abruptly, ''There is no good reason for breaking the divine rule!'' In so doing Jesus is not so much concerned with hypothetical speculations on exceptions as he is zealous for the perfect purpose of God, which does not involve divorce. That Jesus is not seeking to lay down here a legal dictum to cover every situation is understood both by Paul and by Matthew, for Paul does grant an exception (1 Cor. 7:15) as does Matthew. One might, as has been mentioned, see Paul and Matthew as corruptors of Jesus' teaching in this area; but if we believe that Jesus is employing overstatement in this instance, we will instead see the canonical writers as authoritative interpreters who bring out the sense of what Jesus actually means by his teaching.[10]

Another example in which an Evangelist by his redaction clearly indicates that he understands Jesus' teaching to be exaggerated involves the controversial saying of Jesus found in MATTHEW 10:34:

Do not think that I have come to bring peace on earth; I have not come to bring peace, but a sword. [MATT. 10:34]	Do you think that I have come to give peace on earth? No, I tell you, but rather division. [LUKE 12:51]

It is almost certain that the Matthean version of this saying is authentic, for it is far easier to understand why one would change ''sword'' to ''division'' than to understand why one would change ''division'' to ''sword.'' The desire of the church to disassociate itself from anything that could be misconstrued as teaching political revolution or rebellion would have as a consequence a strong inclination to change ''sword'' to ''division'' and an even stronger reluctance to change ''division'' to ''sword.'' That Jesus himself was not a political revolutionary, that is, a Zealot, and had no sympathies in that direction is evident from such passages as MATTHEW 5:38–42 (esp. v. 39); Matthew 26:52; MARK 12:13–17; and LUKE 6:27–29. Furthermore, it is evident from the context, as we shall immediately see, that Jesus was not concerned here with political revolt or rebellion but rather with family divisions. Luke, understanding the exaggerated nature of Jesus' saying and the possibility of its being misunderstood, therefore used "division" to describe the dissension and disruption that Jesus brings to homes in which some believe in him and others do not.

In addition to modifying the wording, another way in which an Evangelist can reveal that he does not interpret a saying of Jesus literally is by means of the context into which he places the saying. An example is the statement just discussed, where Jesus asserts that he did not come to bring peace on earth but a sword (MATT. 10:34). The context that follows clearly indicates that Matthew does not interpret this saying politically or militarily at all, for in what follows we read of family strife (v. 35) and the need to love Jesus more than family (v. 37)! From this it is clear that Matthew interprets the saying he records in 10:34 as a metaphor about the family strife and discord that sometimes result from following Jesus Christ.

In a similar manner the apparently absolute and unconditional "Judge not, that you be not judged" (Matt. 7:1), is followed in the next verse by the warning that God will judge us by the same standard by which we judge others (and for Matthew, God's judgment of the world is inevitable).[11] There follow the warning against seeing a speck in our brother's eye and not seeing the log in our own (vv. 3–5), and the command not to give to dogs what is holy or to throw our pearls before swine (v. 6). This command of course entails making a judgment regarding to whom we are not to give what is holy. Matthew clearly did not see any conflict between the prohibition of judging in verse 1 and the judging described and commanded in the following verses. In addition to these references it must be noted that Matthew 18:15–17 (cf. also LUKE 17:3) prescribes how the church should proceed in matters of church discipline. Obviously the prohibition in Matthew 7:1 does not exclude the church discipline prescribed in Matthew 18:15–17. This is possible only if Matthew 7:1 is understood as an example of overstatement.

CANON 7. A statement which the audience of Jesus did not interpret literally may contain exaggeration

If we assume that Jesus not only sought to communicate certain truths and realities to his listeners, but that he effectively did so, we must also assume that his audience understood, for the most part at least, his teachings. This does not deny the fact that frequently his audience misunderstood his teachings, and that their failure in this regard may even at times have been Jesus' intent (MARK 4:10–12; 7:17–18). Nevertheless the primary purpose of any prophet, teacher, or evangelist is to convey his message to his audience in a way that will enable them to understand what he is trying to say. No one teaches with a goal of being totally incomprehensible! Do we find in the Gospels any occasions when Jesus' audience interpreted a saying of his as being an exaggeration? If so, this may provide a guide for us. But how can we know how Jesus' audience interpreted his teachings? Even if we grant that the Gospels of Matthew and John were written by eyewitnesses, or if we grant that all of the teachings of Jesus recorded in the Gospels came ultimately from eyewitnesses (Luke 1:1–4) who were aware how the audience interpreted his teachings, the fact remains that the Gospel writers were not primarily concerned with recording how his audience interpreted his words. Furthermore, the very arrangement of Jesus' teachings into collections or blocks such as the Sermon on the Mount compounds the problem, for it is impossible in such instances to know how the audience of Jesus reacted to a particular saying in that collection. It must be confessed with all candor, then, that the applicability of this canon is extremely limited.

There are, however, some instances in which the response of Jesus' audience is recorded and provides a clue for us. It is evident from MARK 10:22 that the rich young ruler understood that, for him at least, the command of Jesus to ''go, sell what you have, and give to the poor'' (MARK 10:21) was not an overstatement, but was meant to be taken quite literally, for we read that the young man's countenance fell and he went away sorrowful. On the other hand, the opposition of the Pharisees toward Jesus and his followers would tend to indicate that Matthew 23:2 was not interpreted in a completely literal way by Jesus' audience. Another passage where this canon might be applicable is the conversation of Jesus with the Syrophoenician woman in MARK 7:24–30. To the woman's request that he heal her daughter he replied, "Let the children first be fed, for it is not right to take the children's bread and throw it to the dogs" (MARK 7:27). It is clear that the woman did not understand Jesus' metaphorical language as a literal refusal. On the contrary she understood it as the beginning of a dialogue. She understood his meaning to be: "The children should be fed first, shouldn't they? It is not right to take the children's bread and throw it to the dogs, is it?" In view of the fact that she continued the dialogue and responded both in faith and with wit, "Yes, Lord; yet even the dogs under the table eat the children's crumbs" (v. 28), Jesus granted her request and healed her daughter.

CANON 8. A statement which has not been literally fulfilled may contain exaggeration

There are times when the exaggerated nature of a saying of Jesus suggests itself by the fact that the statement has not been literally fulfilled in history or practice. The exaggerated nature of MARK 13:2—"Do you see these great buildings? There will not be left here one stone upon another, that will not be thrown down"—is evident from history itself. Some of those stones still stand one upon the other! The prophecy's meaning was nevertheless clearly fulfilled in the destruction that befell Jerusalem in A.D. 70. The actual intent of the statement, but not the affective expression used to convey it, has been carried out.

Other examples of non-fulfilment are various sayings on prayer:

> Ask, and it will be given you; seek, and you will find; knock, and it will be opened to you. For every one who asks

receives, and he who seeks finds, and to him who knocks it will be opened. [MATT. 7:7-8]

And Jesus answered them, "Have faith in God. Truly, I say to you, whoever says to this mountain, 'Be taken up and cast into the sea,' and does not doubt in his heart, but believes that what he says will come to pass, it will be done for him. Therefore I tell you, whatever you ask in prayer, believe that you receive it, and you will." [MARK 11:22-24]

To these references can be added Matthew 18:19; Luke 11:5-8; LUKE 11:9-13; and John 14:13; 15:7, 16; 16:23-24. Although some of these promises are qualified (MARK 11:22-24 requires faith—one must not doubt but believe; Matt. 18:19 requires two people agreeing in prayer; John 15:7 requires abiding in Christ; John 14:13; 15:16; and 16:23-24 require asking in Jesus' name), MATTHEW 7:7-8 and the parallel in LUKE 11:5-13 have no qualification at all. The problem which a literal interpretation of these verses creates is self-evident. Christians through the centuries have at times asked and not received, sought and not found, knocked and not been opened unto. Furthermore, at times they have, abiding in Christ and asking in his name, prayed in large numbers (far more than two or three) and with great faith, doubting nothing. But to no apparent avail!

How are we to explain this? One could, of course, say that frequently Christians have prayed wrongly and that God in his mercy and wisdom has not granted their requests. James 4:3 ("You ask and do not receive, because you ask wrongly, to spend it on your passions") can be mentioned in this regard.[12] No doubt Jesus would have agreed wholeheartedly with the teaching of this verse. He in fact expected his listeners to assume certain qualifications. He expected them to assume that they should not ask for anything that would dishonor God or impair their physical-moral-mental-emotional-spiritual growth as children of God. Note, however, that the emphasis of Jesus' teaching concerning prayer is God's loving and gracious desire to bless his children, not a list specifying things that we ought not to pray for. As a result he did not incorporate any qualifications in his teaching on prayer, even though he expected that his hearers would assume them. This omission of qualifications in these sayings of Jesus on prayer signifies that we are dealing here with exaggeration. It is interesting to note that when the Evangelists recorded these examples of Jesus' use of overstatement, they likewise expected their readers to be able to recognize them as such.[13]

Our final example of the principle that a lack of fulfilment of certain sayings of Jesus may be a signal that we are dealing with an exaggerated form of teaching on the part of Jesus is Matthew 26:52 (not all warriors die young!).

CANON 9. A statement which, if literally fulfilled, would not achieve the desired goal may contain exaggeration

We have still another clue to the possible presence of exaggeration if the literal fulfilment of a particular saying would not achieve what Jesus intended.[14] This canon applies primarily to various exhortations given by Jesus. If we were to take the words of Jesus in MATTHEW 5:29–30 literally and mutilate our bodies, would we achieve the goal Jesus sought? Would the removal of the right eye keep one from lusting (note the context of Matt. 5:28)? Would the removal of both eyes accomplish this? From where does lust arise? Can one not lust in the dark with both eyes shut? And are hands the cause of sin? Are they not, rather, simply instruments by which the sinful heart carries out its lusts? To interpret these words literally is to assume that Jesus naively believed that the mutilation of one's eyes or hands could protect us from sin, but this is clearly contradicted by Jesus' teaching elsewhere (canon 2) that it is what comes out of a person, that is, out of his heart, that defiles him (MARK 7:20–23). What Jesus is seeking in MATTHEW 5:29–30 is for us to remove from our lives anything that would keep us from entering the kingdom of God. He is seeking repentance. Repentance does not involve mutilation of our bodily members, which are God-given gifts and vehicles by which he may be served, but mutilation of our fallen Adamic nature. This involves the inner man, not our external members. Literal fulfilment of MATTHEW 5:29–30 would therefore not bring about the desired goal. On the contrary, it could actually cause us to lose sight of the real problem by focusing on the symptoms instead.

Another example is found in Matthew 6:3–4. Keeping one's left hand from knowing what the right hand is doing would not necessarily bring about Jesus' goal of secrecy in our giving. Others still might know. To use a ridiculous illustration: one could perhaps sound a trumpet each time one intends for the left hand to cease paying attention to what the right is doing. With careful conditioning the sound of the trumpet could immediately cause the left hand not to know what the right hand is doing and at the same time signal to all those in the vicinity that they should note our generous giving! Of course, all of this is impossible, but it does demonstrate that a literal carrying out of what Jesus commands in these verses would not bring about what Jesus is seeking. As a result it is reasonable to conclude that we have here a case of exaggeration for effect.

CANON 10. **Statements which make use of particular literary forms are prone to exaggeration**

In the introduction we mentioned that certain literary forms are more prone to exaggeration than are others. Whereas doctors' reports, laboratory analyses, chemistry textbooks, and automobile manuals must be literal, we tend to expect exaggeration in love letters, fish stories, and descriptions of grandchildren. Likewise in both the Old and New Testaments there are certain literary forms which tend to use exaggerated language. They include proverbs, prophecy, poetry, metaphor, and parables.

Exaggeration in proverbs

A proverb is a brief, pithy saying which is known through nature or experience and presents some general truth in a striking manner. These truths are usually available for all to see; thus, wisdom literature is not limited to the Bible. The wisdom literature of the Bible has, in fact, many parallels in nonbiblical literature. The main difference between biblical and nonbiblical proverbs does not lie in their form or even in their content, but rather in the fact that biblical proverbs are presented not only in the light of nature and experience that is available to all, but also in the context of the revelation of God found in the Old and New Testaments.

Proverbs by their very nature are prone to exaggeration because they tend to express a general truth in compressed form and in universal language. They also tend to use sharp contrasts and paradox. "Most proverbs are remembered chiefly, not because of the truth they reveal, but because they are in the form of a general or universal hyperbolic statement not encumbered by exceptions and limitations."[15] Perhaps the best way of demonstrating this character of proverbs is simply to quote a number of them. First we shall present a number of Old Testament proverbs which use universal language to express a general truth and reality:

Honor the LORD with your substance and with the first fruits of all your produce; then your barns will be filled with plenty, and your vats will be bursting with wine. [Prov. 3:9–10]

The LORD does not let the righteous go hungry, but he thwarts the craving of the wicked. A slack hand causes poverty, but the hand of the diligent makes rich. [Prov. 10:3–4]

Misfortune pursues sinners, but prosperity rewards the righteous. [Prov. 13:21]

A soft answer turns away wrath, but a harsh word stirs up anger. [Prov. 15:1]

A slave who deals wisely will rule over a son who acts shamefully, and will share the inheritance as one of the brothers. [Prov. 17:2]

Train up a child in the way he should go, and when he is old he will not depart from it. [Prov. 22:6]

He who oppresses the poor to increase his own wealth, or gives to the rich, will only come to want. [Prov. 22:16]

The wisdom and truthfulness of these proverbs would be accepted by almost all. Hard work does, more often than not, bring prosperity. A soft answer frequently does avoid confrontation and hostility. Even Proverbs 17:2, although not a usual occurrence in life, nevertheless serves as a truthful warning to sons that they should not act shamefully lest they lose their inheritance. (For a servant or slave to share in the inheritance of his master was not impossible in biblical times, although it would have been unheard of in America in the first part of the nineteenth century.) It is also true that individuals taught to love and serve the Lord in their childhood will remain faithful to their God and continue to serve him during their years as adults. Yet this is not always true. There are exceptions. Godly parents who have sought to raise their children in the fear and admonition of the Lord have seen them become reprobate and apostate. Both Eli and Samuel had that experience (1 Sam. 2:12; 8:5). Of course, one could say that Eli and Samuel (and all parents today whose children do not walk in the ways of the Lord) did not train their children perfectly. But which parents whose children have become true followers and servants of God can boast that they trained their children perfectly? Proverbs 22:6 is a general truth expressed in universal language: the normal experience is that children raised to love the Lord will serve him as adults. This is not, however, a law of life which holds 100 percent of the time. It is also obvious that there are hard-working people who do not prosper and tithers who do not possess great wealth. A proverb by its very nature often evokes the response, ''Yes, but...,'' that is to say, ''Yes, I agree in principle that this is true, but there are exceptions.''[16] This response does not nullify the value of the proverb. We must understand that the genre seeks to present in universal language a general truth concerning life in the light of the revelation of God in nature and in his written Word.

With this in mind let us look at some of the proverbs of Jesus:

> Where your treasure is, there will your heart be also. [MATT. 6:21]

> A disciple is not above his teacher, nor a servant above his master. [MATT. 10:24]

> Out of the abundance of the heart the mouth speaks. [MATT. 12:34b]

> All who take the sword will perish by the sword. [Matt. 26:52c]

> A prophet is not without honor, except in his own country, and among his own kin, and in his own house. [MARK 6:4]

> He who is faithful in a very little is faithful also in much; and he who is dishonest in a very little is dishonest also in much. [Luke 16:10]

That these proverbs of Jesus are general truths which are simply confirmed by the exceptions is evident. Most people who are faithful in small matters are indeed faithful in large ones as well. Yet there are people who do not steal the pennies of others but, when a really big opportunity comes, find the temptation irresistible. Some people also speak not out of their hearts but with forked tongue. The same mouth can pronounce blessings and cursings (James 3:10). Although James gives three proverbs in question form which suggest that this is impossible (3:11–12), he nevertheless knows that believers do use their tongues to bring curses as well as blessings. This, he declares, ought not to be (3:10b).

From these examples it is clear that the proverbial form is prone to exaggeration. By its very nature it is so inclined. This is not always true, however, for there are proverbs that are universal and without exception (MATT. 6:27; 10:26; Luke 12:15; 14:11). Nevertheless, we should be aware that many proverbs do use exaggeration, and they should be interpreted accordingly.

Exaggeration in prophecy

Another form inclined toward the use of exaggeration is prophecy.[17] This does not mean that all of the details of prophetic literature are exaggerated. Rather, it means that some prophecy is not so much concerned with an exact literal description of future events as with a picturesque portrayal of those events. Some prophetic literature is not so much a photographic picture of what is to occur as an impressionistic painting. Furthermore, we must also understand that a future prophecy of judgment which appears absolute and irreversible always assumes that if the people repent, the judgment that is prophesied will be stayed. Messages of judgment are proclaimed in the hope that upon hearing them, the people will repent and avoid the judgment foretold. All of these warnings carry with them an unexpressed ''unless they repent.'' In fact many times events are foretold precisely in order that they not come to pass.[18]

An example is Jonah 3:4: ''Yet forty days, and Nineveh shall be overthrown!'' We read shortly thereafter that ''when God saw what [the Ninevites] did, how they turned from their evil way, God repented of the evil which he had said he would do to them; and he did not do it'' (3:10). That Jonah knew that his proclamation entailed this very possibility is clear from 4:1–2: ''But it displeased Jonah exceedingly, and he was angry. And he prayed to the LORD and said, 'I pray thee, LORD, is not this what I said when I was yet in my country? That is why I made haste to flee to Tarshish; for I knew that thou art a gracious God and merciful, slow to anger, and abounding in steadfast love, and repentest of evil.' '' Jonah knew from the beginning that his prophecy was not simply a prediction of future events. If it had been simply a prediction, he would have relished his task. His prophecy, however, was not simply a prediction but rather a warning to Nineveh. This is why he sought to flee from God. He did not want to preach to the people of Nineveh because he knew that they might repent and thus stave off the divine judgment. And Jonah wanted Nineveh damned!

Another example of a prophecy which was capable of being halted even though it appeared in absolute form is found in Isaiah 38:1. Isaiah says to Hezekiah, "Thus says the LORD: Set your house in order; for you shall die, you shall not recover." Yet in the following verses we read that God granted to Hezekiah his request and gave to him fifteen more years of life. Still another example is found in Micah 3:12, where Micah prophesies of the destruction of Jerusalem. We know from Jeremiah 26:16–19 that this prophecy was averted due to the repentance of the people.

These examples demonstrate that all prophecies of judgment must be interpreted in light of the principle found in Jeremiah 18:7–8: "If at any time I declare concerning a nation or kingdom, that I will pluck up and break down and destroy it, and if that nation, concerning which I have spoken, turns from its evil, I will repent of the evil that I intended to do to it" (see also 1 Kings 21:20–29). From this passage and the examples given, it is clear that prophecies of judgment which are stated in absolute form can be reversed if repentance is forthcoming. Similarly, prophecies of blessing can be reversed in case of apostasy (Jer. 18:9–10). By their very nature, then, all such prophecies are exaggerated.

The impressionistic quality of much prophetic literature is another cause of exaggeration. Note the following example:

> Behold, the day of the LORD comes, cruel, with wrath and fierce anger, to make the earth a desolation and to destroy its sinners from it. For the stars of the heavens and their constellations will not give their light; the sun will be dark at its rising and the moon will not shed its light. I will punish the world for its evil, and the wicked for their iniquity; I

will put an end to the pride of the arrogant, and lay low
the haughtiness of the ruthless. [Isa. 13:9–11]

The prophecy given here is addressed to Babylon (13:1, 19).
God will judge Babylon for her many evils. This is certain!
Yet the terminology used is certainly not literal, for the stars
and moon did not cease giving their light and the sun was
not dark in its rising when Babylon fell to the Persians in
539 B.C. We have here, in the idiomatic language of judgment, picturesque descriptions of the impending destruction of the Babylonian Empire. Judgment did indeed come
upon Babylon when it was absorbed by the Persians and
the once mighty kingdom simply ceased to exist. The genre
of prophetic judgment, however, does not demand a literal
fulfilment of every detail of its impressionistic terminology.
Such prophecy finds its fulfilment in the fact that judgment
does indeed take place. Similar examples of exaggeration
and hyperbole in prophetic judgments include Deuteronomy 28:25–46; Isaiah 3:24–4:1; 33:9; 34:1–15; Jeremiah
4:11–13, 23–26; 15:8; Amos 8:9; Nahum 1:4–5; Habakkuk
1:6–9; 3:10–12; and Zechariah 2:4–5. Another factor that
comes into play here is the fact that prophecies of judgment
were seen as a foreshadowing of the final eschatological
judgment which is to come. Each historical judgment was
understood as an adumbration of God's righteous outworking of his justice at the end of history.

Prophetic references to future blessings are also frequently
given in picturesque and exaggerated language. With regard
to Israel's return from exile the prophet Ezekiel uses the
eschatological language of resurrection:

> The hand of the LORD was upon me, and he brought me
> out by the Spirit of the LORD, and set me down in the midst
> of the valley; it was full of bones. And he led me round
> among them; and behold, there were very many upon the
> valley; and lo, they were very dry. And he said to me, "Son
> of man, can these bones live?" And I answered, "O Lord
> GOD, thou knowest." Again he said to me, "Prophesy to
> these bones and say to them, O dry bones, hear the word
> of the LORD. Thus says the Lord GOD to these bones:

Behold, I will cause breath to enter you, and you shall live.
And I will lay sinews upon you, and will cause flesh to come
upon you, and cover you with skin, and put breath in you,
and you shall live; and you shall know that I am the LORD.''
[Ezek. 37:1–6]

With regard to the messianic age, the Old Testament
prophets frequently painted idyllic scenes in which the curse
and hostilities of nature are undone:

The wolf shall dwell with the lamb, and the leopard shall
lie down with the kid, and the calf and the lion and the
fatling together, and a little child shall lead them. The cow
and the bear shall feed; their young shall lie down together;
and the lion shall eat straw like the ox. The sucking child
shall play over the hole of the asp, and the weaned child
shall put his hand on the adder's den. They shall not hurt
or destroy in all my holy mountain; for the earth shall be
full of the knowledge of the LORD as the waters cover the
sea. [Isa. 11:6–9]

For waters shall break forth in the wilderness, and streams
in the desert; the burning sand shall become a pool, and
the thirsty ground springs of water; the haunt of jackals shall
become a swamp, the grass shall become reeds and rushes.
[Isa. 35:6b–7; see also 41:18–19]

For you shall go out in joy, and be led forth in peace; the
mountains and the hills before you shall break forth into
singing, and all the trees of the field shall clap their hands.
Instead of the thorn shall come up the cypress; instead of
the brier shall come up the myrtle; and it shall be to the
LORD for a memorial, for an everlasting sign which shall not
be cut off. [Isa. 55:12–13]

Regardless of how great a renewal occurred with the coming of the messianic age, it is clear that the mountains and
hills did not sing, nor did trees clap their hands. (See also
Isa. 35; 60:15–22; Mic. 4:4.)

That Jesus and the New Testament writers understood
the prophetic literature to contain picturesque and exaggerated language is evident by the way they interpreted cer-

tain Old Testament prophecies. Whereas the main emphasis of a prophecy was usually interpreted in a literal fashion, there was also an awareness that not all of the portrait was to be interpreted literally. A good example is Joel 2:28–32:

> And it shall come to pass afterward, that I will pour out my spirit on all flesh; your sons and your daughters shall prophesy, your old men shall dream dreams, and your young men shall see visions. Even upon the menservants and maidservants in those days, I will pour out my spirit.
>
> And I will give portents in the heavens and on the earth, blood and fire and columns of smoke. The sun shall be turned to darkness, and the moon to blood, before the great and terrible day of the LORD comes. And it shall come to pass that all who call upon the name of the LORD shall be delivered; for in Mount Zion and in Jerusalem there shall be those who escape, as the LORD has said, and among the survivors shall be those whom the LORD calls.

In Acts 2:16 Peter states concerning the events of Pentecost that "this is what was spoken by the prophet Joel" and then proceeds to quote the passage. Apparently Peter (and/or Luke) understood that the astronomical terminology in the prophecy is not to be understood literally but indicates the eschatological nature of the coming of the Spirit and its inauguration of the new age. The nonliteral fulfilment of some of the details in Joel is quite disturbing to many readers. In fact some are so disturbed by this that they deny that the events of Pentecost are in fact the fulfilment (or complete fulfilment) of the prophecy. Not recognizing the impressionistic quality of prophetic language, they argue that what happened at Pentecost resembled what Joel prophesied but was not the actual fulfilment of his words. Yet surely Peter's understanding as recorded by Luke in Acts 2:16—"this is what was spoken by the prophet Joel"— means that the events of Pentecost are the fulfilment of what Joel prophesied.

A similar process is also at work in MARK 9:11–13. In reference to the prophecy in Malachi 4:5 that Elijah will come "before the great and terrible day of the LORD," Jesus is asked, "Why do the scribes say that first Elijah must come?" To this Jesus replies,

> Elijah does come first to restore all things; and how is it written of the Son of man, that he should suffer many things and be treated with contempt? But I tell you that Elijah has come, and they did to him whatever they pleased, as it is written of him.

Jesus maintains that although John the Baptist was not Elijah *redivivus* (John 1:19–23), he nonetheless was the fulfillment of the person and role portrayed in the prophecy of Malachi 4:5.

With this as a background we should not be surprised to find exaggeration in some of the prophetic sayings of Jesus, and indeed we do. Note the following examples:

> Do you see these great buildings? There will not be left here one stone upon another, that will not be thrown down. [MARK 13:2]

> You will be hated by all for my name's sake. [MARK 13:13a]

> But when you see the desolating sacrilege set up where it ought not to be (let the reader understand), then let those who are in Judea flee to the mountains; let him who is on the housetop not go down, nor enter his house, to take anything away; and let him who is in the field not turn back to take his mantle. [MARK 13:14–16]

> But in those days, after that tribulation, the sun will be darkened, and the moon will not give its light, and the stars will be falling from heaven, and the powers in the heavens will be shaken. [MARK 13:24–25]

> The queen of the South will arise at the judgment with the men of this generation and condemn them; for she came from the ends of the earth to hear the wisdom of Solomon, and behold, something greater than Solomon is here. The men of Nineveh will arise at the judgment with this genera-

tion and condemn it; for they repented at the preaching of
Jonah, and behold, something greater than Jonah is here.
[LUKE 11:31–32]

It has already been mentioned that the exaggerated nature
of MARK 13:2 is witnessed to by the fact that some of the
foundation stones of the Herodian temple still remain ''one
stone upon another'' even though the city and temple, in
fulfilment of Jesus' prophecy, were totally destroyed by the
Romans in A.D. 70.

As to MARK 13:13a we need not interpret the expression ''hated by all'' so narrowly as to infer that every one
of the earth's population will hate the followers of Christ.
A good indication of how this verse should be interpreted
can be gleaned from Acts 4. Here, after Peter and John are
released from prison, the church prays,

Sovereign Lord, who didst make the heaven and the earth
and the sea and everything in them, who by the mouth of
our father David, thy servant, didst say by the Holy Spirit,
''Why did the Gentiles rage, and the peoples imagine vain
things? The kings of the earth set themselves in array, and
the rulers were gathered together, against the Lord and
against his Anointed''—for truly in this city there were
gathered together against thy holy servant Jesus, whom
thou didst anoint, both Herod and Pontius Pilate, with the
Gentiles and the peoples of Israel, to do whatever thy hand
and thy plan had predestined to take place. And now, Lord,
look upon their threats, and grant to thy servants to speak
thy word with all boldness, while thou stretchest out thy
hand to heal, and signs and wonders are performed through
the name of thy holy servant Jesus. [Acts 4:24–30]

The church quotes Psalm 2:1–2 to portray the animosity and
hostility of their enemies toward both their Lord and
themselves. In the prayer the enemies mentioned by the
psalmist (the Gentiles, the peoples, the kings of the earth,
and the rulers) are interpreted as being Herod, Pontius
Pilate, the Gentiles, and the peoples of Israel. The latter two
expressions of necessity include everyone on earth! Yet

those who prayed this prayer knew that there were some, themselves included, who had loved Jesus during his ministry. And they also knew that whereas the leadership of Israel opposed the church, the people in general did not (Acts 2:47; 5:13). What we have in Acts 4:24–30 and MARK 13:13a is the use of exaggerated language to stress the persecution and opposition that the church faced and faces. These passages do not describe with literal exactness the number of the enemies of the church; rather, they are impressionistic expressions of the intensity of the persecution and warnings that the future persecution of Christ's followers will indeed be severe.

The language of MARK 13:14–16 also appears to be exaggerated, for if this passage refers to the revolt of the Jewish nation and its destruction in A.D. 70, there certainly would have been time to enter one's house to grab one's mantle. The Roman legions at times moved swiftly but not that swiftly. (Actually the Roman legions tended to move rather slowly and methodically.) If, on the other hand, these verses refer to the great tribulation of the end times, would fleeing to the mountains of Judea do any good? Not at all! Furthermore, the Evangelists (parallel passages appear in Matthew and Luke), in writing for audiences who did not live in Palestine, knew that their readers would not interpret this warning literally. How could they (or we) flee to the mountains of Judea at the time of "the desolating sacrilege"? The very fact that the Gospel writers believed that these verses were meaningful for their non-Judean audiences indicates that they regarded them metaphorically as referring to a tribulation which would involve their non-Judean readers. Similarly, the astronomical language of MARK 13:24–25, a passage which speaks of the coming tribulation, may entail exaggeration as a consequence of its use of idiomatic eschatological terminology.

Finally, although it is not impossible that the queen of Sheba and the people of Nineveh will accuse the men of Jesus' generation on the great day of judgment (LUKE 11:31–32), it seems more likely that Jesus is declaring that if the queen of Sheba and the Ninevites acknowledged the presence of divine wisdom in, respectively, the words of Solomon and Jonah, how much more should his own audience acknowledge the divine message he proclaimed and respond accordingly!

Exaggeration in poetry

Another literary form or genre which frequently contains exaggeration is poetry. We even speak of poetic license or poetic heightening to describe the freedom of the poet to exaggerate. Because of the need for meter and/or rhyme, poets are permitted to use language more freely in order to express their thoughts. Furthermore, the very use of this genre indicates that the writer or speaker is not interested merely in the conveying of literal information; prose would be more conducive for that purpose. Rather, poetry is used to make an impression, to influence, to help people memorize ideas.

Biblical poetry is most readily recognized by the presence of parallelism or rhythmic balance. An expression coined to describe this phenomenon is *parallelismus membrorum* (parallelism in the members). Various types of parallelism can be found in the Bible: (1) synonymous parallelism—the succeeding line or lines repeat essentially the same thought in a balanced cadence but use different words; (2) antithetical parallelism—the second line expresses an opposite thought; (3) synthetic or constructive parallelism—the succeeding line or lines supplement or bring the thought of the first line to completion; (4) step parallelism—the second line advances the thought of the first line one additional step; and (5) chiasmic parallelism—the second line expresses the thought of the first line (or its antithesis) in inverted order (abba).

It should be pointed out that poetry does not require the use of exaggeration but rather is prone to it. Some Old Testament examples should be looked at first. We have already mentioned that proverbs incline toward exaggeration. One of the reasons for this is their frequent appearance in poetic form. Note for instance the following:

A wise son makes a glad father, but a foolish man despises his mother. [Prov. 15:20]

A tranquil mind gives life to the flesh, but passion makes the bones rot. [Prov. 14:30]

In the first instance "despises" does seem a rather exaggerated word, and in the latter "rot" is certainly not a literal description of what actually occurs; but we must remember that in these proverbs we are dealing with poetry, and exaggeration is quite common in this form of literature. In Malachi 1:2–3 two factors betray the presence of exaggeration. First, there is its rhythmic nature: "Yet I have loved Jacob but I have hated Esau." Second, there is the word *hated*. We have already suggested that on occasion "hate" does not mean "to bear malice toward someone," but "to love someone less than another." The idiomatic meaning of the term combines with poetic contrast to form an exaggerated statement which emphasizes God's gracious calling and the covenant which he established with Jacob. (The saying is only tangentially concerned with Esau.)

Contrasting the narrative account of the defeat of Sisera in Judges 4 with Deborah's poetic version in Judges 5 will give us a good idea of poetry's tendency to exaggerate. In the narrative account the battle and the death of Sisera are described in a straightforward manner. Deborah's song, however, is prone to exaggeration:

LORD, when thou didst go forth from Seir, when thou didst march from the region of Edom, the earth trembled, and the heavens dropped, yea, the clouds dropped water. The mountains quaked before the LORD, yon Sinai before the LORD, the God of Israel. . . . The kings came, they fought; then fought the kings of Canaan, at Taanach, by the waters of Megiddo; they got no spoils of silver. From heaven fought the stars, from their courses they fought against Sisera. [Judg. 5:4–5, 19–20]

In the past the poetic nature of this song was frequently ignored by the commentators, and various literal explanations of its assertions were offered (storms, earthquakes, hail). Recognition of the poetic nature of these verses, however, enables us to see that the singer is metaphorically proclaiming that God was with his people in battle and that through his power and might victory was won. We are not being told that the stars literally fought against Sisera.[19] (For a similar poetic description using cosmic terminology, see 2 Sam. 22:8–16, where God's deliverance of David from his enemies is depicted with great exaggeration.)

Still another example of the use of poetry to portray a historical incident in unusually picturesque language is found in Exodus 15. After a straightforward narration of Israel's safe passage through the Red Sea and the subsequent destruction of Pharaoh's armies (Exod. 14:21–29), the victory is described poetically. The metaphorical and exaggerated nature of the poetic version is immediately apparent:

> I will sing to the LORD, for he has triumphed gloriously; the horse and his rider he has thrown into the sea. . . . Pharaoh's chariots and his host he cast into the sea; and his picked officers are sunk in the Red Sea. . . . In the greatness of thy majesty thou overthrowest thy adversaries; thou sendest forth thy fury, it consumes them like stubble. . . .
> Sing to the LORD, for he has triumphed gloriously; the horse and his rider he has thrown into the sea. [Exod. 15:1, 4, 7, 21]

Whereas the narrative account reports that the chariots of Pharaoh followed after Israel (14:23) and the waters came back over them (14:26–28), in the poetic version the Lord, who is seen as a mighty warrior (15:3), picks up his enemies and casts them into the sea (15:1, 4, 21). All the time, however, it is evident from 15:8–10 that the poet is aware of what actually happened: the waters which had been made to part for the children of Israel returned to cover the forces of Pharaoh. It is interesting to note that in the midst of the poem an entirely different metaphor is used to speak of the Lord's destruction of Pharaoh's armies, a metaphor which seems at first glance highly inappropriate. In 15:7b the destruction of Pharaoh's armies by drowning is likened to fire consuming stubble. Yet the poet is not troubled by the mixed figures. Remember that we are dealing with poetry and not historical narrative; both drowning and the burning of stubble are metaphors of judgment and destruction, and judgment and destruction did in fact come upon the armies of Pharaoh. (Still another example of the difference between the more sober nature of narrative and the more picturesque and exaggerated nature of poetry can be seen by comparing the creation narrative in Gen. 1 with its poetic counterpart in Ps. 104.)

Within the Gospels we find a large number of examples of poetry. By far the most numerous kind is antithetical parallelism; one author lists 138 instances in the Synoptic Gospels alone.[20] To these can be added about seventy-five cases of the four other kinds of parallelism.[21] Let us consider just a few examples of poetry in the teachings of Jesus:

> No one can serve two masters; for either he will hate the one and love the other, or he will be devoted to the one and despise the other. You cannot serve God and mammon. [MATT. 6:24]

> Ask, and it will be given you; seek, and you will find; knock, and it will be opened to you. For every one who asks receives, and he who seeks finds, and to him who knocks it will be opened. [MATT. 7:7–8]

> Do not think that I have come to bring peace on earth; I have not come to bring peace, but a sword. [MATT. 10:34]

Although there are other signals of exaggeration in all three of these examples, the fact that they are in poetic form is also a signal and may help explain in part the presence of exaggeration, for poetry is conducive to exaggeration. Other examples of exaggeration in the poetical utterances of Jesus include MATTHEW 5:39–41; Matthew 6:5–6; MARK 2:21–22; and Luke 16:10.[22]

Exaggeration in metaphor

Another literary form that must be mentioned is

metaphor. By its very nature metaphor involves exaggeration, for it does not say that something is like something else, which can be true, but that something is something else, which cannot be true. A simile is a comparison of two different things which is introduced by the word *like* or *as*. By the use of this introductory word, a simile avoids any absolute identification of the objects compared. A metaphor, on the other hand, is an absolute comparison of two unlike things, and this as a matter of course involves exaggeration. Consider the following examples:

> But I am a worm, and no man;
>   scorned by men, and despised by the people.
> [Ps. 22:6; see also Ps. 102:3–11]

> I am a rose of Sharon,
>   a lily of the valleys. [Song of Sol. 2:1]

> There shall come forth a shoot from the stump of Jesse,
>   and a branch shall grow out of his roots. [Isa. 11:1]

> You are the salt of the earth; but if salt has lost its taste, how shall its saltness be restored? [MATT. 5:13]

> You serpents, you brood of vipers, how are you to escape being sentenced to hell? [Matt. 23:33]

> At that very hour some Pharisees came, and said to him, "Get away from here, for Herod wants to kill you." And he said to them, "Go and tell that fox, 'Behold, I cast out demons and perform cures today and tomorrow, and the third day I finish my course.' " [Luke 13:31–32]

In these examples it is evident that the persons referred to in the metaphor are not, respectively, a worm, a rose, a stump or branch, salt, vipers, or an actual fox. In one way or another they resemble the object used to describe them, but they are not identical with the object. We must be aware, then, that metaphors by their very nature entail exaggeration.

Exaggeration in *mashal*/parable

Closely related to two forms already mentioned, proverbs and metaphors, are the Old Testament *mashal* and its New Testament equivalent, the parable. Actually, under the term *mashal* or parable can be included not only proverb and metaphor, but also riddle, allegory, taunt, similitude, story and example parables.[23]

Exaggeration is commonplace within the Old Testament *mashal*. Consider, for example, Ezekiel 20:49–21:5:

> Then I said, ''Ah Lord GOD! they are saying of me, 'Is he not a maker of allegories?' ''
> The word of the LORD came to me: ''Son of man, set your face toward Jerusalem and preach against the sanctuaries; prophesy against the land of Israel and say to the land of Israel, Thus says the LORD: Behold, I am against you, and will draw forth my sword out of its sheath, and will cut off from you both righteous and wicked. Because I will cut off from you both righteous and wicked, therefore my sword shall go out of its sheath against all flesh from south to north; and all flesh shall know that I the LORD have drawn my sword out of its sheath; it shall not be sheathed again.

Other examples of exaggeration in the Old Testament *mashal* are 2 Samuel 12:1–4; Isaiah 5:1–4; and Ezekiel 17; 24:2–5.

It is not surprising, then, that despite the real-life and down-to-earth nature of Jesus' parables we frequently encounter exaggeration in them. To be sure, the parables are not fablelike in quality, for trees and animals do not talk and people do not fly, but the parables nevertheless do use exaggerated language. A good example is the parable of the unforgiving servant:

> Therefore the kingdom of heaven may be compared to a king who wished to settle accounts with his servants. When he began the reckoning, one was brought to him who owed him ten thousand talents; and as he could not pay, his lord ordered him to be sold, with his wife and children and all that he had, and payment to be made. So the servant fell

on his knees, imploring him, "Lord, have patience with me, and I will pay you everything." And out of pity for him the lord of that servant released him and forgave him the debt. But that same servant, as he went out, came upon one of his fellow servants who owed him a hundred denarii; and seizing him by the throat he said, "Pay what you owe." So his fellow servant fell down and besought him, "Have patience with me, and I will pay you." He refused and went and put him in prison till he should pay the debt. When his fellow servants saw what had taken place, they were greatly distressed, and they went and reported to their lord all that had taken place. Then his lord summoned him and said to him, "You wicked servant! I forgave you all that debt because you besought me; and should not you have had mercy on your fellow servant, as I had mercy on you?" And in anger his lord delivered him to the jailers, till he should pay all his debt. So also my heavenly Father will do to every one of you, if you do not forgive your brother from your heart. [Matt. 18:23–35]

The exaggerated nature of this parable is apparent in the huge sum which the unforgiving servant was forgiven. It was 10,000 talents. In comparison, the entire tribute of Galilee and Perea for 4 B.C. was only 200 talents and the entire yearly income of Herod the Great was only 900 talents![24]

Other examples can also be listed. Is it not strange that all ten maidens were asleep when the bridegroom came (Matt. 25:5)? And is it not strange that all those invited to the banquet made excuses and did not attend (LUKE 14:18)? And certainly not all Samaritans were as good as the one in the story or all priests and Levites as bad (Luke 10:30–35). As for the rich man who forgave the dishonest steward (Luke 16:1–9), surely his behavior was quite unusual; and, alas, fathers like the father of the prodigal son are all too rare (Luke 15:11–32). Although of a real-life quality, the parabolic form by its very nature permits and even encourages the unusual and the exaggerated, for we are not dealing here with history but story!

In concluding our discussion of the various literary forms which are prone to exaggeration and which should therefore alert us to the possibility of hyperbolic language, it should be pointed out that these forms (except for metaphor) do not inevitably contain exaggeration. Some instances of these forms contain exaggeration and some do not. Each individual example must be examined in the light of all the canons which we are discussing in this volume. It should also be pointed out that whereas one may take exception as to whether a specific example we have given does indeed contain exaggeration, we have in the case of each canon presented a sufficient number of other examples to warrant regarding it as a signal of possible exaggeration.

Canon 11. A statement which uses idiomatic language may contain exaggeration

It is a characteristic of every language that certain terms and phrases become part of a storehouse of idioms whose meaning is no longer determined by their literal sense and grammatical relationships, but rather by the way they are used and function in everyday speech. One of the greatest problems in learning a new language is the existence of idioms. Beginners always stumble over this problem, for what seems like a harmless statement in the new language may turn out to be idiomatic and have nuances that can be quite embarrassing. For example, to translate into German a simple statement of how one is being affected by the temperature can be disastrous. The English "I am hot" cannot be literally translated "Ich bin heiss," but must be translated "Mir ist es heiss" (i.e., "to me it is hot"), for whereas the latter German sentence refers to the temperature, the former is idiomatic and actually refers to sexual temperature (arousal)!

In English we use idioms all the time to express ideas and thoughts which are quite different from the literal meaning of the individual words and the grammatical construction. "Have a good day" is not literally a command which the hearer is to obey, but a simple farewell. "How are you?"

many times is simply a greeting; often the last thing the speaker wants to hear is how the person really is. Even an atheist will use the idiom ''God bless you,'' which for him is equivalent to the idiom ''Gesundheit'' (literally, ''good health''). Some idioms exaggerate in order to describe certain feelings: ''If I don't get something cold to drink, I'll die of thirst''; ''If that happened to me, I would be embarrassed to death''; ''His best friend kicked the bucket''; ''Yesterday when I went shopping, I just ran around in circles''; ''She's really gone off the deep end''; ''He must have eyes in the back of his head.'' These are all idioms whose meanings today have little correlation with the precise grammatical relationships and the literal meanings of the terms employed. Furthermore, there appears to be in all cultures a host of universal archetypal symbols which quickly take on idiomatic significance: fire, water, bread, light, darkness, blood, up, down, plowing, reaping, washing.

In interpreting the teachings of Jesus, as well as all literature and speech, it is therefore clear that we must be alert to the use of idiomatic language. To complicate the matter even further we must be aware that the meanings of idioms are not static but fluid. They change. This is especially true in our society and time. In the past, to be described as ''square'' was a compliment; today it is an insult! We must, then, make sure to interpret a biblical idiom in light of its meaning at the time it was written. Fortunately, drastic changes in meanings were far less frequent in ancient societies than they are today. Nevertheless, the root definition of terms (i.e., their etymology) may be of little significance in seeking to understand the meaning of a phrase, for what is needed is not a knowledge of the history of the terms found therein, but rather a knowledge of the usage of the phrase at the time it was written or uttered. (To use more technical terminology, we are primarily interested in the synchronic dimension of a term rather than its diachronic evolution.)

Within the Old Testament we find a number of terms and phrases which, interpreted literally, mean something totally different from what they meant in actual practice and usage. Some of these idioms use exaggerated language. A good example is the love-hate antithesis:

> If a man have two wives, one beloved, and another hated, and they have born him children, both the beloved and the hated; and if the firstborn son be hers that was hated: Then it shall be, when he maketh his sons to inherit that which he hath, that he may not make the son of the beloved firstborn before the son of the hated, which is indeed the firstborn: But he shall acknowledge the son of the hated for the firstborn, by giving him a double portion of all that he hath: for he is the beginning of his strength; the right of the firstborn is his. [Deut. 21:15–17, KJV]

> "I have loved you," says the LORD. But you say, "How hast thou loved us?" "Is not Esau Jacob's brother?" says the LORD. "Yet I have loved Jacob but I have hated Esau; I have laid waste his hill country and left his heritage to jackals of the desert." [Mal. 1:2–3]

In both these references the idiomatic love-hate antithesis actually signifies a contrast between loving more and loving less. In the Deuteronomic passage what we have is not an absolute love for one wife and an absolute hatred for the other, but rather a favoring of the one wife over the other. In fact, the Hebrew word which the King James renders "hate," the Revised Standard renders "dislike." Two other examples of this idiom are 2 Samuel 19:6 (v. 7 in the Hebrew text) and Proverbs 13:24. The true nature of this idiom is perhaps most apparent in Genesis 29:30–31:

> So Jacob went in to Rachel also, and he loved Rachel more than Leah, and served Laban for another seven years. When the LORD saw that Leah was hated, he opened her womb; but Rachel was barren.

Here it is clear that Leah's being hated (v. 31) does not mean that Jacob was malevolent or harbored malice toward her. What it means is that Jacob loved Rachel more than Leah (v. 30), that is, he loved Leah less. (In the poetry of the ancient Near East numerous terms were paired together. In such instances the meaning of these terms is far more dependent upon their idiomatic usage together than upon their literal meaning in isolation.)[25]

An idiom frequently used to express the loss of courage is the figure of a melting heart (Josh. 2:11; 5:1; 7:5; 2 Sam. 17:10; Ps. 112:10). Here a literal interpreting of the idiom would, of course, be absurd.

Over the centuries many Christians have been offended by Psalm 137:8–9 because they have not understood its idiomatic nature:

> O daughter of Babylon, you devastator!
>   Happy shall he be who requites you
>   with what you have done to us!
> Happy shall he be who takes your little ones
>   and dashes them against the rock![26]

How could the psalmist wish such terrible and hateful revenge upon the Babylonian children? How could such verses be included in the Scriptures? Once we realize, however, that what we have in this passage is an idiomatic picture of divine retribution and judgment upon an evil nation for their sins, much of the problem disappears. What the psalmist is seeking is not an actual smashing of Babylonian children against the rocks, but rather an earthly manifestation of divine judgment through which God will demonstrate his righteousness. The reference is not meant to be taken literally, but is to be understood as idiomatic language for the establishment of divine judgment and righteousness upon the earth.[27] If these verses are understood in this way, their seeming offensiveness disappears.

Some areas have their own special cluster of idioms. For instance, a number of idiomatic phrases are associated with the theme of judgment, the horror of the divine wrath. The same idioms are used for the temporal chastenings of Israel, Judah, and other biblical nations, and for the final judgment which will occur at the end of history.[28] We read that the sun will no longer give its light (Isa. 13:10; 24:23; Ezek. 32:7–8; Joel 2:10, 31; 3:15; Amos 8:9). We read of earthquakes (Zech. 14:5; 2 Baruch 27:7; 70:8; 2 Esdras 9:3), of fire (2 Baruch 27:10; 70:8; 2 Esdras 5:8), of drought (1 Enoch 80:2), of famine and sword and pestilence (Jer. 11:22; 14:12; 16:4; 21:9; Ezek. 6:11). We read that the land will become a wilderness (Isa. 64:10; Jer. 9:12; 23:10; Joel 2:3). Of course some of these figures (e.g., fire, famine, sword, and pestilence) are naturally associated with war and siege, but as time progressed they came to be associated with virtually any type of judgment.

In a similar manner the themes of future deliverance from one's enemies and the blessing and bliss of the new age also have their cluster of idioms. We read, for example, that the lamb and the wolf (or lion) will exist side by side (Isa. 11:6-9; 65:25) and that the wilderness and desert will turn into forests and fruitful fields where water abounds (Isa. 32:15; 35:1, 6-7; 41:18-19; 43:19-20). The promise made to Abraham that his seed will be as numerous as the sand of the sea is yet another common idiomatic exaggeration (Gen. 22:17; cf. 32:12; Josh. 11:4; Judg. 7:12).

It is not surprising, then, to find in Jesus' teaching concerning the judgment to come similar idiomatic language:

> For nation will rise against nation, and kingdom against kingdom; there will be earthquake in various places, there will be famines; this is but the beginning of the sufferings. [MARK 13:8]

> But in those days, after that tribulation, the sun will be darkened, and the moon will not give its light, and the stars will be falling from heaven, and the powers in the heaven will be shaken. [MARK 13:24-25]

> The Son of man will send his angels, and they will gather out of his kingdom all causes of sin and all evildoers, and throw them into the furnace of fire; there men will weep and gnash their teeth. [Matt. 13:41-42]

> So it will be at the close of the age. The angels will come out and separate the evil from the righteous, and throw them into the furnace of fire; there men will weep and gnash their teeth. [Matt. 13:49-50]

And cast the worthless servant into the outer darkness; there
men will weep and gnash their teeth. [Matt. 25:30]

The idiomatic nature of the terminology in MARK 13:8 and
24–25 is quite apparent from the Old Testament references
already given. "To weep and gnash the teeth" is a favorite
expression of Matthew (8:12; 13:42, 50; 22:13; 24:51; 25:30).
Although the same combination is found elsewhere only
in LUKE 13:28, the expression "to gnash one's teeth" was
a common idiom for rage, mockery, or pain (Job 16:9; Pss.
35:16; 37:12; 112:10; Lam. 2:16; Acts 7:54). That "the fur-
nace of fire [hell]" had also become an idiom by New Testament times is evident from 2 Esdras 7:36; 1 Enoch 10:13;
and 4 Maccabees 16:21.

There are other exaggerations which appear to be idiomatic: a camel going through the eye of a needle (MARK
10:25; cf. b. Berachoth 55b; b. Baba Metzia 38b) and faith
which can remove mountains (MATT. 17:20; 21:21; 1 Cor.
13:2) or cast a tree into the sea (Luke 17:5–6). If we are correct in claiming that these are idioms, the hearers of Jesus
would no more have interpreted them literally than we
would interpret a reference to "Rev. Jones's faith which can
remove mountains" literally. The faith which can remove
mountains is great faith in God, not an ability to eliminate
Mount Everest from the face of the earth. Once we become
aware of the presence of idioms in the teachings of Jesus,
we should be on guard not to interpret them literally.

CANON 12. A statement which uses universal language may contain exaggeration

The presence of universal language in a statement is also
an indication that the saying may be an exaggeration. In
everyday speech we frequently use universal language to
express general truths, yet for such statements there will
almost always be exceptions. We have already noted this
in regard to proverbs. Some people, however, believe that
a universal or all-inclusive statement is by definition an
exaggeration. They are wrong, for there are, of course, all-

inclusive statements that are literally true. When Paul says, "All have sinned and fall short of the glory of God" (Rom. 3:23), he is literally correct. All in Adam have sinned. There is none righteous, no, not one (Rom. 3:10).[29] Similarly, Paul intends for his readers to take the universal statement in 2 Corinthians 5:10 literally: "For we must all appear before the judgment seat of Christ, so that each one may receive good or evil, according to what he has done in the body." Jesus also makes universal statements which must be taken in a literal way. There is no trace of exaggeration when he says, "Unless you repent you will all likewise perish" (Luke 13:3, 5).

Nevertheless, it is more often true than not that unqualified general propositions found in the Bible are exaggerated statements.[30] There are numerous instances where Jesus used universal language in ways which make it clear that he did not intend for his words to be interpreted literally. Instead he intended that the all-inclusive language be understood as making his basic point all the more emphatic. There are many precedents in the Old Testament; the writers expected their audience to understand that some of their universal statements were not to be taken literally.[31] Consider, for example, Jeremiah 6:13, where the prophet condemns the corruption in Judah:

> For from the least to the greatest of them, every one is greedy for unjust gain; and from prophet to priest, every one deals falsely.

Surely Jeremiah is not claiming that there is not a single priest or prophet who is not greedy and does not deal falsely. After all, he himself is a prophet!

It is not surprising, then, that Jesus uses universal language in a similar way:

> And Jesus said to him, "If you can! All things are possible to him who believes." [Mark 9:23]

> Give to every one who begs from you; and of him who takes away your goods, do not ask them again. [LUKE 6:30]

But woe to you, scribes and Pharisees, hypocrites! Because
you shut the kingdom of heaven against men; for you
neither enter yourself, nor allow those who would enter to
go in. [MATT. 23:13]

Are all things indeed possible to him who believes? Is the
believer really omnipotent? Surely many qualifiers are
assumed in Mark 9:23. The believer cannot become God nor
cause God to cease existing. The believer cannot violate the
laws of logic, and in particular the law of contradiction, nor
change the fate of the dead. It is also clear from the teachings
of Scripture that we should not give to every person who
begs from us, for Paul in 2 Thessalonians 3:6–13 forbids giving to lazy Christians who refuse to earn their own living.
Furthermore, every parent knows it is his duty at times not
to give his children what they ask. Not only common sense
but love demands this. Nevertheless, such exceptions
should not lessen the impact of Jesus' teaching in LUKE
6:30: the believer is to be generous to the point of giving
up all his goods, if God so wills. In the reference to the
Pharisees and scribes in MATTHEW 23:13 we see another
use of all-inclusive language, but certainly not every Pharisee
and scribe was like the hypocrites described here and in
MATTHEW 23:5–7, 23, 27, 29–30; Matthew 23:15, 24. After
all, Nicodemus was a Pharisee (John 3:1), and in Luke 13:31
we read of certain Pharisees who warned Jesus of the danger
posed by Herod. Yet a large number of Pharisees were
hypocrites, so that Jesus in his rebuke of them could
justifiably use all-inclusive language. Any Pharisee present
could have profited from the warning and rebuke of Jesus,
even as any American tourist can profit from the rebuke
and castigation of all American tourists as ugly Americans.
Such a rebuke makes those Americans who are a credit to
their country all the more determined not to be ugly
Americans. Other passages where Jesus' use of universal
language is to be interpreted as exaggeration include MAT-
THEW 10:32 (cf. 7:21–22); 23:35; Matthew 23:3; MARK
2:21–22; 10:11–12; 13:30; and Luke 5:39.

CANON 13. **A statement which deals with subject matter prone to exaggeration may contain exaggeration**

Within the biblical materials, as well as in life in general, there are a number of subject areas which characteristically involve the use of exaggeration. We shall mention and illustrate only a few of them. One such area is descriptions of a person's emotional disposition. The Semite was certainly not one to hide feelings of misery or grief but expressed them openly for all to know.

> My flesh is clothed with worms and dirt; my skin hardens, then breaks out afresh. My days are swifter than a weaver's shuttle and come to their end without hope. [Job 7:5-6]

> I am weary with my moaning; every night I flood my bed with tears; I drench my couch with my weeping. My eye wastes away because of grief, it grows weak because of all my foes. [Ps. 6:6-7]

The exaggeration present in these examples is most apparent. Job's flesh was surely not covered with worms, nor did his days pass as quickly as a weaver handles a shuttle. As for the psalmist, it is doubtful that his tears flooded his bed and that his grief caused his eye to waste away (literally, to be moth-eaten). Similar examples of exaggeration to express grief and misery can be found in Job 6:2-4; 9:17-18; 16:11-16; Psalms 22; 38; 69; 88:3-9; 102:3-11; Isaiah 21:3-4; and Lamentations 3:1-21. To these Old Testament examples we can add Jesus' words in Gethsemane:

> And he said to them, ''My soul is very sorrowful, even to death.'' [MARK 14:34]

Another area in which we frequently encounter the use of exaggeration is promises or words of encouragement. Note, for instance, how God encouraged Abraham and his descendants:

> I will make your descendants as the dust of the earth; so

that if one can count the dust of the earth, your descendants also can be counted. [Gen. 13:16]

"Look toward heaven, and number the stars, if you are able to number them." Then he said to him, "So shall your descendants be." [Gen. 15:5]

I will do you good, and make your descendants as the sand of the sea, which cannot be numbered for multitude. [Gen. 32:12]

One need only reflect upon the impossibility of counting the dust of the earth, the stars, and the sand of the sea to see the exaggerated nature of these promises. Consider also God's description of the Promised Land into which Moses would lead the people of Israel:

Then the LORD said, "I have seen the affliction of my people who are in Egypt, and have heard their cry because of their taskmasters; I know their sufferings, and I have come down to deliver them out of the hand of the Egyptians, and to bring them up out of that land to a good and broad land, a land flowing with milk and honey, to the place of the Canaanites, the Hittites, the Amorites, the Perizzites, the Hivites, and the Jebusites. . . . I promise that I will bring you up out of the affliction of Egypt, to the land of the Canaanites, the Hittites, the Amorites, the Perizzites, the Hivites, and the Jebusites, a land flowing with milk and honey." [Exod. 3:7–8, 17]

Closely related to these promises are the numerous prophetic passages which in extravagant terminology encourage Israel with hopes of cosmic renewal as well as of judgment for her oppressors.[32] It is not surprising, therefore, to find that Jesus also used exaggeration as a means of encouragement for his disciples and as a medium for the divine promises:

But even the hairs of your head are all numbered. [MATT. 10:30]

Behold, I have given you authority to tread upon serpents

and scorpions, and over all the power of the enemy; and nothing shall hurt you. [Luke 10:19]

Among other passages that could be mentioned are MATTHEW 6:33; MARK 10:29–30; and LUKE 17:5–6.

Other areas could be named as well, for we often find exaggeration in passages containing numbers (Gen. 24:60; Exod. 1:7–9; Num. 10:36; Judg. 7:12; Ps. 3:6; 144:13), descriptions of size (Gen. 11:4; Deut. 1:28), or praise for heroes (Judg. 20:16; 2 Sam. 1:23). The reader of Scripture should keep in mind the almost universal tendency to exaggerate in such matters.

In concluding this chapter it will be profitable to comment in general on the various canons that have been discussed. Not all the canons listed are of equal value, and not every canon is applicable in every instance. Certain canons are, furthermore, less accessible to most readers of the Gospels. Most lay persons will find it more difficult to ascertain if a saying contains idiomatic language (canon 11) than to check if other sayings of Jesus contradict the literal meaning of the saying in question (canon 2). The following clues to the possible presence of exaggeration would appear to be serviceable for people with an elementary biblical understanding and a few minimal tools such as a Bible dictionary and concordance:

1. Statements which are literally impossible.
2. Statements which conflict with what Jesus says elsewhere.
3. Statements which conflict with the behavior and actions of Jesus elsewhere.
4. Statements which conflict with the teachings of the Old Testament.
5. Statements which conflict with the teachings of the New Testament.
7. Statements which the audience of Jesus did not interpret literally.
8. Statements which have not been fulfilled literally.
9. Statements which, if literally fulfilled, would not achieve the desired goal.

12. Statements which use universal language.

The remaining canons are more technical in nature and are accessible primarily to people with theological training:

6. Statements which are interpreted by another Evangelist in a nonliteral way.
10. Statements which use particular literary forms prone to exaggeration.
11. Statements which use idiomatic language.
13. Statements which deal with subject matter prone to exaggeration.

7

Purposes of Exaggerated Language

In chapter 1 of this volume we sought to demonstrate the presence of exaggerated language in the teachings of Jesus. We then sought in chapter 2 to establish certain canons by which such exaggeration can be detected. We listed thirteen canons and gave examples of how they can be used to detect exaggeration in Jesus' teachings and, for illustrative purposes, in the literature of the Old Testament as well. It is now time to deal with the function of exaggeration in literature in general and in the teachings of Jesus in particular.

The Various Kinds of Language

The purpose of language varies according to the intention of the speaker or writer. One may, for instance, use language to instruct, to reason, to command, to stimulate, or to express feelings. To put it simply, we might say that language is essentially either referential or "commissive" in nature.[1] The primary aim of referential language is description. It seeks to convey and clarify information. In so doing it seeks to bring about a rational thinking process; it is more concerned with one's reason than with one's emotions. As a result it tends to be characterized by nonemotive or "steno-" words rather than "depth" or "tensive" words. Commissive language, on the other hand, seeks to cause things to happen (i.e., to persuade one to perform and do certain tasks rather than simply to inform of certain facts) or to elicit certain feelings. Commissive language seeks primarily to affect the hearer rather than to provide him with information. As a result it tends to be characterized by tensive and emotive words which challenge and bring about decision and empathy. It needs to be pointed out, however, that even as referential language, while conveying information to the mind, may also affect the emotions, so also commissive language, while seeking to affect the emotions, may at the same time convey information to the mind. The difference is one of emphasis. The prime goal of referential language is to convey information; the prime goal of commissive language is to affect the hearer's emotions.

Referential language tends to be literal and cognitive in nature and to take the form of declarative sentences. It appeals primarily to the mind and the thought processes. At times it intentionally refrains from the use of any terminology which may arouse the emotions, for it wants the recipient to think clearly and objectively. In order to realize this goal, it seeks to get rid of all ambiguity and achieve semantic precision.[2] As a result it may merely present the facts and nothing but the facts. An example of referential language is Dr. Robert H. Stone's letter to Dr. Anderson (p. 138). In this letter Dr. Stone used referential language as devoid of emotive terminology as was possible. It is, of course, debatable whether any communication can be completely free of emotional language. Certainly the description of the patient's heart condition would raise some emotional response from the patient. "Paroxysmal atrial tachycardia" can be a very emotional term even if the patient does not understand precisely what it entails. Naked facts can and frequently do stir emotions. A report on what transpired at Auschwitz may use only the sterile referential language of historiography, but the information conveyed will stir the emotions of the reader and result in a definite response. A straightforward presentation of pure facts can at times challenge, stir emotion, and bring about action. The reason for this is that certain information, even if presented in noncommissive language, will, upon encountering a related need or attitude in the individual, produce an affect of one sort or another. The facts of the gospel, even when presented in referential language, are nevertheless "the power of God for salvation" (Rom. 1:16). Referential language, however, has as its primary goal the conveying of information. It can therefore be evaluated as either true or false, because the information conveyed either corresponds to reality or it does not.

Commissive language, on the other hand, while it also conveys information, seeks not merely or principally to inform, but to affect the recipient in some way. One type of commissive language—"performative"—seeks in particular to effect some sort of performance from the hearer. In seeking to bring about performance, it frequently makes use of commands or imperatival sentences. Such commissive language seeks to get something done and carries with it a demand for decision and response. In seeking to achieve this aim, persuasive, emotional, and exaggerated language is frequently used, for such language has the capacity to stir the emotions. Of course we cannot evaluate the command itself as being true or false; rather, it must be evaluated as to whether it is valid or invalid in the light of our presuppositions. Performative language, then, seeks not so much to *de*scribe, but to *pre*scribe and bring about a response.

Another kind of commissive language—expressive—seeks to state certain facts in ways that will elicit specific feelings and attitudes. We saw an example in Dr. Stone's letter to Joan (p. 138). Here Dr. Stone not only sought to convey certain information (his love for Joan), but also to arouse her emotions by the use of exaggerated language. A bare, factual usage of referential language could not convey the feelings of Dr. Stone nearly as well as his use of figurative and exaggerated language. By the use of such language he sought not merely to convey to Joan knowledge and information concerning his attitude toward her, but also to communicate his feelings, his longings, his deep love for her as well. No doubt he also hoped that his choice of language would so affect Joan that she would respond towards him in kind. Language which seeks to make an impression frequently takes on poetic or metaphorical form. Like performative language, expressive language cannot usually be judged as being either true or false. A different evaluative description is required; for example, adequate or inadequate, effective or ineffective. There is a sense, however, in which expressive language can be judged to be true or false. If a speaker or writer is purposely deceitful and uses expressive language to mislead, then it would seem reasonable to conclude that the language is not merely inadequate or ineffective, but false as well. It does not truly express one's feelings or attitudes. If Dr. Stone loved Joan and expressed his love poorly, we might say that his language was inadequate and ineffective; but if he did not love Joan at all, his language was false.

In the teachings of Jesus we find all the forms of language we have just discussed. We find referential language in the places where Jesus is seeking primarily to convey information and to appeal to reason. A good example is MARK 3:22–27:

> And the scribes who came down from Jerusalem said, "He is possessed by Beelzebul, and by the prince of demons he casts out the demon." And he called them to him, and said to them in parables, "How can Satan cast out Satan? If a kingdom is divided against itself, that kingdom cannot stand. And if a house is divided against itself, that house will not be able to stand. And if Satan has risen up against himself and is divided, he cannot stand, but is coming to an end. But no one can enter a strong man's house and plunder his goods, unless he first binds the strong man; then indeed he may plunder his house."

In this passage Jesus clearly sought to reason with his opponents. Now it is of course true that Jesus was seeking ultimately some sort of a response from them and was not seeking here only to convey bare facts and to demonstrate a sterile, unemotional logic. Few religious teachers are ambivalent as to whether their students respond to what they are saying. Jesus always hoped for a positive response to everything he said and did. Here, however, the primary purpose of his language was to convey certain information and logical reasoning in a way which would appeal to his listeners' rational processes, to their minds rather than to their hearts. Other examples in which the referential dimension is dominant in the teachings of Jesus can be found in MARK 8:31; 9:9–13; 12:18–27, 28–34, 41–44; and Luke 17:20–21.

On the other hand, there are many instances in which Jesus' language was primarily performative. By nature every command or imperative is basically performative in function. Unless a command has become an idiom, it seeks to cause something to happen. "Have a good day" and "Enjoy yourself," although imperatival in form, no longer seek a response, but are simply idiomatic expressions for "Good-bye" (which itself is, literally, a contraction of "God be with you" and a simple idiom used at times of departure). Jesus issued a great number of commands, some explicit, some merely implied. True, many of them do not contain exaggeration. The commands to repent (MARK 1:15), to keep his words (MATT. 7:24–27), and to believe (MARK 1:15; John 14:1) are unadorned by exaggerated terminology. Yet on numerous occasions Jesus heightened the affective nature of his commands by using exaggeration. The commands to hate father and mother (LUKE 14:26), to cut off one's hand and pluck out one's eye (MARK 9:43–47), to refrain from judging (MATT. 7:1) and swearing (Matt. 5:34), all contain exaggerated language which serves to startle the hearer and make him reflect on the nature of Jesus' command and the performance demanded.

At times Jesus also used exaggerated language in order to create a greater impression and to stir his hearers to reflect upon the reality which he was teaching. Again numerous examples are available. "It is easier for a camel to go through the eye of a needle than for a rich man to enter the kingdom of God" (MARK 10:25) by its exaggerated language challenges anyone with possessions to reflect seriously upon his relationship with God and the danger of the love of money (1 Tim. 6:10). Calling the scribes and Pharisees hypocrites because they strain out gnats but swallow camels (Matt. 23:24) is clearly hyperbolic.[3] While the figure is impossible, it is a striking and unforgettable picture of the behavior of the scribes and Pharisees. Similarly, the warning to take the log out of one's own eye before seeking to remove the speck from a brother's (MATT. 7:5) is a vivid portrayal of the hypocrisy involved in judging the faults of others while ignoring one's own.

The Value of Exaggerated Language

At times exaggeration serves a most useful function in speech and literature. It frequently has great mnemonic value since it creates a picture that is unforgettable. Who can forget the figures of a speck in one eye and a log in another, a camel going through the eye of a needle, straining gnats and swallowing camels? Such pictures are long remembered. No doubt Jesus intended such language to aid his hearers in remembering what he taught, for without access to pencil and paper or cassette recorders the vast majority of his audience had no means of preserving what he taught other than to memorize his words. The use of exaggeration made the task of remembering easier.

Another valuable function of exaggerated language is that it facilitates decision and change by impressing upon the hearer the seriousness of what the speaker is teaching. LUKE 14:26 teaches that following Jesus does not involve some cheap and easy faith; rather, it involves hating one's parents! Following Jesus is not, as Dietrich Bonhoeffer pointed out, a "cheap grace." No, it involves placing Jesus before all else. The many woes pronounced upon the Pharisees and scribes in Matthew 23 use harsh exaggeration (note the universal condemnation of all the Pharisees and scribes—they make proselytes children of hell [v. 15]; they strain out gnats but swallow camels [v. 24]; they are full of extortion and rapacity [v. 25]) and various graphic similes and metaphors (like whitewashed tombs [v. 27]; serpents, brood of vipers [v. 33]) in order to emphasize the gravity of their hypocrisy and the need to repent and change. In this way exaggeration functions in literature much as does verbal intonation in speech. A soft, mild "Watch out!" does not in any way affect the hearer as does a "WATCH OUT!" screamed as loudly as possible. Exaggerated language can serve as a scream of warning to bring the hearer's attention to the subject at hand and facilitate the appropriate response. Exaggeration is far more forceful and compelling in this regard than any literal statement can ever be.

A third purpose for the use of exaggerated language is to help communicate exactly how the speaker feels concerning the issue at hand. The psalmist revealed by his use of exaggeration his great love for the city of Jerusalem:

> His holy mountain, beautiful in elevation, is the joy of all the earth. [48:1–2]

> If I forget you, O Jerusalem, let my right hand wither! Let my tongue cleave to the roof of my mouth, if I do not remember you, if I do not set Jerusalem above my highest joy! [137:5–6]

In like manner Jesus frequently revealed his innermost feelings by the use of exaggerated language. Note how the following examples enable us to catch a glimpse of his deepest emotions. When asked for his essential thoughts on the matter of divorce, he replied:

> Whoever divorces his wife and marries another, commits adultery against her; and if she divorces her husband and marries another, she commits adultery. [MARK 10:11–12]

Having decried the use of prayer as a means of gaining public applause and recognition, he enjoined:

> But when you pray, go into your room and shut the door and pray to your Father who is in secret; and your Father who sees in secret will reward you. [Matt. 6:6]

And having denounced those who fasted in order to be seen and admired by others, and not in order to please God, he taught:

But when you fast, anoint your head and wash your face,
that your fasting may not be seen by men but by your Father
who is in secret; and your Father who sees in secret will
reward you. [Matt. 6:17–18]

Finally, as he faced the agony of the cross he said, ''My soul
is very sorrowful, even to death'' [MARK 14:34]. Perhaps
nowhere do we feel the heartbeat of Jesus more fully than
we feel it in his use of exaggerated language.[4]

A final function of exaggeration in language is to stimulate
our interest and hold our attention. Exaggeration makes one
sit up and take notice. Literal language unbroken by metaphor or exaggeration tends to be monotonous or at least
dull, but hyperbole or overstatement creates a certain tension which awakens not only the interest of the hearer but
also his thinking process. It teases the hearer into wrestling
with the underlying meaning of what is being said. Because
exaggerations contradict our ordinary way of thinking, they
raise questions. The greater the exaggeration, the more we
are challenged to arrive at the real intention of the author
or speaker: What exactly does he mean? Can he really expect
us to understand him literally, to carry out his instructions
to the letter? If not, what is he driving at? Needless to say,
this attention-getting purpose of exaggeration may be present in combination with its mnemonic, performative, and
expressive purposes. Use of exaggeration for one purpose
does not automatically exclude the others.

Conclusion

We have noted a number of reasons why Jesus chose to use exaggerated language in his teachings. It must be pointed out here that he never did so in order to deceive. The doctoring of business ledgers, so that the assets look greater than they really are, and the distorting of facts by a totalitarian state are not legitimate uses of exaggerated language. Jesus always assumed that his readers, either through intuition or logic, would understand that exaggeration was being used and would interpret his sayings accordingly. Exaggeration is a legitimate device in speech or literature only if the audience recognizes it as such. In most instances this is no major problem. But in our scientific age it is important to remind ourselves that Jesus frequently made use of the picturesque language of metaphor and exaggeration. As a result, we must take care to understand not merely the lexical meaning of Jesus' words, but also the underlying intent in his particular use of these figures of speech. This is a most important step in interpreting the teachings of Jesus, for in such passages the language used does not always correspond with the intended meaning. We must be careful to distinguish between the *referent* of a verbal symbol, that is, the object to which it literally refers, and the *sense*, that is, the mental image the verbal symbol is intended to convey.

More often than not, our intuition will keep us from interpreting Jesus' metaphors and exaggerations literally. This is especially true if we are well acquainted with the teachings of Jesus in general. The canons which have been listed in chapter 2 can serve as additional tools in the hermeneutical process. While they will not always enable us to determine with absolute certainty whether a saying is an exaggeration, they will allow us nevertheless to base our interpretation on more than intuition.

Recognition that a particular text contains exaggeration, however, does not end the hermeneutical process. Having noted the presence of exaggeration, we must seek to understand why Jesus used exaggeration in this particular instance. That an exaggeration which occurs in a command is performative in function is readily apparent. In such cases Jesus was emphatically seeking to bring about a decision of some sort. But we must also determine the precise decision expected of the original audience (the first *Sitz im Leben*), the original readers of the Gospel (the third *Sitz im Leben*), and the present reader as well. Furthermore, we must bear in mind that the presence of exaggeration in the teachings of Jesus in no way lessens the radical nature of their demand. To interpret LUKE 14:26 to mean not that we should hate our parents, but that love for Christ must take precedence over all human love, even the love of a husband for a wife or of parents for their children, does not lessen the radical nature of the demand at all. Abraham knew this (Gen. 22)! Likewise repentance, correctly understood, is even a more radical demand than the plucking out of an eye or the cutting off of a hand (MARK 9:43–47), for it involves a fundamental change of the entire person, not simply the violent removal of one part of the body!

Due to the present abundance of writing materials, the mnemonic value of exaggeration may not be as important today as in Jesus' day. The attention-getting purpose of an exaggeration may also be less important today for some; but the expressive purpose of such sayings is still very significant, for they reveal Jesus' innermost feelings on vital issues. While all the teachings of Jesus are important for the Christian, Jesus used exaggeration to highlight those to which he wanted to give additional emphasis. It is therefore incumbent on the Christian reader today to give special attention to and scrupulously heed those teachings.

Part 3

Difficult Passages in the Epistles

Introduction to Part 3

The difficulties which a reader encounters in the Epistles tend to be quite different from those encountered in the Gospels. One reason for this is the difference in their literary genre. In the Gospels we encounter the genre of historical narrative. Along with the task of understanding what the author is seeking to teach by the historical materials, there enters into consideration the historicity of these materials. How do the accounts recorded in these works correspond to what actually happened? Was Quirinius really governor of Syria, and was there really a census under Quirinius when Jesus was born? Was Jesus really tried before the Sanhedrin, Herod, and Pilate? By their very nature the study of the Gospels brings historical issues to the surface.

The Gospels also present the reader with certain difficulties in that there are multiple accounts of various events. At times we have four separate accounts of an incident. At times we have close parallels in the three Synoptic Gospels. Yet these accounts are never exactly the same word for word. It is clear that the Evangelists thought of themselves as inspired interpreters of the life and teachings of

Jesus and not simply as stenographic secretaries, and thus the differences do raise questions for the reader. Along with these problems we also encounter difficult sayings, actions, and predictions that come from the lips of Jesus.

In the Epistles (or Letters) of the New Testament we encounter a different set of issues. We are not involved so much here in asking, ''What really happened?'' as in seeking to understand the meaning of the author in his historical context. We are, of course, interested to learn all that we can about the thought-world of the first century and especially of the early church, but there are far fewer allusions to historical circumstances and events in a book like Romans than in a book like Luke. And for the most part the questions that parallel accounts raise in the Gospels are absent from the Epistles. The issues we meet in the Epistles are more linguistic in nature, and in this work we shall seek to illustrate how one can come to understand the meaning which an author gave to his words. In "Difficult Passages in the Gospels" it was pointed out that many of the difficulties that we encounter in reading are resolved once we understand what the author meant by his words. This is equally true in the case of difficulties encountered in the Epistles.

In this book we shall begin with the most basic building block used by the writers. We shall look at how we can understand the meaning an author gave to *words*. This will be our area of concern in chapter 8. In chapter 9 we shall deal with how to understand the statements in which these words are found. Here we shall point out the importance of the *grammatical syntax* which an author gives to his words within the statement. In chapter 10 we shall emphasize the importance of the *authorial context*. By the words, sentences, and paragraphs with which an author surrounds his statements, he gives important clues and hints as to what those statements mean. We shall look at how the authorial context helps us to understand various difficult statements found in the Epistles. In chapter 11 we shall look at the *larger context* of the entire biblical canon and see how our knowledge of this context enables us to understand and resolve various difficulties. In the final chapter we shall look at an example in which we can apply each of the principles learned in the first four chapters as well as consider how to deal with an example which seems to defy a successful resolution.

8

Understanding Words

The basic building blocks of all statements are words. Since all statements are constructed of these basic building blocks, an incorrect understanding of the meaning of an important word in a sentence will inevitably lead to an incorrect understanding of the sentence. As a result, one of the primary tasks of interpretation is to understand what the words of a statement mean, or as one author has stated, we must "come to terms." Only then can we proceed to the meaning of the statement itself. Since, however, one cannot spend a great deal of time investigating every individual word in each sentence, the interpreter must focus attention upon the key terms. These are fairly apparent by the frequency with which they appear in the sentence and its immediate context as well as by their importance in the argument.

People have used a number of methods in order to understand the meaning of words. One such method is the study of the etymology of the word. What is the root meaning of the word? The reader may even have heard sermons in which reference is made to the root meaning of the English word which is used to translate the Greek or

Hebrew term: "Webster's Dictionary tells us that this word comes from a root which means . . ."! Such a procedure is obviously faulty. The writers of Scripture were not thinking about the root meaning of English words that would be used to translate their texts millennia later. Yet, in a more academic fashion, scholars have also at times built on the root meaning of a Greek or Hebrew term in their text. In the vast majority of instances this is likewise an erroneous procedure. An example will demonstrate this. When speakers use words such as "nice" or "let," are they thinking of their root meanings? Or are they thinking of how these words are being used at the present time? Surely it is the latter. They are not thinking that the word *nice* comes from the Latin *nescius*, which means "ignorant," nor that in the eighteenth century "nice" meant "precise." And when they use "let," are they thinking of its Middle English root *lette*, which means "hinder" or "obstruct"? Note, for instance, Romans 1:13 in the King James Version: "I purposed to come unto you, (but was let hitherto)." Here "let" is used in its old sense of being hindered, but today we do not use this word in this manner except in playing tennis, where a "let" hinders the game from proceeding. The complete detachment of the present meaning of words from their etymology is most apparent in the attempt to understand the meaning of idioms. Idiomatic phrases have little connection with the root meanings of their words. This is why trying to understand the meaning of idioms in a foreign language is so difficult.

In general the etymology of a word is of little or no importance in understanding the meaning of that word in a statement. Writers usually have little interest in the root meaning of a word or the history of how the word has been understood in the past. They are interested only in how it is understood in the present. Using more technical terminology, we can say that writers pay attention not to the diachronic or past meaning of a term, but to its synchronic meaning at the time when they write. The etymology of a word is useful in two instances, however. One such instance occurs when an author intentionally plays on the etymological meaning of the word. Paul does this in Philemon when he plays on the name *Onesimus*, whose root meaning is "useful," and refers to the fact that once Onesimus was "useless" but now he is "useful" (v. 11). There are many times when the biblical authors play on the root meaning, that is, the etymology, of a name (e.g., Gen. 2:23; 3:20; 4:1; 17:5; Matt. 1:21, 23). The second instance in which the etymology of a word may be useful occurs when a word appears only once or twice in literature, and we do not know what its meaning is. In such cases when the synchronic or contemporary meaning of the term is unknown, the only possibility left for the scholar is the hope that when the author used this term, it still bore a meaning closely resembling the meaning of its root. Today this is not very likely, for the meanings of words change so quickly. Think of how such terms as "a square guy" (a compliment if my father said it), "gay," and "pot" have changed or taken on new meanings in the past few decades. On the other hand, ancient languages and society tended to be far more stable and traditional, so that biblical terminology did not experience such rapid and radical changes. Nevertheless, we should always remember that the use of etymology for understanding the meaning of a word, unless the author clearly indicates a play on the etymology of the word, is a last-chance attempt at trying to discover the meaning of the word in the author's time. It is in a sense a last resort. Certainly one would not want to build a theological argument on the supposition that a word bore the exact meaning of its ancient root.

There are several other pitfalls that can ensnare readers in their pursuit after the meaning of the words in a text. One pitfall is to assume that a word that looks and sounds alike in two different languages has the same meaning in both languages. This is less a problem for the biblical languages than for modern languages. (A friend of mine immigrated as a young child from Germany to the United States. He was frightened by the experience, especially when upon arrival he and his parents met a large, black immigration official, for the boy had never seen a black man before. The immigration official was a kindly gentleman and tried to befriend the lad. Offering him a candy bar, he urged, "Take it. It's a gift. Gift." Now my friend's fright turned to sheer terror, for in German "Gift" means poison!) A more serious problem lies in assuming that the range of meanings of an English word corresponds exactly to the range of meanings of the biblical word it translates. For instance, the word *pneuma* is translated by "spirit" in English and "Geist" in German, but the English word has potential meanings not possible in either Greek or German. Alcoholic "spirits" is possible only in English. (For an example of this kind of problem see pp. 233–38.) An even more serious problem encountered in seeking the meaning of biblical words is created by the false assumption that a word possesses the same meaning everywhere it is found. Essentially this assumes that biblical words are technical terms whose meaning is constant for all biblical authors. (For an illustration see pp. 243–48.)

Individual words possess a range of possible meanings, and the same word can be used to mean quite different things. Five minutes' reading in a dictionary will demonstrate this. The word *love*, for instance, does not mean the same thing in every statement. In one sentence it can mean "affection"; in another it can mean "sexual intercourse"; and in still another "a score in tennis." The context alone determines which particular meaning (out of the whole range of possible meanings) the word has in a given statement. When using a word, an author generally chooses one specific meaning out of the possible range of meanings of that word. It is only through the context in which the word is found that we can understand the specific meaning of the word. Using more technical terminology, we can say that a word in the "norms of language" has a finite range of meanings. A dictionary provides us with this range of meanings or the *langue* of a word. In a statement, however, a word has a particular or singular meaning. The "norms of the utterance" limit these possibilities to a singular meaning or the *parole*. Thus whereas the *langue* involves all the possibilities which language permits (all the dictionary possibilities), the *parole* limits the meaning of the word to the single, particular meaning of the author (the one specific dictionary meaning the author intended, such as "a score in tennis").

The process by which the meaning of an individual word is determined by the context, and the meaning of the context is at the same time determined by the meaning of the individual word, is called the hermeneutical circle. Although it seems extremely difficult, in practice the process is quite simple. Within the mind the reader or listener is able to clarify the precise meaning of a word by understanding what the context reveals about the specific meaning of the word. At the same time the preliminary understanding of what the word can and may mean is helping clarify what the context means. As I write on my word processor, I see time and time again the light switching back and forth from one disc to another. In the interpretative process the mind does the same, switching back and forth from the word to the context, and from the context to the word, until the context reveals the specific meaning of the word, and the word clarifies the meaning of the context.

There are three basic tools available for understanding the meaning of a word in a statement. The first is a dictionary or lexicon, which reveals to us the possible range of meanings or the "norms of language." Unless an author reveals to the reader otherwise, the desire to be understood causes the author to use words within this possible range of meanings. If a word is used in a way in which it has never been used before and the reader has no indication of this use, communication is impossible. This is revealed quite nicely in the conversation between Alice and Humpty Dumpty in Lewis Carroll's *Through the Looking Glass*:

> "There's glory for you!"
>
> "I don't know what you mean by 'glory,'" Alice said.
>
> Humpty Dumpty smiled contemptuously. "Of course you don't—till I tell you. I meant 'there's a nice knockdown argument for you.'"
>
> "But 'glory' doesn't mean 'a nice knockdown argument,'" Alice objected.
>
> "When *I* use a word," Humpty Dumpty said, in a rather scornful tone, "it means just what I choose it to mean—neither more nor less."
>
> "The question is," said Alice, "whether you can *make* words mean so many different things."
>
> "The question is," said Humpty Dumpty, "which is the master—that's all."

Can Humpty Dumpty make a word mean whatever he wants it to mean? In his writings he can. *But* if he wants to communicate something to his readers, he is bound to abide by the norms of language and assign to words meanings within the acceptable range or boundaries. Although he may choose to give to certain words meanings outside those boundaries, he must reveal this to his readers, if he wishes to communicate. And since most writers seek to communicate their thoughts to their readers (why else would they write?), we can assume that the words they use have meanings lying within the norms of language. A dictionary or lexicon reveals to us the *langue* or possible meanings of each word.

The second basic tool is a concordance, which is most helpful in understanding what a particular word means in a specific instance. It helps by showing where an author uses this same word elsewhere. This in turn helps us to see if the author tends to use this term in a specific way. By this procedure we can narrow the scope of possible meanings to the specific range of meanings which an author gives to this word. It may even reveal instances in which the author uses this word in parallels whose meaning is quite clear. The third basic tool for understanding the particular meaning of a word is a grammar. Through this tool we better learn how a word functions in a particular statement. (Grammar will be the focus of chapter 9.)

Is New Testament "Wine" the Same as Today's Wine?

A good example of how misunderstanding develops by assuming that the meaning of a term in English corresponds exactly to the Greek or Hebrew word it translates is the word translated "wine" in the Bible. Does what we mean by the term *wine* correspond exactly to what the ancient writers meant by this word? Is the wine referred to in the Bible the same as that bottled today by Christian Brothers or Château Lafitte-Rothschild or Mogen David? The answer to this question is, "Not exactly." It is obvious that the term *wine* in the Bible does not mean unfermented grape juice, for the command "Do not get drunk with wine" (Eph. 5:18) and the numerous warnings against wine in Scripture (e.g., Lev. 10:9; Prov. 20:1; 21:17; 23:29–35) make no sense at all if the word refers to a nonalcoholic beverage. On the other hand, it is also clear that the term does not correspond exactly to what we mean by wine today.

In ancient Greek culture, wine was usually stored in large pointed jugs called *amphoras*. When wine was to be used, it was poured from the amphoras into large bowls called *kraters*, where it was mixed with water. This became clear to me when I had the privilege of visiting the great archaeological museum in Athens, where I saw dozens of these large kraters. At the time it was not clear what their use signified about the drinking of wine in biblical times. From these kraters, cups or *kylikes* were then filled. What is important to note is that before wine was drunk, it was mixed with water. The kylikes were filled not from the amphoras but from the kraters.

The ratio of water to wine varied. Homer (*Odyssey* 9.208–9) mentions a ratio of twenty parts water to one part wine. Pliny (*Natural History* 14.6.54) mentions a ratio of eight parts water to one part wine. In one ancient work, Athenaeus's *Learned Banquet*, written around A.D. 200, we find in book 10 a collection of statements from earlier writers about drinking practices. An exchange from a play by Aristophanes reads: "'Here, drink this also, mingled three and two.'/'Zeus! But it's sweet and bears the three parts well!'" The poet Euenos, who lived in the fifth century B.C., is also quoted: "The best measure of wine is neither much nor very little;/For 'tis the cause of either grief or madness./It pleases the wine to be the fourth, mixed with three nymphs." Here the ratio of water to wine is three to one. Other writers mentioned include Hesiod (three to one), Alexis (four to one), Diocles (two to one), Ion (three to one), Nicochares (five to two), and Anacreon (two to one). Sometimes the ratio goes down to one to one (and even lower), but it should be noted that such a mixture is referred to as "strong wine." Drinking wine unmixed, on the other hand, was looked upon as a Scythian or barbarian custom. Athenaeus quotes Mnesitheus of Athens:

> The gods have revealed wine to mortals, to be the greatest blessing for those who use it aright, but for those who use it without measure, the reverse. For it gives food to them that take it and strength in mind and body. In medicine it is most beneficial; it can be mixed with liquid and drugs, and it brings aid to the wounded. In daily intercourse, to those who mix and drink it moderately, it gives good cheer; but if you overstep the bounds, it brings violence. Mix it half and half, and you get madness; unmixed, bodily collapse.

It is evident that wine was seen in ancient times as a medicine (and as a solvent for medicines) and of course as a beverage. Yet as a beverage it was always thought of as a mixed drink. Plutarch (*Symposiacs* 3.9), for instance, states, "We call a mixture 'wine,' although the larger of the component parts is water." The ratio of water might vary, but only barbarians drank wine unmixed, and a mixture of wine and water of equal parts was seen as "strong drink" and frowned upon. The term *wine* or *oinos* in the ancient Greek world, then, did not mean wine as we understand it today, but wine mixed with water. Usually a writer simply referred to the mixture of water and wine as "wine." To indicate that the beverage was not a mixture of water and wine one would say "unmixed [*akratesteron*] wine."

One might wonder whether the custom of mixing wine with water was limited to the ancient Greeks. The burden of proof should probably be upon anyone who argues that the pattern of drinking wine in Jewish society was substantially different from that of the examples already given. And we do have examples in both Jewish and Christian literature and perhaps in the Bible that wine was likewise understood as being a mixture of wine and water. In several instances in the Old Testament a distinction is made between "wine" and "strong drink." In Leviticus 10:8–9 we read, "And the LORD spoke to Aaron, saying, 'Drink no wine nor strong drink, you nor your sons with you, when you go into the tent of meeting.'" Concerning the Nazirite vow Numbers 6:3 states that the Nazirite "shall separate himself from wine and strong drink." This distinction is found also in Deuteronomy 14:26; 29:6; Judges 13:4, 7, 14; 1 Samuel 1:15; Proverbs 20:1; 31:4, 6; Isaiah 5:11, 22; 28:7; 29:9; 56:12; and Micah 2:11. The 1901 *Jewish Encyclopedia* (vol. 12, p. 533) states that in the rabbinic period at least, "'yayin' [wine] is to be distinguished from 'shekar' [strong drink]: the former is diluted with water ('mazug'); the latter is undiluted ('yayin hai')."

In the Talmud, which contains the oral traditions of Judaism from about 200 B.C. to A.D. 200 (the Mishnah) and later commentary on those traditions (the Gemara), there are several tractates in which the mixture of water and wine is discussed. One tractate (Shabbath 77a) states that wine which suffers from being mixed with three parts of water is not wine. The normal mixture is said to consist of two parts water to one part wine. In a most important reference (Pesahim 108b) the writer states that the four cups every Jew was to drink during the Passover ritual were to be mixed in a ratio of three parts water to one part wine. From this we can conclude with a fair degree of certainty that the fruit of the vine used at the institution of the Lord's Supper was a mixture of three parts water to one part wine. In another Jewish reference from around 60 B.C. we read, "It is harmful to drink wine alone, or again, to drink water alone, while wine mixed with water is sweet and delicious and enhances one's enjoyment" (2 Macc. 15:39).

In ancient times there were not many beverages that were safe to drink. The danger of drinking water alone raises another point. The ancients could make water safe to drink in several ways. One method was boiling, but this was tedious and costly. They also tried different methods of filtration. The drinking of wine (i.e., a mixture of water and wine) served therefore as a safety measure, since often the water available was not safe. (I remember all too well drinking some water in Salonica, Greece, that would have been much better had it been mixed with sufficient wine or some other purifying agent.)

When we come to the New Testament, we find that the content of the wine is never discussed. The burden of proof, however, is surely upon anyone who would say that the wine of the New Testament is substantially different from the wine mentioned by the Greeks, the rabbis during the Talmudic period, and the early church fathers. In the writings of the early church fathers it is clear that "wine" means wine mixed with water. Justin Martyr around A.D. 150 described the Lord's Supper in this way: "Bread is brought, and wine and water, and the president sends up prayers and thanksgiving" (*Apology* 1.67.5). Some sixty-five years later Hippolytus instructed the bishops that they should "eucharistize [bless] first the bread into the representation of the Flesh of Christ; and the cup mixed with wine for the antitype of the Blood which was shed for all who have believed in Him" (*Apostolic Tradition* 23.1). Cyprian around A.D. 250 stated in his refutation of certain heretical practices:

> Nothing must be done by us but what the Lord first did on our behalf, as that the cup which is offered in remembrance of Him should be offered mingled with wine.... Thus, therefore, in considering the cup of the Lord, water alone cannot be offered, even as wine alone cannot be offered. For if anyone offer wine only, the blood of Christ is disassociated from us: but if the water be alone, the people are disassociated from Christ.... Thus the cup of the Lord is not indeed water alone, nor wine alone, unless each be mingled with the other. [Epistle 62.2, 11, 13]

Here it is obvious that unmixed wine and plain water were both found unacceptable at the Lord's Supper. A mixture of wine and water was the norm. Earlier (the latter part of the second century) Clement of Alexandria had stated: "It is best for the wine to be mixed with as much water as possible.... For both are works of God, and the mixing of the two, both of water and wine, produces health, because life is composed of a necessary element and a useful element. To the necessary element, the water, which is in the greatest quantity, there is to be mixed in some of the useful element" (*Instructor* 2.2.23.3–24.1).

Within the New Testament itself, we have only one example in which it is obvious that the author's understanding of *oinos* ("wine") differs from ours. This is found in Revelation 14:10 where the writer speaks of "the wine of God's wrath, poured unmixed (*akratou*) into the cup of his anger." Here it is clear that the author is speaking of an unusual display of the wrath of God. There is nothing normal about this display of God's wrath. It will not be mitigated by his graciousness. Rather, the "unmixed" pure wine of God's wrath will be manifested. If the author thought that the word *wine* meant what we mean by wine today, that is, pure wine unmixed with water, the use of the term *unmixed* would not have been necessary. However, since "wine" was normally a mixture of water and wine, he had to add the term *unmixed* to describe the undiluted wrath of God. It is evident from this example that in seeking to understand the meaning of a word we must seek to understand what it meant in the context of the author. The meaning of the English word used in the translation may not correspond perfectly with the meaning of the original word.

Can an Unbeliever Understand the Gospel? (1 Cor. 2:14)

One passage that has frequently been misinterpreted because of the misunderstanding of key words is 1 Corinthians 2:14. Here Paul states,

> The unspiritual man does not receive the gifts of the Spirit of God, for they are folly to him, and he is not able to understand them because they are spiritually discerned.

Frequently this verse has been interpreted to mean that according to Paul the non-Christian cannot understand the gospel message. An example of such interpretation is found in a recent work in which the author states, "Although God desires to communicate to all men, not just anyone can understand Scripture. . . . *Faith* is the prerequisite for truly understanding God's Word."

In order to understand exactly what Paul meant by his words, we must note the context in which they are found. This context is made up of numerous elements, including the historical period and the cultural milieu, but the most important element for narrowing down the range of possible meanings of Paul's terms is the author's own writings and in particular the immediate context. In regard to 1 Corinthians 2:14 this means that we should seek to understand what the terms in this verse meant in first-century Greek and in the situation of the early church of that period, but above all we must try to understand how Paul in his letters and particularly in 1 Corinthians used these terms.

With regard to 1 Corinthians 2:14 it will be especially important to note how Paul uses the terms *receive, folly, understand,* and *discern* if we are to interpret this passage correctly. For many people the term *folly* refers to "something which is not understandable, incapable of comprehension, unintelligible." Yet does "folly" deal with the mind's inability to conceptualize certain doctrinal statements, or does it involve an evaluative judgment of some sort? A closer look at how Paul uses this term elsewhere in 1 Corinthians is enlightening.

> Where is the wise man? Where is the scribe? Where is the debater of this age? Has not God *made foolish* the wisdom of the world? [1:20, italics added]

> For the wisdom of this world is *folly* with God. [3:19, italics added]

In the first example the apostle uses the verb form of this term (*emōranen*) whereas in the second example he uses the noun (*mōria*), but it should be observed that in both instances we are not dealing with a lack of comprehension or understanding. Surely Paul is not claiming that God is not able to understand the wisdom of this world. The omniscient God is certainly able to understand anything that the finite human mind is able to grasp. No, God understands the wisdom of this world, but he has judged and evaluated it as being foolish. To interpret "made foolish" and "folly" as evaluative judgments on God's part makes far better sense than to interpret them as meaning that God cannot understand the wisdom of this world, for Paul certainly believed that God is all-knowing.

First Corinthians 2:14 should be understood in a similar way. From experience it is evident that unbelievers can understand the doctrinal teachings of the Bible. In fact some unbelievers can describe and explain Christian doctrines better than some believers can. They can even get better grades on biblical and theological examinations. But (and this is no small "but") the unbeliever in evaluating these doctrines thinks that they are "folly." Such a person judges them as unrealistic, primitive, superstitious, mythical, unscientific. In other words the unbeliever, although capable of understanding what these doctrines teach, is incapable of appreciating their truthfulness and significance. The believer, on the other hand, is convinced of their veracity and ascribes to them great significance, for to him these doctrines are truths from God himself. They are for him divine wisdom.

Another term that needs to be understood more clearly in this verse is the Greek word which is translated "receive." In the Pauline Letters we find several instances in which it is used in the same sense as we find it here.

> And you became imitators of us and of the Lord, for you *received* the word in much affliction, with joy inspired by the Holy Spirit. [1 Thess. 1:6, italics added]

> And we also thank God constantly for this, that when you received the word of God which you heard from us, you *accepted* it not as the word of men but as what it really is, the word of God, which is at work in you believers. [1 Thess. 2:13, italics added]

> Working together with him, then, we entreat you not to *accept* the grace of God in vain. [2 Cor. 6:1, italics added]

In these examples the Greek word translated "receive" in 1 Corinthians 2:14 is rendered "received," "accepted," and "accept." It is evident that in these examples to "receive" does not mean to comprehend or understand, but rather to welcome or to receive eagerly. Thus what Paul is saying in 1 Corinthians 2:14 is that the unbeliever does not receive the gospel message in the sense of welcoming it. This does not mean that he cannot understand the gospel message, but rather that his attitude toward and reception of it is hostile.

In a similar way the term "understand" (*gnōnai* in the Greek, "know" in the KJV) can mean more than to "understand conceptually." The range of meanings of this word in different contexts can be seen in the following passages:

> For although they *knew* God they did not honor him as God or give thanks to him, but they became futile in their thinking and their senseless minds were darkened. [Rom. 1:21, italics added]

> For since, in the wisdom of God, the world did not *know* God through wisdom, it pleased God through the folly of what we preach to save those who believe. [1 Cor. 1:21, italics added]

In both these instances the apostle uses the term which is translated "understand" in 1 Corinthians 2:14. In the first example Paul states that there is a sense in which the world possesses a conceptual knowledge of God's existence and power as witnessed to by his creation. In this sense the unbeliever "knows" God. Yet in a deeper sense the unbeliever chooses not to "know" God because the world does not delight in the gospel message. The world's wisdom has no room for the truth of its sin, its depravity, its helplessness. The wisdom of God, the cross, is simply folly to the world, and thus it chooses not to "know" God.

And so, in the context of this letter, to "understand" in 1 Corinthians 2:14 does not mean to "conceptualize" or to "intellectually comprehend," but rather to "grasp the truthfulness of" and to "recognize as fact." In this verse "understand" is used in conjunction with "discerned," which means "evaluated" or "judged." (See how the Greek word translated "discerned" here is rendered in

1 Cor. 2:15; 4:3–4; 9:3; 10:25, 27; 14:24.) To "understand" therefore means to evaluate positively. It is in this sense that the unbeliever cannot "understand" the things of the Spirit. Only when one possesses the Spirit can one evaluate correctly the truthfulness of the gospel message.

As a result of a proper understanding of various words in 1 Corinthians 2:14, we have interpreted this verse as meaning that the unbeliever, being unable to evaluate correctly the gospel message, judges it to be foolish, rather than as meaning that the unbeliever cannot intellectually understand Christian doctrines. This interpretation also accords well with the context of 1 Corinthians 1:18–2:5. Here Paul contrasts the wisdom of God, which the world denigrates as folly (1:18), with the wisdom of the world, which despite its cleverness (1:19) and lofty words (2:1) God has exposed as truly foolish (1:20). The issue in the first chapters of 1 Corinthians does not involve the ability of believer and unbeliever to conceptualize the Christian teaching concerning the death of Christ, but rather the unbeliever's attitude to this divine truth and God's rejection of the human-centered wisdom of this world. Paul does not deprecate wisdom in the true sense, for true wisdom does not stem from this world but from God (2:6–7). Paul, like the psalmist, deprecates a so-called wisdom that lacks reverence and submission to God, for he realizes that "the fear of the LORD is the beginning of wisdom" (Ps. 111:10). Apart from such reverence and submission the gospel message becomes a stumbling block to Jewish expectations and folly to Gentile philosophical reasoning (1 Cor. 1:23).

Perhaps what Paul teaches in 1 Corinthians 2:14 can be summarized by way of the following example. Imagine that a great professor, the world's leading Pauline scholar, is delivering a lecture on the apostle's doctrine of justification by faith. It is the most brilliant lecture ever given on the subject. In fact, if the apostle Paul had been present, he would have responded, "Thank you, Professor, for helping me to understand." However, after explaining what Paul meant by his teaching on justification, the professor adds, "But you know, of course, that this is pure nonsense!" It is clear that the professor as an unbeliever does understand Paul's doctrine of justification by faith. He can brilliantly conceptualize and explain this biblical teaching, but he does not welcome it. On the contrary, he rejects it as folly. What he lacks is the believer's Spirit-given conviction of the truthfulness and reality of this teaching.

On the other hand, imagine that a believer who lacks academic training is also asked to explain what Paul means by the doctrine of justification by faith. This individual apologizes for not being a theologian and, as tears form in the eyes, states, "I guess it means that Jesus did it all for us." Now it is evident that there is a sense in which the latter individual "understands" (i.e., is able to conceptualize) this great biblical doctrine far less than does the great professor, but there is also a sense in which the believer "discerns" it (i.e., recognizes its truthfulness) far better. "The unspiritual man does not receive the gifts of the Spirit of God, for they are folly to him, and he is not able to understand them because they are spiritually discerned."

Does James Disagree with Paul on Justification? (James 2:14–26)

The one biblical passage that has probably caused more theological difficulty than any other is James 2:14–26, for it seems to conflict with and contradict the Pauline doctrine of justification by faith. We need only place the two teachings side by side to see the problem:

> For if Abraham was justified by works, he has something to boast about, but not before God. For what does the scripture say? "Abraham believed God, and it was reckoned to him as righteousness." [Rom. 4:2–3]

> Was not Abraham our father justified by works, when he offered his son Isaac upon the altar? [James 2:21]

And

> For we hold that a man is justified by faith apart from works of law. [Rom. 3:28; see also 4:5]

> You see that a man is justified by works and not by faith alone. [James 2:24]

It is not surprising that Martin Luther, in seeking to make clear the Pauline doctrine of justification by faith, thought that the Epistle of James was "a right strawy Epistle" which contained no gospel.

The proper application of the basic principle that words possess a certain elasticity and therefore a range of possible meanings, so that the same word may be used in varied ways in different contexts, helps to alleviate the problem. For example, the English word *faith* can mean any of the following: a religion (the Hindu "faith") or a branch thereof (the Protestant "faith"); a specific set of theological doctrines (a church's statement of "faith"); a living, vital trust in God (she has a real "faith"); a set of intellectual tenets one ascribes to with varying degrees of commitment (one's "faith" in a number of causes); something which one believes is true but to which one nevertheless remains uncommitted or opposed (the "faith" of demons); an assured hope and trust (Heb. 11:1). The word *faith* can mean any of the above and more. As in the case of Humpty Dumpty (p. 232), the elasticity of a word, however, has its limits, for if we seek to communicate with others, the meaning we give to a word must lie within the accepted norms of language held by the community with which we are seeking to communicate. If we use a word in a totally new way, so that it means something outside the common norms of meaning, we must reveal this clearly to our audience if we want communication to occur. The word *faith*, for example, may mean any of the possibilities listed above, but it cannot mean "hamburger."

It is a false and dangerous assumption to believe that a word must always mean the same thing. Words can have a variety of meanings according to the context in which we find them. This is most evident when we look up a word in a dictionary. Usually there are a number of possible meanings for any given word. On the other hand, when a word is used in a specific context, it loses its elasticity and takes on one specific meaning. (In some instances a word can mean more than one thing, as in the case of a pun, but this is the exception to the rule.) A good example of how a word loses its elasticity in a context is the use of a sentence in a dictionary definition to illustrate one of the possible meanings of a word. In the sentence the word is no longer elastic but takes on a singular meaning. In view of the multiplicity of possible meanings caution must be exercised when we use a Bible concordance. It is indeed a most valuable tool, but we must not conclude that a word means the very same thing in all of its appearances in the Bible. The specific meaning of a word depends upon the specific context in which it is found. This is true for the Bible as well as for any other literary work.

Keeping this principle in mind, we shall now consider whether the terms *faith* and *works* have identical meanings for Paul and James. Looking first at the use of "faith," we see that Paul speaks of an obedient trust (Rom. 1:5), a faith like Abraham's (Rom. 4:9, 16), a faith from the heart (Rom. 10:9), a faith involving discipleship (2 Cor. 5:7), and a faith that is accompanied by the gift of the Holy Spirit (Gal. 3:2, 14). On the other hand, we find that in James "faith" means something quite different. He speaks of a faith unaccompanied by works (2:14), a faith that can see Christians in dire need of food and clothing and not provide them with these necessities of life (2:15–17), an intellectual assent to a fact (2:19a), and a faith that even demons possess (2:19b).

We should also note the differences between the use of the word *works* by Paul and by James. For Paul "works" are antithetical to faith (Rom. 4:2–5) and to the grace of God (Rom. 11:6), involve the keeping of the Jewish law and in particular the rite of circumcision (Gal. 5:2–4), are a legalistic attempt to achieve a right standing before God by one's keeping of the law (Rom. 3:20; 4:2), permit one to boast before God (Rom. 4:2), and seek to place God in one's debt (Rom. 4:4). For James, however, "works" are acts of compassion done in obedience to faith, such as clothing the naked and feeding the hungry (2:15–17), are intimately associated with Abraham's faith (2:22), involve obeying God's direct command (2:21), and include protecting God's messengers (2:25).

It is evident that although both Paul and James use the terms *faith* and *works* within the norms of meaning for their day, in the specific context in which they wrote they selected different meanings for these terms. When Paul talks about faith, he means the believer's wholehearted trust in and sole dependence on the grace of God in Christ for salvation. James, however, means an intellectual assent to doctrine which neglects works of Christian love and which even demons possess. Clearly they are not talking about the same thing. As for "works," in Paul the term refers to self-righteous acts done legalistically in order to merit or earn salvation, whereas in James it refers to loving acts of kindness done by a believer who already has exercised saving faith.

So then, although the words of Romans 4:2–3 appear to conflict with those of James 2:21, and Romans 3:28 with James 2:24, in actuality they do not, because they do not bear the same meanings. Paul is attacking the view that one may be justified on the basis of works done legalistically in order to merit favor with God. Can we by our works place God in our debt? Paul argues vigorously that we are saved on the basis of God's grace and through faith alone. On the other hand, James in his epistle is attacking a totally different view. He is arguing against the position that mere intellectual assent without an accompanying rebirth issuing into newness of life can bring salvation.

Think for a moment how we might counsel identical twins, one of whom thinks that he must earn his salvation and will get to heaven only when he becomes good enough, and the other of whom thinks that despite all of his immorality and sin he will still get to heaven because ten years ago he made a "decision" for Christ. Would not we tend to share the Pauline emphasis with the former and the emphasis of James with the latter? Actually Paul's statement, "For in Christ Jesus neither circumcision nor uncircumcision is of any avail, but *faith working through love*" (Gal. 5:6, italics added), is quite similar to what we find in James 2:14–26. By understanding the principle that words contain a range of possible meanings and that the specific meaning of a word is determined by the context in which it is used, we alleviate much of the alleged tension between James and Paul.

There are at least two other reasons why this passage in James should not be interpreted as contradicting the teachings of Paul. These might better be dealt with in chapter 2 since it deals with the importance of grammar and syntax in interpreting a text. For convenience' sake, however, since we are dealing with this passage, we shall discuss them here. One additional argument in favor of our understanding of this passage is found in the hypothetical nature of James 2:14, "What does it profit, my brethren, *if* a man says he has faith but has not works? Can his faith save him?" [italics added]. In the original Greek we find a conditional statement in the subjunctive rather than in the indicative mood. Such a statement in the subjunctive mood deals with possibility rather than actuality. This means that James is not assuming that one can in fact have faith without works. Rather he is dealing with a hypothetical situation. To word this in another way, James is not implying that in reality a person can have faith but not works, for he assumes that this is impossible. A true faith is always associated with works of love (see James 2:18, "Show me your faith apart from your works, and I by my works will show you my faith"). Hypothetically, but only hypothetically, will he entertain the possibility of faith without works.

Second, we should note that in verse 14 James raises a question not concerning faith in the true sense but concerning the faith just spoken about, that is, the faith that has no works. In the Greek text there is an article present in the question, "Can his [lit., the] faith [we have just spoken about] save him?" This means that James is not talking about genuine faith as he understands it, but about an inauthentic faith—a faith without works. James asks, "Can the faith just referred to, that is, a faith which is unaccompanied by works of love and compassion, can this kind of faith save him?" The answer is, of course, no! Such a faith cannot save anyone. We are indeed saved by faith alone, but as one scholar has put it, the faith that saves is never alone. It always results in acts of loving obedience. As Paul states, only a faith which works through love can save (Gal. 5:6).

While no attempt has been made to explain all the difficulties that James 2:14–26 raises, the above insights alleviate some of the difficulties associated with this passage. Once we recognize that although the same terms are used by both James and Paul, these terms mean quite different things in their respective contexts, then we are well on the way to resolving some of the problems. This receives additional support from the hypothetical nature of the argument in verse 14 and the fact that James makes clear that *the* faith he is referring to is a counterfeit faith unaccompanied by good works, which is a faith even demons possess.

It is clear from the passages discussed in this chapter that a proper understanding of a biblical statement depends on a correct understanding of the meaning of the basic building blocks of that statement. Only when we understand what the author means by the words he uses can we come to understand what he means by his combination of those words into sentences. In seeking to understand the meaning of a word, the first step must be to delimit the range of possible meanings that a word may have. What is the semantic range of possibilities, or to phrase this differently, what do the norms of language allow as meanings for this word? A dictionary or lexicon is most useful at this point, for it will delimit the semantic range. Next we must eliminate various possibilities until we ascertain the specific meaning of the word in the sentence. Here a concordance, which helps us see how the author uses this same word elsewhere, and a grammar, which helps us to understand the grammatical construction of the immediate context, are most useful. When we know the specific meaning of various key words, we can go on to investigate the meaning of the statement or proposition in which these words are found.

9

Understanding Grammar

After we have come to understand the meaning of the individual words which make up a statement, we can proceed to the interpretation of the statement itself. A statement consists of a number of words which the author has put into some sort of grammatical relationship in order to express his or her thought. To understand the author's statement, the reader must decipher the grammatical code tying these words together. Although the reader might know precisely what each word in a sentence means, there is the additional problem that different combinations of these words can mean different things. For instance, the words *Joan, Bob,* and *loves* permit all sorts of possible meanings. We can say (1) Joan loves Bob; (2) Bob loves Joan; (3) Bob, Joan loves; (4) Joan, Bob loves; (5) Loves Joan Bob; and (6) Loves Bob Joan. These possibilities can be further increased by the way in which the sentence is punctuated. If we end them with a question mark, a period, or an exclamation point, we have additional possibilities of meaning.

Different languages use different grammatical codes. In English, word order is of paramount importance. The question of whether "Joan" is the subject or the object of the verb depends on its position in the sentence. In other languages, word order is of minor importance, and the relationship of a noun to the verb is determined not by word order but by its specific ending. Other aspects such as tenses, moods, and cases may be indicated by prefixes or suffixes. Often key relationships between parts of sentences are indicated by conjunctions or particles such as "if," "because," "when," and "in order that." Without a correct understanding of the grammatical code used by the author, misinterpretation is all too likely to occur. On the other hand, interpretative difficulties can frequently be resolved by a correct analysis of the grammar which binds words together. Whereas in the understanding of words, a dictionary/lexicon and a concordance are the most helpful tools, here the primary tool is a grammar. For the student of the Greek New Testament this will include a basic grammar of New Testament Greek and an intermediate or advanced grammar which deals with Greek syntax. For the student of the English Bible, the primary tool will be an English grammar. In this chapter we shall look at several examples in which a knowledge of Greek grammar plays a most important role.

What Does It Mean to Work Out Your Own Salvation? (Phil. 2:12)

One of the most precious teachings of the Christian church is the doctrine of justification by faith. In contrast to the idea that salvation comes through one's own works or through a combination of faith and works, the Reformers proclaimed that justification is a gift of God and that it is appropriated "by faith *alone*."

That this is a biblical teaching is evident. Above all, it was made clear by the apostle Paul, who struggled against the teaching of certain Judaizers. These Judaizers claimed that justification results from a combination of faith and works, and insisted that the Gentile converts to Christianity had to perform certain works, such as submitting to circumcision and keeping various Old Testament food regulations, if they were to be saved/justified (Acts 15:1-5). Paul argued vehemently against this teaching by pointing out that since the Gentile believers had by faith alone received the Holy Spirit, who is the firstfruits and seal of salvation, they did not need to do anything more. God had accepted them, and this was confirmed by his having given them his Spirit (Gal. 3:1-5; see also Acts 11:2-18; 15:7-11). Paul also pointed out that Abraham, the father of the faithful, was justified by faith alone (Gal. 3:6-9). Paul made several other statements to the same effect:

> For by grace you have been saved through faith; and this is not your own doing, it is the gift of God—not because of works, lest any man should boast. [Eph. 2:8-9]

> Therefore, since we are justified by faith, we have peace with God through our Lord Jesus Christ. [Rom. 5:1]

> And to one who does not work but trusts him who justifies the ungodly, his faith is reckoned as righteousness. [Rom. 4:5]

The biblical nature of the doctrine of justification by faith alone is clear from these and many similar passages. There are, however, a few New Testament texts which seem to conflict with this teaching. One of them is Philippians 2:12. In this instance, however, some of the same principles of interpretation which helped us to understand why James 2:14-26 does not conflict with this great doctrine will show that Philippians 2:12 does not conflict either.

Paul states in Philippians 2:12:

> Therefore, my beloved, as you have always obeyed, so now, not only as in my presence but much more in my absence, work out your own salvation with fear and trembling.

At first glance this passage seems to conflict with what Paul states in Ephesians 2:8–9 and Romans 4:5; 5:1. How can you "work out your own salvation" if salvation/justification is by faith alone? Is it possible that Paul teaches something here which contradicts justification by faith alone? There are at least three powerful reasons why it would be incorrect to interpret this verse as standing in contradiction to what Paul teaches elsewhere concerning the doctrine of justification by faith.

First, our emphasis on the careful analysis of words should cause us to note the meaning of the key word *work out*. (It is a single word in Greek.) This term is different from the one Paul uses when arguing against the belief that we can earn justification by works. In those passages the terms used are the noun *ergon* and the derivative verb *ergazomai*, but here he uses *katergazomai*. This is, of course, clear in the Greek text, but it is also clear in numerous English translations as well, especially those in the King James tradition, which includes not only the King James, but also the English Revised, the American Standard, the Revised Standard, and the New American Standard. The New English Bible and the New International Version also join in and translate *katergazomai* "work out" and not "work for" or "work to get." Unfortunately not all biblical versions translate the Greek term this carefully.

It is critical at this point to observe just how the apostle uses this term elsewhere in his writings. It appears twenty times in the Pauline Letters: Romans 1:27; 2:9; 4:15; 5:3; 7:8, 13, 15, 17, 18, 20; 15:18; 1 Corinthians 5:3; 2 Corinthians 4:17; 5:5; 7:10, 11; 9:11; 12:12; Ephesians 6:13; and Philippians 2:12. It should be noted that in each of these passages there is no idea of meriting or earning something, for the law does not earn wrath (Rom. 4:15), sin does not earn covetousness (Rom. 7:8), nor does generosity earn thanksgiving (2 Cor. 9:11). The way Paul usually uses and understands this term can be seen even more clearly in the following instances:

> For I will not venture to speak of anything except what Christ *has wrought* through me to win obedience from the Gentiles, by word and deed. [Rom. 15:18, italics added]

> The signs of a true apostle *were performed* among you in all patience, with signs and wonders and mighty works. [2 Cor. 12:12, italics added]

It is clear that in these two instances there is no idea of meritorious works in view. There is no concept of earning something. Christ did not "earn" obedience from the Gentiles through Paul, nor did Paul earn the "signs of a true apostle." Rather these signs were manifested or demonstrated to the Corinthians. Paul's apostleship was a fact. It was the outworking of that fact and reality which was manifested to the Corinthians. In a similar way Paul is not telling the Philippians to merit or earn their salvation, but rather to manifest (demonstrate or live out) the salvation which they already possess.

Second, we should note the context in which Philippians 2:12 is found. Actually the clause we are discussing, "work out your own salvation," is neither a complete verse nor, more importantly, a complete sentence. In seeking to understand what Paul means here the best commentary is not some other passage in the Bible, but the rest of the sentence. Philippians 2:12–13 is the complete sentence in which the words "work out your own salvation" are found.

We note here that verse 13 begins with the word "for" (*gar*). This means that the reason for Paul's exhortation in verse 12 is to be found in verse 13. To word this a little differently, the "for" of verse 13 reveals that the ground or basis of Philippians 2:12 is the reality spoken of in verse 13. It is because "God is at work" in the hearts and lives of the Philippian Christians that Paul tells them to work out their own salvation. It is, in other words, because the Philippian Christians have already been justified/saved (1:28); it is because they are already saints (1:1); it is because they are already "in Christ" (1:1) and are therefore a "new creation" (2 Cor. 5:17); it is because of all this that Paul tells them to live out (manifest, demonstrate, work out) the salvation which they already possess.

The basis of this Pauline exhortation is the reality that the God the Philippians believe in has already transformed them into a new creation. They have through the regenerating work of the Holy Spirit been born again. They have died to sin and have been raised to newness of life (Rom. 6:1–5). The basis of this exhortation to the church, and for that matter the basis of all the commands given to God's people, is the great truth that God has transformed and is transforming them through the Holy Spirit into the image of his Son. This teaching must never be forgotten, for it is a continual theme of Scripture (see, e.g., Rom. 7:5–6; 8:1–4). No wonder Paul has the confidence to say to the Philippians, "And I am sure that he who began a good work in you will bring it to completion at the day of Jesus Christ" (1:6).

Finally, and this could well have been mentioned first, it is the same author who wrote, "By grace you have been saved through faith" (Eph. 2:8), and "Work out your own salvation"! We are not dealing with the teaching of two different authors but rather with the same person. Since the apostle Paul himself argues most forcefully and eloquently that justification is by faith alone, it would appear that for him this cardinal teaching and the meaning of Philippians 2:12 do not conflict. It is true, of course, that at times people are inconsistent, but Paul by any standard was a brilliant theologian. For him to be inconsistent on this crucial point for which he fought so hard is extremely unlikely. (For the evangelical the doctrine of inspiration also argues strongly that Paul's teachings are consistent.) It would seem far more likely, then, that our understanding of the meaning of Philippians 2:12 is incorrect rather than that the apostle has made a major error in his theology at this point.

This is confirmed by a closer look at the whole Book of Philippians. Paul is not writing an evangelistic treatise seeking to show the Philippians how they can be saved/justified. Nor is he endeavoring to defend this doctrine against a misunderstanding by the Judaizers. On the contrary, he is writing to "saints" (1:1) who can "rejoice in the Lord" (3:1). Furthermore, in this very letter Paul teaches clearly that justification does not come out of one's own doing, but comes rather as a gift from God *through faith* (3:9). In light of this it is extremely unlikely that "work out your own salvation" should be interpreted as teaching the very opposite. It is best, then, to interpret our passage as follows, "Since you Philippians have been justified by faith alone and since you have experienced a rebirth by the Holy Spirit, who is continually working in your lives both to change your innermost being to desire his good pleasure and to enable you to carry it out, live out [manifest or demonstrate] with fear and trembling the salvation you possess."

In seeking to understand the meaning of this difficult passage of Scripture we have again found the basic hermeneutical principle discussed in the previous chapter helpful. This principle emphasizes the importance of understanding the meaning of the key building blocks which make up a sentence. In this instance we must understand what the key term *work out* means. To do this we looked first at other writings of the apostle where he uses the same word. Since elsewhere he does not use this term to mean "earn" or "merit" but rather "manifest" and "demonstrate," it probably means the same in this instance as well. Second, and this is the main emphasis of this chapter, we examined the grammatical context in which the term is found. The little word *for* clearly indicates that Paul is not speaking of earning one's salvation: the ground of the command ("for") is the fact that the Philippians were already the children of God and that God was through his Spirit already working his good pleasure in them.

A third principle which we found helpful in understanding this verse, and which will be the theme of the next chapter, is that we should always seek to understand a passage in the context of what its author says elsewhere. Any teaching of Paul (or of any other author) should be interpreted in light of what Paul (or the other author) teaches elsewhere. Since Paul more than any other writer in the New Testament emphasized that salvation is a matter of grace and comes by faith alone, it is very unlikely that he would be saying the very opposite in this passage. It is highly improbable that Philippians 2:12 conflicts with what Paul teaches elsewhere concerning justification by faith. We shall deal in greater detail with this principle in the next chapter. It might also be pointed out here in passing that Philippians 2:12 reveals a continuity between Paul and James in that Paul also sees a need for one's salvation, which is by grace through faith alone, to be demonstrated and manifested by good works.

What Does It Mean to Be Filled with the Spirit? (Eph. 5:18)

Various passages in the Epistles of the New Testament are troublesome for different reasons. At times we encounter difficulty because an author may assume certain knowledge on the part of his readers which we today do not possess. Two examples of this are Paul's reference to being baptized for the dead (1 Cor. 15:29; see pp. 152–57) and the bodily ailment which caused him to preach the gospel to the Galatians (Gal. 4:13). Unlike the original readers of these letters, who understood exactly to what the apostle was referring, we today do not have access to this information. Another reason why certain passages cause difficulty is the complexity of the subject matter (e.g., predestination) or the apparently contradictory nature of the material (e.g., divine predestination and human responsibility). In a few rare instances the presence of textual variants can cause difficulties as well (Rom. 5:1; Col. 2:2).

On numerous occasions, however, passages are difficult to understand not so much because of the text itself, but because of the popular and erroneous interpretations associated with it. Rather than modify or give up these precious interpretations, we prefer to force the text to fit them. In actuality, however, no biblical text can be forced to fit an interpretation. The text has meant, means, and will always mean exactly what the author consciously willed it to say. As a result we can never force a text to mean what the author did not mean. It means today what the author meant when he wrote it. And this cannot be changed. We can, however, consciously or, more often than not, unconsciously misinterpret the text to fit our own views, but in so doing we do not change the meaning of the text but only place on it an alien meaning.

One example of a text associated with an erroneous understanding is Ephesians 5:18, where Paul states, "And do not get drunk with wine, for that is debauchery; but be filled with the Spirit." A popular interpretation of this passage is that being "filled with the Spirit" refers to an experience which raises a believer to a new stage in the Christian life. Another name given to this supposed experience is the baptism of (or more correctly "in") the Spirit. This experience is seen as enabling the believer to arrive at a new level of discipleship in which God gives to him or her various spiritual gifts such as are mentioned in 1 Corinthians 12:4–11. Usually there is an accompanying sign which verifies that the individual has truly had this experience, and that sign is speaking in tongues.

Although the charismatic movement, in which this theology is so dominant, is a recent phenomenon, the underlying thought has ancient roots. There are similarities with the idea of a "two-level" ethic found in the early church, particularly in the writings of Tertullian and Origen in the second and third centuries. Here we find a two-level view of Christian experience in which certain believers attain only the first level of the Christian life and are concerned with such things as the Ten Commandments, the golden rule, and the love commandment. On the other hand, there is a higher ethic or level, which only certain individuals attain. At this level a person surrenders such things as material possessions, marriage, and family. We can see in such an ethical system the beginnings of a two-level system in which laity and clergy are distinguished.

A far more significant and influential predecessor of this theology is found in the Methodism of John Wesley, who envisioned two distinct levels in the Christian life. Through faith in Jesus one enters the level of justification. Here one is saved, justified, forgiven, and granted eternal life. Subsequently, however, one should seek the second level of sanctification. Although Wesley himself never claimed to have obtained this level of Christian perfection, he preached it. This basic two-stage understanding of the Christian life has spread widely and has had numerous offshoots. We see variations of it when we speak of receiving Jesus as our Savior and then later making him Lord, of having Christ dwell in our hearts but later placing him on the throne of our hearts, of being saved and then later receiving the baptism of/in the Spirit, of being justified and then later being sanctified, of being saved and then later finding some sort of a spiritual secret for the deeper life.

One major problem that has frustrated many of those involved in this kind of theology is how a person can know or prove that he or she has experienced this second blessing or level. What is the sign which verifies that a person has indeed experienced sanctification or, as it is more popularly called, the baptism of/in the Spirit? Some have argued that the sign of this experience is swooning or being slain in the Spirit, that is, fainting because of this second work of the Spirit. Others argue that the sign is a shaking which the Spirit brings on an individual in this experience. Still others argue that the sign is "treeing the devil," that is, chasing the devil out of one's life. In 1901 in Topeka, Kansas, and in 1906 in Los Angeles, there came to the forefront a different sign, which soon became the clear proof of having been baptized in the Spirit. This was the sign of speaking in tongues.

The phenomenal rise and growth of the Pentecostal movement at the beginning of this century and the more recent charismatic movement have brought about the spread of this theology throughout the Christian world. Ephesians 5:18 is seen as an important support of this theology. It is actually a more useful text than the seven passages in the New Testament which refer to the baptism of/in the Spirit (Matt. 3:11; Mark 1:8; Luke 3:16; John 1:33; Acts 1:5; 11:16; 1 Cor. 12:13), for whereas Christians are never commanded to be baptized in the Spirit, they are commanded here to be filled by the Spirit. Yet on closer examination, this text does not fit the charismatic teaching of a two-level Christian experience. This is clear from the grammar in this verse.

The clearest indication that Paul is not commanding the Ephesian Christians to enter into a second level of the Christian experience is the fact that the command is in the present tense. In Greek one uses either the present tense or the aorist tense with the imperative mood, that is, with commands. The present tense generally indicates that the command is to be continually obeyed. This means that Paul is saying in Ephesians 5:18, "Be *continually* filled with the Spirit." It is clear from the tense of this command that Paul is not urging his readers to have an experience once and for all which places them on a new level in the Christian life, but rather to be continually filled with the Spirit. The command therefore does not refer to a one-time experience as in charismatic teaching, but to a continual everyday experience in which Christians are being ruled by the Spirit. Grammatical considerations reveal that Paul's command cannot be interpreted as urging a once-in-a-lifetime experience which will initiate the individual into a second level of the Christian life.

The question of how one is to be continually filled with the Spirit is more difficult to answer. If the participles found in Ephesians 5:19–21 are to be interpreted as instrumental in nature, Paul is explaining in these verses how Christians are to be filled with the Spirit. It is by addressing one another in psalms and hymns and spiritual songs, by singing and making melody to the Lord with all our heart, and by giving thanks always and for everything. Most scholars, however, do not see these participles as being instrumental but as describing the manner in which being filled with the Spirit should be manifested. But how, then, are we to be filled with the Spirit? Most suggestions tend to focus on what the believer must do: we must empty ourselves of all personal ambition, we must "pray through" until God blesses us with his Spirit, we must cleanse ourselves of every sin, and we must dedicate ourselves totally to Christ. Regardless of whether or not there is value in such suggestions, the emphasis is a dangerous one. It focuses on what works we must do in order for God to bless us with his Spirit. It almost gives the impression that we must persuade a reluctant God who does not want to bless us with his Spirit to nevertheless do so. Thus we must talk God into being willing to fill us with his Spirit.

Perhaps two additional Pauline passages concerning the believer's relationship to the Spirit may be of help. In Ephesians 4:30 Paul states, "And do not grieve the Holy Spirit of God, in whom you were sealed for the day of redemption." In a similar manner he declares in 1 Thessalonians 5:19, "Do not quench the Spirit." Is it possible that instead of needing to persuade God to fill us with his Spirit, we need rather to stop hindering (i.e., grieving, quenching) the work that the Spirit is already seeking to do in our lives? Jesus said that God is much more willing to give his Spirit to those who ask than human fathers, who are evil, are willing to give good things to their children (Luke 11:13). It is true that we have for the moment stepped out of the Pauline Epistles, but surely the apostle Paul would agree with Luke that God is eagerly seeking to fill us with his Spirit. If this is true, it may be that instead of concentrating on how we may somehow entice God to fill us with his Spirit, we need to concentrate rather on no longer hindering the work which the Spirit is already seeking to do in our lives. The reason why so many of us are not filled with the Spirit is that we grieve and quench what he is seeking to do in our lives.

How do we grieve and quench the Spirit? It is significant that the command in Ephesians 4:30 is located in the middle of a paragraph of ethical commands. It is unlikely that Ephesians 4:30 was meant to be read in isolation from the other injunctions. It may well be, therefore, that rather than seeking some experience which will automatically fill us with the Spirit, we should put away falsehood, speak truth to each other, refrain from anger and stealing, perform honest work, avoid evil talk, and put away malice (see Eph. 4:25–32).

We possess within the Scriptures the will of God for us; we have his commandments to us. We should not search heaven and earth for some special experience which will automatically fill us with the Spirit. If we keep his commandments, then we shall find that day after day we are filled with his Spirit. Having begun a good work in us, God is eager to bring that work to completion (Phil. 1:6). And he has already given us his Spirit to assist us in this. The God of all grace is not looking for us to perform some mighty act by which we arrive at some second level in the Christian life. He wants us only to stop hindering the work of the Spirit which is already going on in our lives. As we seek by his grace to obey him and keep his commandments, we shall be filled with his presence. On the other hand, just as a parent-child relationship is hindered and grieved by disobedience on the part of the child, so do we by disobedience hinder and grieve the work which the Spirit seeks to accomplish in us.

In Ephesians 5:18 Paul is not urging us to have an experience which will result in what Wesley called sanctification or what charismatics today call the baptism in the Spirit. Rather he is commanding us to be continually filled with the Spirit. This does not refer to a one-time experience but to a continual relationship with the Spirit in which we no longer quench what he is trying to do in our lives. God through his Spirit is already at work in us, seeking to make us desire and do his perfect will. To know his will we need not ascend into heaven to bring Christ down, for the word is close by (Rom. 10:6b–8). Jesus said, "If you love me, you will keep my commandments" (John 14:15). As we trust in the grace of God and keep his commandments, we shall be filled with the Spirit.

Do God's People Not Sin? (1 John 3:6, 9)

In the first letter of John we are confronted with statements which at first glance seem to conflict with both experience and the teachings of the Scriptures elsewhere. In 1 John 3:6 and 9 we read:

> No one who abides in him sins; no one who sins has either seen him or known him. . . . No one born of God commits sin; for God's nature abides in him, and he cannot sin because he is born of God.

The problem raised by these verses is immediately apparent, for believers even in their best moments still sin. Our experience seems to give the lie to what these verses claim. One can, of course, so redefine sin that it may be possible for a Christian not to commit sin as it is newly redefined, but the Bible does not redefine sin in such a manner. A denial of sin in the life of the believer can be built only on a naiveté concerning the magnitude of the problem of sin and depravity in the human heart and a misconception of what has and what has not yet been effected in our redemption. The resurrection of the body is still future, and so is our ultimate deliverance from sin and death. More important, however, the apparent meaning of 1 John 3:6 and 9 conflicts with what the Scriptures teach elsewhere concerning our being justified sinners, but sinners nonetheless. Did not our Lord teach us to pray, "Forgive us our sins, for we ourselves forgive every one who is indebted to us" (Luke 11:4)? Was the apostle Paul simply talking about his preconversion sins when at the end of his life he referred to himself as the "foremost of sinners" (1 Tim. 1:15)? The way the Scriptures speak of sin in the Christian life (see Rom. 14:23; 1 Cor. 6:18; 15:34; James 2:9; 4:17) clearly assumes the presence of sin in the life of the believer.

Even if we were to ignore our experience and the rest of Scripture, 1 John 3:6 and 9 would raise problems with what we find in the rest of this brief letter. There are several instances in which the author refers to sin in the life of the believer. Among the verses in which it is evident that the author believes that Christians sin:

> If we say we have no sin, we deceive ourselves, and the truth is not in us. If we confess our sins, he is faithful and just, and will forgive our sins and cleanse us from all unrighteousness. [1 John 1:8–9]

> My little children, I am writing this to you so that you may not sin; but if any one does sin, we have an advocate with the Father, Jesus Christ the righteous. [1 John 2:1; see also 1:6; 5:16–17; and the exhortations not to sin found in 2:15; 3:11–12]

It is clear from these references that the same author who writes, "No one who abides in him sins," and "No one born of God commits sin," also writes that those who do sin have Jesus Christ as their advocate before God (2:1) and that if they confess these sins, God will in his faithfulness and righteousness forgive them of all their sin (1:9).

Numerous attempts have been made to resolve this problem. One such attempt is to speak of two different kinds of Christians: the one literally does not sin and the other does. First John 3:6 and 9 speak of the former, whereas passages like 1 John 1:8–9 and 2:1 speak of the latter. Such a view is often found in Holiness, Methodist, and Pentecostal literature. According to this view, 1 John 3:6 and 9 are to be interpreted literally, that is, the former group of Christians in fact do not sin. They are referred to as those who have been ''sanctified,'' ''baptized in the Holy Spirit,'' and ''filled with the Spirit.'' They are believers who truly abide in Christ. When, and only when, a Christian has had this second experience are 1 John 3:6 and 9 literally true. (Usually along with such views there is of necessity a redefinition of sin as well.)

Our text, however, gives no hint of a division of Christians into two such classes. Actually verse 6 speaks of all humanity as being divided into two classes. Either one does not sin and thus is abiding in Christ, or one sins and has not seen or known him. It is also clear that the latter group is of the devil (3:8). This would be a rather harsh classification for Christians who are not perfect. Such an explanation, then, is not permitted by our text, for there is no hint anywhere that the author is making some sort of a distinction between two groups of believers. Furthermore, the author's classification of himself as one who confesses his sins (note the ''we'' in 1 John 1:9) refutes such a view.

Another attempted explanation sees in the word *abides* of 1 John 3:6 the key for understanding these passages. According to this explanation, Christians do not sin when they abide in Christ. When Christ dwells and reigns in them, they do not sin. The problem arises when Christ no longer abides in believers, for then they can and do sin. There are two difficulties with such an interpretation. For one, there is no hint in 1 John that a Christian can pop in and out of an ''abiding'' state. John does not say ''whenever one abides'' or ''at those times when one abides,'' but simply speaks of those who abide, that is, those who are in an abiding relationship with Christ. Second, to abide in Christ is explained further in 3:6 as knowing him. To abide in Christ means to know Christ, to be a Christian. It means to keep his commandments (3:24), to confess Jesus as the Son of God (4:15), to abide in love (4:16), and to break bread at communion (John 6:56). Clearly, to abide in Christ refers simply to being a Christian and not to being an élite Christian who possesses a unique holiness.

Other attempts which try to explain our passages state that the author is inconsistent and that what he says here cannot be reconciled with what he says elsewhere, or that our passages must be understood as hyperbolic and as an exaggerated presentation of a desired goal that unfortunately cannot be attained. It should be noted that the author gives us no hint at all concerning the latter view. We should not assume that an author is exaggerating unless there are some clues in the text or in his other teachings that he is doing so. John does not give us the slightest hint that he is using hyperbole in these passages. As to the former explanation, is it likely that the author of 1 John was so illogical that in his own mind he did not reconcile the statements of 1 John 3:6 and 9 with what he says elsewhere? This does not seem very likely.

How then can we explain these passages? At this point the issue of syntax plays a cardinal role. Probably the most helpful procedure is to note carefully the tenses used in these verses. In describing past actions the Greek language has four specific tenses: the aorist, imperfect, perfect, and pluperfect. In general it can be said that the imperfect tense indicates the continual doing of some past action ("They *were driving* for two days"). The perfect indicates an action which took place in the past and has continuing consequences in the present ("They *have been married* for ten years"). The pluperfect indicates an action which took place in the past and had continuing consequences in the past ("They *had been married* for ten years when this happened"). The aorist is the least precise of the four past tenses and is the one normally used to refer to something in the past without emphasizing anything about the past action ("He *saw* an accident"). Unfortunately, in describing present actions there is only one tense available in Greek; and it must serve to describe present actions that are punctiliar in nature ("Jesus *heals* you"), present situations that have continuing consequences ("We *are* God's children"), and present actions that are continually being done ("He *is* always *praising* God").

In 1 John 3:6 the verb "sins" is in the present tense, and in 3:9 "commits" is also in the present tense. These can be and probably should be translated as "continually sins" and "continually commits." With regard to 3:9 it should be noted that the New American Standard Bible translates this verb as "practices" sin, and the New International Version translates it "will continue to" sin. The grammar clearly permits this translation, and two important factors argue in its favor. The first is that interpreting the verb as indicating a continual practicing of sin will allow us to harmonize the author's teaching here with what he says elsewhere in the letter concerning the fact that Christians do sin. All things being equal, an interpretation that harmonizes the data should be chosen over one that does not, for writers desire to be consistent in their works. A second and more important syntactical reason for interpreting the verbs in this manner is found in 3:9, where we read "he cannot sin." In Greek this consists of the verb "to be able" (*dunatai*) and the present infinitive "to sin" (*hamartanein*). In Greek the present infinitive is usually used when a continuing activity is being referred to, whereas the aorist infinitive is used when one does not wish to refer to a continuing action, or when one wishes to refer to a punctiliar action. If John wanted to emphasize that individuals begotten of God are not able to sin *ever*, he would have used the aorist infinitive rather than the present infinitive we find in 3:9. What our passage states is that those who are begotten of God are not able to continue sinning or to abide in sin. By the use of the present infinitive the author reveals that he is not referring to an act of sin but to a practicing of sin. The use of the present participle in 3:6 (*hamartanōn*, "no one who [continually] sins") and 3:8 (*poiōn*, "he who [continually] commits sins") supports this understanding.

The problem encountered in our text is resolved once we understand the grammar, specifically, the tense of the verb, and thus see that John is referring not to acts of sin, but to the continuing practice of sin. As believers we do sin, yet John tells us that although we should not, if we do, we have Jesus Christ as our advocate before God (2:1), and if we confess our sins, God will graciously forgive us (1:9). To live in sin, however, is something else. The person who abides in Christ cannot continue to abide in sin also. To abide continually in sin means that one is associated with the devil, who sinned from the beginning (3:8), rather than with the God of righteousness.

In this short chapter we have looked at some problem passages in the Epistles whose difficulties were resolved by a close examination of their syntax (grammar). Needless to say, we have done so in a superficial manner, for we did not even explain the rules of Greek syntax. To do so would require a much larger and different work. What we have attempted to demonstrate is that, in the interpretative process, just as there is a need to understand correctly what individual words mean, so there is also a need to understand the syntax by which these words are related to one another.

This can, of course, be best done by a careful analysis of the syntax of the Greek New Testament, for the authors wrote in that language. On the other hand, we should also carefully analyze a good translation of the Greek text. We have been richly blessed in our generation with numerous excellent translations of the Bible; perhaps no generation of the English-speaking world other than the sixteenth century has witnessed such a wealth of translations. In translating the Greek text for us, the translators made judicious selection not only of the words which they chose, but also of the grammar. Their selections of tenses, conjunctions, and punctuation were carefully weighed and discussed. They took great care in seeking to represent accurately the words and thoughts of the New Testament writers. To profit most from their efforts, we must look carefully at the words and the syntax they used to express the thoughts of the inspired writers. We need likewise to come to our texts with both reverence and care as we seek to understand the revelation of God found in the New Testament.

10

Considering the Context
The Author's Writings

In seeking to understand the meanings of terms and the syntax in which they are found, our biggest aid is the context which the author gives them. We have already referred to the hermeneutical circle and the fact that the precise meaning of a word is determined by the meaning of the statement in which it is found, and that the meaning of the statement is of course dependent on the meaning of the word. The meanings of words and statements are also determined by the meaning of the paragraph in which they are found, which in turn is determined by the meaning of the statements, which in turn is determined by the meaning of the words. Fortunately all of this goes on simultaneously and often unconsciously in the mind of the interpreter. Since we are interested in understanding what authors mean by the words and sentences they write, we must study the context in which they write.

The specific context that we shall look at in this chapter is the context of an author's writings. The words in a given writing should always be interpreted in the light of what the author says elsewhere. Unless there is proof to the contrary or a specific statement that the present material is at odds with what was written previously, an author should be granted the premise of being relatively consistent. This should be granted to any author of reasonable intelligence. For thoughtful and careful authors it should be granted even more readily.

In seeking to understand the apostle Paul's statements, then, we should assume that what he says in one setting will be reasonably consistent with what he says elsewhere. Thus if Paul is speaking about the law in one passage, it is helpful to know what he says elsewhere on the same subject. Yet an even greater certainty as to an author's thought can be obtained if we narrow the context. For instance, what Paul says on a subject in 1 Thessalonians will be helpful in understanding what he means when he speaks about the same subject in Romans. But knowing what Paul says elsewhere in Romans on this same subject will be more useful. And what Paul says in the same chapter will be even more useful. And what Paul says in the same paragraph will be still more useful. And what Paul says in the sentences immediately before and after is even more useful than that. And what Paul says in the rest of the sentence is most useful of all!

In this chapter we shall look at several difficult passages in the Epistles and seek to interpret them in light of their authorial context.

Does God Remain Faithful When We Are Faithless? (2 Tim. 2:11–13)

Within the Scriptures we encounter a number of instances where in the midst of a passage we are totally surprised by the way the argument turns. We are anticipating that the argument will proceed in a certain manner when, lo and behold, the author ''throws us a curve.'' An example of this is found in Romans 9, where Paul is talking of God's having loved Jacob and hated Esau (v. 13), of his having mercy on whomever he wills and hardening whomever he wills (v. 18). Then in verse 19 Paul raises the question, "Why does he still find fault? For who can resist his will?" At this point the reader tends to agree with the question and respond, "Yes, Paul, that is a good question. What about this?" The next verse clearly catches the reader by surprise, for instead of proceeding to answer the question he has raised Paul states, "But who are you, a man, to answer back to God?"

Another passage in which the apostle catches us by surprise is the poetic form of 2 Timothy 2:11–13:

The saying is sure:

[1] If we have died with him, we shall also live with him;
[2] if we endure, we shall also reign with him;
[3] if we deny him, he also will deny us;
[4] if we are faithless, . . .

At this point we expect something like what we have just found in line [3]—"he also will deny us"; but instead we find in line [4] "he remains faithful—for he cannot deny himself." Here we are taken somewhat by surprise, for line [4] seems to deny what line [3] says.

As we compare the first two lines, it is obvious that there is close agreement in both form and content. The subject in both parts of each line is "we," and our doing something positive is said to result in future blessing—we shall live and we shall reign with Christ. The only difference in these two lines is the change in tense from the past "have died" (a culminative aorist) to the present "endure" (a durative present). The third line differs in tense as well, for here we have a future tense "[shall] deny," but the more important difference is one of form. Here, although the subject of the protasis (the subordinate "if" clause) is still "we," the subject of the apodosis (the independent clause) is "he," that is, God. Yet the meaning is still quite close: "if we deny him, we shall be the recipients of God's denial [lit., he will deny us]." In the third line just as in the first two lines what we do results in a corresponding consequence of good or evil. It may well be that the form of the third line has been changed to make it more compatible with the well-known saying of Jesus, "Whoever denies me before men, I also will deny before my Father who is in heaven" (Matt. 10:33). This is probably the reason why line [3] was written as we find it rather than as "if we deny him, we shall also be denied."

The fourth line, however, raises numerous questions and problems. Its form after the protasis is totally different, for in contrast to the first three lines, there is no mention of "we" or "us" in the apodosis or second clause. Even more puzzling than the change in form is the question of the meaning of this line. Is the last clause ("for he cannot deny himself") to be understood as a threat or a promise? We shall address ourselves to this question shortly, but it would be better to deal with the meaning of each statement in order.

After mentioning his own suffering for Christ (vv. 9–10), Paul introduces the hymn of verses 11–13 with a well-known idiom, "The saying is sure." (For other examples see 1 Tim. 1:15; 3:1; 4:9; Titus 3:8.) The first line has frequently been interpreted as referring to a martyr's death. But in view of the parallel in Romans 6:8, where Paul states, "But if we have died with Christ, we believe that we shall also live with him," it would be better to interpret this line as referring to the experience of baptism, which was intimately associated with conversion. The tense of the verb (an aorist) supports this interpretation. The second line, which refers to enduring for Christ, has caused little difficulty. The consequence of reigning with Christ brings to mind such passages as Revelation 5:10; 20:4, 6; and 22:5—"and they shall reign for ever and ever."

The third line speaks of denying Christ. As already mentioned, it is probable that behind this statement lie the words of Jesus in Matthew 10:33. (It is also probable that a parallel to denying Christ is being ashamed of him and his words [Mark 8:38].) It is interesting to note the progression of tenses in the protasis of the first three lines. In line [1] we have a past tense (an aorist) which refers back to the experience of conversion and baptism; in line [2] we have a present tense (a durative present) which refers to a present continual patient endurance for Christ's sake; and in line [3] we have a future tense which refers to a possible future renunciation, denial, or repudiation of our faith. Such questions as to whether a true Christian can ever deny Christ or whether believers will always persevere in their faith are not in the mind of the author. This text is not interested in such speculation. The author in this hymn is simply repeating the words of Jesus that to deny him will result in being denied on the final day of judgment.

This brings us to line [4]. There are two basic ways of interpreting this line. If we interpret it as a continuation of the thought of line [3], we see this line as containing a threat: "If we are unfaithful [in the sense of becoming apostate], God will remain true to his holiness and right-eousness and bring upon us his holy wrath and eternal judgment, for God is not able to deny his holy character and nature [lit., himself]." This interpretation has the merit of following the thought pattern of the previous lines. In each of them either good behavior results in good consequences or bad behavior in bad consequences. One logically expects therefore that the bad behavior of line [4] (being unfaithful) will result in a bad consequence. As a result of reading the first three lines, one expects the apod-osis of line [4] to be a threat.

On the other hand, there are several problems with this interpretation which suggest that line [4] should be in-terpreted as a promise rather than a threat. One reason involves the verb which is translated "are faithless" (*apistoumen*). This verb can mean "to be unbelieving" in the sense of not ever having put one's faith in Jesus Christ (see Rom. 3:3; 1 Pet. 2:7; cf. also the noncanonical Mark 16:11). However, the verb can also mean "to be faithless" in the sense that some Christians lack the kind of faith they ought to have. (It is so used in Luke 24:41.) The noun (*apistia*) can also be used in this sense, as in Mark 9:24 where a father cries out to Jesus, "I believe; help my unbelief!" By contrast, in Romans 3:3; 11:20 and 23 it is used to describe the unbelief of non-Christians. It is evident, therefore, that although this verb and its corresponding noun can be used to refer to unbelief in the sense of not ever having placed one's faith in Christ, these terms can also be used to refer to a Christian's lack of trust. The verb "are faithless" can within the norms of language mean to lack saving faith or to lack the kind of faith we as Christians ought to have, that is, to be weak in faith. The former would require that line [4] be interpreted as a threat; the latter would require that it be interpreted as a promise.

A second problem with interpreting line [4] as a threat is in the apodosis "he remains faithful." In the Pauline literature the expression "God is faithful" occurs five other times. In each of these instances we find some positive statement or promise with regard to the issue at hand: "God is faithful, by whom you were called" (1 Cor. 1:9); "God is faithful, and he will not let you be tempted beyond your strength" (1 Cor. 10:13); "He who calls you is faithful" (1 Thess. 5:24). (See also 2 Cor. 1:18; 2 Thess. 3:3; cf. Heb. 10:23; 11:11; and 1 John 1:9.) As a result of the positive contexts in which this expression occurs in the New Testament, and especially in Paul, it seems reasonable to assume that it should be interpreted in a similar manner, that is, as a promise, in 2 Timothy 2:13 as well.

Finally, we need to look at the expression "for he cannot deny himself." Although there is no clear linkage in terminology, this statement calls to mind the words of God when he affirmed his promise to bless Abraham and multiply his seed and swore an oath to this purpose (Gen. 22:16–18). Since there was no one greater than himself to swear by, God swore by himself (Heb. 6:13). When God bestows his gracious promises on his people, he has indeed "sworn and will not change his mind" (Heb. 7:21). The reason for this is evident—God cannot deny himself! He must keep the oath which he has sworn to himself. If this is indeed the way that this expression is to be understood, then line [4] is to be interpreted as a promise rather than a threat.

In light of the above, we should interpret the hymn as progressing in this way:

> [1] A statement of reassurance that reminds the readers that when they died with Christ in their conversion, they passed from death into life and shall one day live eternally with Christ;
>
> [2] A promise that patient endurance for Christ in time of tribulation will one day result in our reigning with him eternally;
>
> [3] A solemn warning which recalls the words of Jesus in Matthew 10:33 that the act of denial, which is a repudiation of our faith, will result in the Son of man's repudiating us before the throne of God in the great day of judgment;
>
> [4] A word of comfort and reassurance for sensitive Christians who are burdened with their failures and shortcomings: God's faithfulness is not dependent on the degree of our faithfulness. He will abide faithful to his covenant promises, for he has sworn an oath to this effect; he cannot be untrue to his sovereign promises to us.

It is evident that line [4] was never meant to open the door for possible apostasy. It is not a charter to unfaithfulness. Rather it is meant to serve as consolation for troubled souls. It is meant as a reassuring word that God is faithful to his people far above all that we could ever ask or think. Great indeed is the mercy of our God: "As a father pities his children, so the LORD pities those who fear him" (Ps. 103:13). Even when we prove faithless, he in his grace and mercy remains true to his promises. He has sworn us an

oath that he will never fail us nor forsake us (Heb. 13:5).
This is "Amazing Grace" indeed! "O the depth of the
riches and wisdom and knowledge of God! How unsearch-
able are his judgments and how inscrutable his ways!"
(Rom. 11:33).

Did Paul Learn His Gospel? (Gal. 1:12)

In the opening chapters of Galatians Paul seeks to demonstrate that he is a true apostle in the fullest sense. Apparently his opponents had raised questions with regard to his
credentials as an apostle. They claimed that if he was an
apostle at all, his apostleship possessed less authority than
that of the Jerusalem apostles and that whatever authority
he did possess had been given to him by those apostles. To
answer his critics Paul points out that he is an apostle "not
from men nor through man, but through Jesus Christ and
God the Father" (1:1). This was borne out, among other
things, by the independent course he took from the beginning (he never went to Jerusalem until three years after his
conversion, and then he saw only Peter and James [1:18–
19]), and by the fact that when he went to Jerusalem
fourteen years later (2:1), the Jerusalem apostles acknowledged his apostolic authority among the Gentiles (2:9) as
being equal to Peter's apostolic authority among the Jews
(2:7–8).

Another argument Paul uses to prove his apostolic authority is the fact that his gospel came to him directly from
God. In Galatians 1:11–12 he states:

> For I would have you know, brethren, that the gospel
> which was preached by me is not man's gospel. For I did
> not receive it from man, nor was I taught it, but it came
> through a revelation of Jesus Christ.

These verses have caused considerable confusion, for elsewhere Paul speaks of having "received" and "delivered"
certain traditions, terminology usually used to describe the

process of receiving from predecessors various traditions and in turn passing them on to successors. We have a number of examples of this in Paul's letters. In 1 Corinthians 11:23 the words of the Lord's Supper are introduced by Paul with, ''For I received from the Lord what I also delivered to you.'' Likewise in 1 Corinthians 15:3 Paul introduces what is generally recognized as a pre-Pauline christological formula with, ''For I delivered to you as of first importance what I also received.''

Where and how did Paul ''receive'' this gospel which he tells the Corinthians he delivered to them (1 Cor. 15:3)? No doubt this took place in much the same manner as the Corinthians ''received'' it, that is, by learning it from Christian teachers. This appears to be correct in light of the immediate context, where the same term (*paralambanō*) is used to describe how the Corinthians received the gospel: ''Now I would remind you, brethren, in what terms I preached to you the gospel, which you received, in which you stand, by which you are saved'' (1 Cor. 15:1–2a). If the reception of the gospel by the Corinthians was by the process of teaching and preaching (15:1), then it would appear that Paul's reception of the gospel, which is described by the exact same word (15:3), must have taken place in a like manner. It appears, then, that the term *received* in 15:3 does not refer to a direct divine revelation from heaven, but rather to a mediated delivering of the divine message by Christian teachers.

There are other reasons for believing that Paul in his letters reproduces certain traditions which he had learned from other Christians. These traditions can usually be discerned in Paul's letters by the presence of much un-Pauline vocabulary, an un-Pauline literary style, an atypical (this does not mean contradictory!) theological emphasis, a unique rhythm and balance, or a string of relative clauses. Such clues have led most Pauline scholars today to believe that, among other passages, 1 Corinthians 15:3–7; Philippians 2:6–11; Colossians 1:15–20; Romans 1:3–5; and

3:24–26 witness to early Christian formulations that Paul "received" and incorporated into his letters and preaching.

Besides this reference to Paul's having received certain traditions in the same way that the Corinthians had received them, it is most difficult to assume that the apostle learned nothing about the Christian faith during his career as a persecutor of the church. Certainly as a persecutor Paul must have known something about what Christians believed, for his persecution of the early church was not based on racial or economic considerations but theological ones. Something that Christians were saying and teaching clearly offended him. Obviously, Paul must have known what Christians basically believed and stood for. A dedicated persecutor would seek to know all that he could about the group he was victimizing in order to be better able to refute them.

It is also important to note that Paul acknowledges that three years after his conversion he went up to Jerusalem and spent fifteen days with Peter and James (Gal. 1:18–19). As one commentator has aptly put it, it is quite unlikely that during all this time they talked about nothing but the weather. Surely they must have talked about Jesus and the faith which all of them proclaimed.

It seems clear, therefore, that Paul did acquire considerable information about the Christian faith in a nonsupernatural manner both before and after his conversion. How can we reconcile this with his statement that his gospel did not come from man, that he was not taught it, but that on the contrary it came to him through a revelation of Jesus Christ? While it is true that both before and after his conversion Paul acquired certain facts about the Christian faith, it must be pointed out that the gospel which Paul preached was not simply certain bare facts or information about Jesus. It involved the interpretation of those facts and their theological implications, that is, the kerygmatic interpretation of those facts. It was only through the revelation of Jesus Christ on the road to Damascus that the truthfulness of these facts and their theological implications became known to him. Both the truthfulness of the gospel and some of its major theological implications, as well as his apostolic commission, came to Paul through divine revelation. These were revealed not learned; they came from the Lord not man. It was not through human teaching but through Paul's encounter with Jesus Christ that Pauline theology originated.

All the theological implications of the gospel which were revealed to Paul on the way to Damascus cannot be discussed here, but it may be profitable at this point to mention a few in order to demonstrate why he could say that his gospel came through the revelation of Jesus Christ.

1. One area revealed to Paul on the way to Damascus involved soteriology, or the doctrine of salvation. Paul learned from this revelatory experience that salvation cannot be obtained through the keeping of the law. Even his "blameless" keeping of the law (Phil. 3:6) was useless, for as he learned from his encounter with Jesus Christ, his zeal for the law had made him the very enemy of God! His righteousness melted away when he realized that although he was as a Pharisee blameless according to the law, he was in fact oppressing the people of God. Yet God in his grace saved him. By grace and grace alone God had forgiven him and bestowed on him the very righteousness of Jesus Christ. On the road to Damascus God revealed to him that justification is not of works but by grace alone, and that this justification can be appropriated only by faith.

2. With regard to Christology Paul learned that the one he opposed and ridiculed was indeed alive. The resurrection of Jesus authenticated for Paul all the teachings of Jesus. Jesus of Nazareth was indeed the Christ of God, but he was more than that. In the Old Testament the Voice from heaven was never the voice of a human; it was not even the voice of an angel. It was the voice of God! Yet the one who spoke to Paul was Jesus. Therefore this Jesus must

truly be Lord, the God of the Old Testament. It is not surprising, therefore, that we find in Pauline theology a high Christology indeed. Paul can speak of Jesus' preexistence and lordship over all creation; it is before him that every knee will one day bow and confess that he is both Christ and Lord (Phil. 2:10–11).

3. Concerning eschatology or the doctrine of last things, it was also clear to Paul, as he reflected on his encounter with the risen Christ, that since Jesus had truly been raised from the dead the messianic age had indeed begun. The end of the ages had come (1 Cor. 10:11). The resurrection of the dead had begun. Christ was the firstfruits of the resurrection (1 Cor. 15:23). Another fact that would have given support to this conclusion was the coming of the promised Spirit. The promise of Joel had been realized. The days of the outpouring of the Spirit (Joel 2:28), to which the prophets looked forward, were already present. The presence of the Spirit in the life of the church was the firstfruits of the age to come (Rom. 8:23), the guarantee of our inheritance (Eph. 1:14; see also 2 Cor. 1:22; 5:5). The end times were not simply some far distant hope, for the messianic age had already begun.

There are a number of other theological implications that were revealed to Paul through his encounter with Jesus Christ. One of these would appear to be the doctrine of the church as the body of Christ (''Saul, Saul, why do you persecute me?'' [Acts 9:4]). Another is the universal offer of the gospel to both Jew and Greek. Stephen and the Hellenists had hinted at this earlier, and now it was confirmed as true. Stephen's preaching would later be supported by Paul's reflection on the fact that the promised Spirit fell on both Jew and Greek on the basis of faith alone. It is not surprising, therefore, that Paul above all others proclaimed to both Jews and Greeks the great doctrine of justification by faith alone.

There does not seem to be any conflict, therefore, between, on the one hand, Paul's having learned certain things about the Christian faith both from and through men and, on the other hand, his claim that his gospel came supernaturally by the revelation of Jesus Christ. Clearly it was on the road to Damascus that Saul of Tarsus recognized the truth of the Christian message as well as many important theological consequences of the work of Jesus Christ. Here, too, he was commissioned to be the apostle to the Gentiles. All of this did not come through men, nor was he taught it. On the contrary, it came through the divine revelation of Jesus Christ. As a result Paul could say, "For I would have you know, brethren, that the gospel which was preached by me is not man's gospel. For I did not receive it from man, nor was I taught it, but it came through a revelation of Jesus Christ."

Are We to Praise God for All Things? (Rom. 8:28)

One of the favorite Bible verses of the Christian church throughout the centuries has been Romans 8:28. From this text Christians have drawn strength and encouragement in times of deepest despair and gloom. Despite the experience of tragedy, pain, and disappointment, there has come through this verse a word of reassurance and comfort from God. God has not forsaken his children. He has not failed them. No, on the contrary,

> We know that in everything God works for good with those who love him, who are called according to his purpose.

Yet despite the blessing that this statement has been in the history of the church, what Paul is actually saying has frequently been misunderstood. Some people unfortunately have read into this verse some strange and unchristian concepts. A certain woman who had not been feeling well was hospitalized, certain tests were made, and the resulting diagnosis was cancer. It was an extremely malignant form of cancer, and the prognosis was bleak. She had in fact but a few months to live. The shock was great, and she wept a great deal, not so much for herself but for her family. She was afraid for her husband and children because she felt they needed her. A friend from church visited her during this time of grief and turmoil. After the usual chitchat, the friend said, "Let's thank God for your cancer." The supposed grounds for such a suggestion were texts like 1 Thessalonians 5:16 ("Rejoice always"), Philippians 4:4 ("Rejoice in the Lord always"), and Romans 8:28 (see also Eph. 5:20 and 1 Thess. 5:18). The dying woman's friend believed that Romans 8:28 teaches that all things which happen to a Christian are good, and therefore we should praise God for everything that occurs.

Apart from the question of whether this approach is therapeutic or wise in counseling people experiencing such grief, the real issue is the soundness of the theology underlying such a view. For those familiar with philosophy, the friend's reasoning sounds very much like Greek Stoicism, a philosophy founded by Zeno. It received its name from Zeno's teaching his ideas in the Painted Porch (i.e., the Stoa) of Athens. Stoicism is essentially pantheistic in that it believes that God permeates all things. He is the rational, active cause of all. Hence, the Stoics argued as follows: God is in all things; God is reason; therefore, all things that happen are ultimately reasonable. The Stoics believed that all things that occur are to be accepted as essentially good. As a result, in times of distress and disappointment they found courage in their belief that all things are good; acceptance of this truth brought comfort and peace to them. Many Christians have unknowingly interpreted Paul's theology in Romans 8:28 in the context of a Stoic framework.

But does Paul teach that all things are good or that for Christians all things that take place are good? A number of considerations oppose such a position. One difficulty with this view is that it ignores the problem of sin. This is not the best of all possible worlds. In the opening chapters of

Genesis we read that one of the results of sin is that the creation is under a curse (Gen. 3:17–19). Paul speaks of this in the immediate context of Romans 8:28:

> For the creation waits with eager longing for the revealing of the sons of God; for the creation was subjected to futility, . . . the creation itself will be set free from its bondage to decay and obtain the glorious liberty of the children of God. We know that the whole creation has been groaning in travail together until now; and not only the creation, but we ourselves, who have the first fruits of the Spirit, groan inwardly as we wait for adoption as sons, the redemption of our bodies. [Rom. 8:19–23]

Disease and death are part of the curse under which the present world groans. This is why the believer prays constantly for the time when the creation will be renewed beyond its original perfection, when God will wipe away all tears, and when death and sin will be no more. Thus we pray, "Thy kingdom come" (Matt. 6:10), and "Our Lord, come!" (1 Cor. 16:22). When disease and death befall a believer, they cannot be good. To praise God for cancer, therefore, is to praise him for what is evil and a curse. To praise God *while* we have cancer is indeed appropriate, for because of his nature and deeds God is worthy of praise; but to praise him *for* cancer is to praise him for evil, and this is far from appropriate.

It should also be noted that Romans 8:28 is beset with several textual and exegetical difficulties. The textual problem involves the question of whether "God" is the subject of the verb *works*. In three extremely important Greek manuscripts (Codices Vaticanus and Alexandrinus and the Chester Beatty Papyrus) "God" is the subject. While it is true that the majority of the Greek manuscripts do not have "God" as the subject, it should be remembered that most of them originated many centuries later. If the reading *God* is followed, the exegetical difficulties disappear for the most part, for Paul is not saying that all things work together for our good, but rather that God is at work in all things (good or evil) for our good. On the other hand, if the majority text, which does not have "God" as the subject, is followed, the subject of the verb *works* is unclear. The difficulty of this particular reading is an argument in favor of the majority reading. (A basic rule in textual studies is that the more difficult reading is probably the original one; the less difficult presumably reflects an editor's attempt to clarify.) In this case the two most likely possibilities are that the verse is to be interpreted, "He [i.e., God] works all things for good," or "All things [the Greek allows this word to be either the subject or the object of the verb] work together for good."

The various English translations reveal this uncertainty. The King James Version reads, "All things work together for good." On the other hand, the modern translations all have God as the subject of the verb:

RSV—"We know that in everything God works for good."

NIV—"And we know that in all things God works for the good."

NASB—"And we know that God causes all things to work together for good."

NEB—"and in everything, as we know, he co-operates for good."

Now it is true that the modern translations include a notation to the effect that "other ancient authorities read 'in everything he works for good,' or 'everything works for good'" (RSV), but these are seen as less likely to be correct.

It is a wise hermeneutical principle not to build theological systems on disputed texts, for the likelihood of any interpretation's being correct can never rise above the combined probabilities of each part. In our text this means that if there is a 50 percent probability that Paul did not write "God" as the subject of the verb *works*, and if the linguistic probability that "all things" is the subject rather than the object of the verb is also 50 percent, then the probability that "all things work together for good" is the correct translation is only 25 percent. (The percentages given are, of course, purely hypothetical.)

The textual and exegetical problems associated with this verse should guard us against building too great a theological structure on it. And when we add to the textual and exegetical uncertainty the Christian understanding of the fall, sin, and the curse on creation, it becomes clear that we should not try to build on this passage the idea that all things that befall believers are good and worthy of praise. It should also be noted that no matter how we translate Romans 8:28, the reason or ground for the Christian assurance found in it is given in verses 29 and 30. Here we read nothing about all things being good, but we read rather about the goodness of God who chose (i.e., "foreknew"), predestined, called, justified, and glorified his children. Surely what Paul is saying is that the God who chose, predestined, called, justified, and glorified his children is present and working with us in all circumstances (whether they are good or evil), seeking our good. Because of this we can truly be thankful.

How should a Christian respond to the tragedies of life and to the command to "rejoice always"? With regard to the latter we should note that not only did the apostle Paul write this command, but he also wrote, "Rejoice with those who rejoice, weep with those who weep" (Rom. 12:15). We find that even our Lord wept with others over the death of his friend Lazarus (John 11:35). That the dominant disposition of the Christian should be one of rejoicing and praise goes without saying. Our sins have been forgiven (Rom. 4:7); we have God as our Father (Rom. 8:15); we have the assurance of life everlasting (John 3:16, 36); and our Lord has risen from the dead and ever lives to beseech the Father on our behalf (Heb. 7:25). We already have the firstfruits and guarantee of our salvation, the Holy Spirit (2 Cor. 1:22), and this assures us that God, having begun a good work in us, will one day bring it to completion (Phil. 1:6). We have the assurance that our Lord will never fail us nor forsake us (Heb. 13:5), and that he will be with us until the end of history (Matt. 28:20). How can the Christian not be joyous and full of praise in the light of all this? Yet we still groan inwardly as we await the consummation of all things, and there are even times when we are actually commanded to weep and share the grief of others, even as we are to rejoice and share in their joy (Rom. 12:15).

As to the tragedies in life, we must remember that the wickedness of the human race, death, and disease are evils brought about by the fall. These cannot be called "good." This is evident from the fact that before the fall they did not exist, and in the world to come they will not exist either. To call these good or to praise God for them is to insult the character of a holy and just God. To say that Auschwitz, Treblinka, and Sobibor; cancer, Parkinson's disease, and AIDS; and death itself are good, and to praise God for them cannot but cause us to wonder what kind of a God is being envisioned. Is this the God who loves the world and gave his only Son for its redemption? It is hard to see any great similarity.

How, then, should Christians respond to tragedy and pain? Can we praise God in Auschwitz? Can we rejoice when dying of cancer or when experiencing the death of someone greatly loved? Yes, *in* Auschwitz the believer can still praise God, but not *for* Auschwitz, for it was one of the greatest evils that sinful humans have ever created. What it stood for is forever condemned. Yet in Auschwitz the believer can still rejoice that even amid the most evil attempts to create hell on earth, God will never leave nor forsake. The most that evil persons can do is to take away our physical life, but they can never alter the fact that we are headed for a place which has eternal foundations whose builder and maker is God (Heb. 11:10). Even in

Auschwitz the believer is assured that tribulation, distress, persecution, famine, nakedness, peril, or the gas chamber can never separate one from the love of God in Christ Jesus (Rom. 8:35). Even there we can praise heaven that God is at work shaping and molding us to be more like Jesus, and in the light of eternity this is what really counts.

Similarly, we do not thank God for cancer. We do know, however, that in heaven there is no cancer. This result of the curse will be removed forever. So then, if we experience cancer, we can rejoice that this momentary affliction will one day give way to an eternity of bliss in the presence of Jesus. In a sense we can even rejoice that we will see our Lord sooner than will others, and that "to die is gain" (Phil. 1:21).

In Romans 8:28 Paul was reminding the Roman Christians, who loved God and were called according to his divine purpose, that God is present with his children and works with them in all circumstances. Elsewhere Paul also assured his readers that God would not permit them to suffer or be tempted above what they were able to bear (1 Cor. 10:13). These words of the apostle are still valid today. If the time comes in which we must take up the cross of suffering, we need to remember that even here (indeed, above all here) God is at work in and for us. And it may very well be, as saints have found throughout the centuries, that in such circumstances we shall experience the presence and grace of God as never before.

Is Every Government from God?
(Rom. 13:1–7)

Another passage that has caused ongoing problems in the history of the church is Romans 13:1–7. Here Paul states:

> Let every person be subject to the governing authorities. For there is no authority except from God, and those that exist have been instituted by God. Therefore he who resists

the authorities resists what God has appointed, and those who resist will incur judgment. For rulers are not a terror to good conduct, but to bad. Would you have no fear of him who is in authority? Then do what is good, and you will receive his approval, for he is God's servant for your good. But if you do wrong, be afraid, for he does not bear the sword in vain; he is the servant of God to execute his wrath on the wrongdoer. Therefore one must be subject, not only to avoid God's wrath but also for the sake of conscience. For the same reason you also pay taxes, for the authorities are ministers of God, attending to this very thing. Pay all of them their dues, taxes to whom taxes are due, revenue to whom revenue is due, respect to whom respect is due, honor to whom honor is due.

We become uneasy with this apparent blanket commendation of all governments when we recall how the Nazi regime (and others like it) used this passage in the 1930s and 1940s to promote loyalty and support for itself and its policies from both Protestants and Catholics.

It is not surprising, therefore, that through the centuries Christians have struggled with this passage and how it applies to their immediate situations. Already Origen (185–254) raised the question of whether a power which persecuted the church, fought against the faith, and destroyed religion was truly of God. In the sixteenth century the Reformers took a number of positions on how this passage was to be interpreted. For John Calvin any resistance to lawfully constituted authority was damnable, and not even a persecuting and unbelieving ruler could be forcibly resisted. Christians had no defense against a corrupt government other than prayer and flight, but if commanded by such a government to do what God forbids, they would have to disobey and remain true to God. On the other hand, the Magdeburg Confession, written by Lutherans fighting for their faith against a Roman Catholic emperor, saw it as a positive duty to resist all attacks against the true religion—their Lutheran faith. John Knox, a disciple of Calvin, went still further and claimed that it was the duty of a believer to rebel and seek the overthrow of idolatrous princes.

In seeking to understand the teaching of our text it is important to distinguish two questions: What did Paul mean by Romans 13:1–7? and what is the present-day significance of what Paul meant? It is clear that what the text means is that the Roman Christians who received this letter in A.D. 56 should obey their Roman leaders and give them the respect and taxes which were their due. Our text, then, is very much like Mark 12:13–17; 1 Peter 2:17–19; 1 Timothy 2:1–2; and Titus 3:1 in this regard. The reason behind Paul's admonition is that all authority comes ultimately from God and that rulers are servants of God for their people's good. (Here Paul is also in agreement with such Jewish writings as Wisdom 6:1–3 and Josephus *History of the Jewish War* 2.140.) We should remember that for the most part Nero had been a good emperor up to this time, that Roman law and justice had a positive effect on society, and that the government had frequently come to the defense of the church. The last-mentioned fact is evident from such incidents as are recorded in Acts 16:35–39 and 18:12–16, and there is no reason to think that situations like those we find in Acts 21:31–36; 22:22–29; 23:16–35; and 25:6–12, which took place after Paul wrote Romans, did not occur earlier as well. The *pax Romana* was also most conducive to the spread of the gospel throughout the world, since travel everywhere within the Roman Empire was now safer and more rapid.

On the other hand, Paul was not naive about the Roman government. After all, its leaders were unregenerate, and his writing of Romans 8:35 (''Who shall separate us from the love of Christ? Shall tribulation, or distress, or persecution. . . or sword?'') indicates that he was well aware of a negative role that government could play. When Paul wrote Romans, however, he was not concerned with hypothetical possibilities or exceptions to the rule. He could write as he did because the Roman government functioned within the guidelines which he gives in our passage. Rome had not yet asked the church to give to Caesar the things that were God's. There might well come a time when the words of Peter must be heeded—"we must obey God rather than men" (Acts 5:29)—but this was not yet a significant problem. The Roman government of A.D. 56 was far from perfect, but it was nevertheless an instrument of God in support of peace and justice instead of chaos. In general those who did evil were punished and those who did right were, if not always praised, at least left alone. This was far better than a situation in which "every man did what was right in his own eyes" (Judg. 21:25). Paul may also have believed it important to emphasize this need for obedience because in A.D. 49 there had been a serious clash in Rome between believing and unbelieving Jews. As a result, Emperor Claudius had expelled all the Jews from Rome (Acts 18:2). Concerning this event Suetonius wrote around A.D. 120, "Since the Jews constantly made disturbances at the instigation of Chrestus [this is undoubtedly an error and should be read "Christus"], he [Claudius] expelled them from Rome" (Lives of the Caesars 25).

The main problem Christians face in our passage is not so much the meaning of the text, but rather the significance of that meaning for today. It is understandable why Paul would have commanded the Roman Christians to obey their government in A.D. 56, but the abuse of this text in Nazi Germany and in other totalitarian systems makes us most uneasy, for Paul seems to be giving a blanket blessing on all governments. Yet clearly there are times when we cannot give Caesar what he asks, for example, when he asks for that which belongs to God alone. Furthermore, it is surely incorrect to assume that Paul naively thought that all governments were legitimate. The Roman government of A.D. 56 was, but he was well aware of evil governments in the history of Israel. He knew of many rulers of Israel and Judah who did evil in the sight of the Lord. He was not unaware of such evil rulers as Ahab, Jeroboam, Joash,

Zechariah, and Pekah, as well as Sennacherib and Antiochus Epiphanes. Furthermore, he had even warned of the coming of the Antichrist (see 2 Thess. 2:1–12). As a result, he knew of instances where to obey the government would have been to deny God. He was also well aware of the Roman involvement in the crucifixion of his Lord.

It is often overlooked that Paul in discussing the need to obey authority because of its being ordained of God describes that authority. The authority that he envisions as ordained of God is "not a terror to good conduct, but to bad" (Rom. 13:3). It is an authority which gives its approval to those who do good (v. 3). It is an authority which is "God's servant for your good" and which executes God's "wrath on the wrongdoer" (v. 4). This is how Paul describes governments which possess God's divine approval and which Christians are to obey. In general, Rome in A.D. 56 met this description. It is likewise clear that numerous governments such as Nazi Germany do not. To expect Paul, however, to be concerned with teaching when one must disobey government would clearly be wrong. The need at hand, in light of A.D. 49 and other events of which we are perhaps not aware, was to emphasize the Christians' duty to obey and not rebel against the legitimate authority of Rome.

In my own experience this text became relevant and significant when in the 1970s I was being urged to protest against the Vietnam War by not paying my taxes or at least by not paying the portion of my taxes which went for the military budget. In wrestling with this passage I asked myself several questions: In general does my government punish evil and reward good? Did the Roman government of A.D. 56 use the taxes it collected for nonsocial purposes? Did Rome use the tax moneys of believers for its militaristic aims? Does my government demand for itself that which rightly belongs to God alone? and, finally, Was the Roman government which Paul commanded his readers to obey a better government than mine? After answering yes to the first three questions and no to the last two, it became clear that if the Roman Christians were to obey the Roman government of A.D. 56 and pay it the taxes due, how much more ought I do the same with regard to my government! In light of the meaning of the text in A.D. 56 its significance for my own situation in the 1970s became quite clear. Other areas of protest were still available, but nonpayment of taxes seemed to be excluded by the text.

The time may come, of course, when in our own country the state turns against the people of God. It did not take long for the "Hosanna" of Palm Sunday to change to the "Crucify him" of Good Friday. God's people were persecuted in Old Testament times by outside powers (Assyria, Babylon, Syria, etc.) and from within as well (various rulers of Israel and Judah). The church has also experienced persecution from without as well as from within. To say that this can never happen in our own country is to ignore both the teachings of Scripture and the lessons of history. If the time ever comes when our government in general rewards evil and punishes good, and when it demands for itself what only God is entitled to, then we shall have to say boldly and clearly, "We must obey God rather than men." But this was not the situation in Paul's day when he wrote Romans 13:1–7, and it is not the situation in which we find ourselves today.

Did Paul's Theology Develop?
(1 Thess. 4:13–18)

In discussions of Pauline theology it is not uncommon to read about the development of Paul's thought. That Paul's theology developed in one sense is certainly true. Surely his theology at the end of his life was not identical with his theology ten minutes after his conversion. Over the years God granted Paul additional revelation (2 Cor. 12:7), and as he reflected on the gospel which God had revealed to him, met with Peter and the other disciples, and studied the Old Testament Scriptures, he must have gained additional insights. There is a sense, therefore, in which Paul's theology did indeed develop.

What most scholars mean when they talk about development in Paul's theology, however, is something quite different. Many insist that Paul's theology changed over the course of years, so that what he taught in his early letters (such as 1 Thessalonians) he no longer accepted in his later ones (such as Romans or Colossians). (Most scholars who hold this view do not accept the Pauline authorship of 1 and 2 Timothy and Titus.) Paul is supposed to have changed his view on such things as the resurrection and the parousia. With regard to the former, Paul's original view of a merely physical resurrection to take place at the parousia (1 Thess. 4:13–18) changed to a more spiritual view of a resurrection (1 Cor. 15:35–50) which takes place at death (2 Cor. 5:1–3). With regard to the parousia Paul supposedly changed from the view that Jesus would return in Paul's own lifetime (1 Thess. 4:15, 17) to the view that the second coming would not take place in his lifetime (Phil. 1:19–26).

Probably the one passage that has most often been cited as proof that Paul changed his view as to the time of the parousia is 1 Thessalonians 4:13–18. Here Paul seems to be teaching that Jesus would return in Paul's lifetime:

> For this we declare to you by the word of the Lord, that we who are alive, who are left until the coming of the Lord, shall not precede those who have fallen asleep. [v. 15]

Such a view as to the time of the parousia was clearly incorrect, so Paul later changed and taught that the parousia would not come in his own lifetime. Sometimes a major crisis such as Paul's facing death (2 Cor. 1:8–9) is suggested as having caused this change.

The basic question involves whether Paul did in fact teach at one time that the parousia would take place in his own lifetime. This is not the same as asking whether Paul

personally believed at one time that he would be alive
when Jesus returned. Paul may very well have believed
that he would be alive, yet never have taught this in his
letters. We have no access into Paul's mind as to what he
may have believed but not taught. As a result, we must
narrow the question to, Did Paul ever assert in his letters
that the parousia would take place in his lifetime? Since the
passage most often cited as proof that he did is 1 Thessalonians 4:15, 17, we can reword our question as follows:
Does Paul teach in 1 Thessalonians 4:15, 17, that Jesus
would return in the apostle's own lifetime? For some
people the fact that Jesus did not return in Paul's lifetime is
proof that he did not teach this. Such reverence for the
Scriptures and their infallibility is praiseworthy in one
sense, but in another sense such a view places one's own
doctrinal presuppositions above the meaning of the biblical
text itself. As one who holds the view that the Bible is the
only infallible rule of faith and practice, I believe that we
must let the text speak for itself. We cannot tell the
text what it can or cannot say. True reverence for the
Word of God is to listen to it. Rather than predetermining
what 1 Thessalonians 4:15, 17, can or cannot mean, we
must reverently seek to understand what Paul meant by
this text.

There are a number of philosophical and historical objections that could be raised against the view that Paul's
theology developed (in the sense of "changed") between
his earlier and later writings. These are helpful and will be
examined later, but priority must always be given to the
text itself. The immediate context of 1 Thessalonians 4:15,
17, involves the fact that certain Thessalonian Christians
have died since Paul founded the church there. From Timothy Paul has heard (probably in Corinth) that some of the
Thessalonians are troubled over the fate of those who have
died since Paul's departure. Will they miss out on the
"blessed hope, the appearing of the glory of our great God
and Savior Jesus Christ" (Titus 2:13)? Paul seeks to assure

the Thessalonians that they will not. He does not want his readers to be ignorant and as a result grieve like nonbelievers who have no hope (1 Thess. 4:13), so he declares to them that those who have died in Christ will rise from the dead to meet the returning Jesus. They will therefore not miss out in any way on sharing the glory of the parousia. Then "we who are alive, who are left until the coming of the Lord...shall be caught up together with them ...and so...always be with the Lord" (vv. 15, 17). Paul then applies this great theological truth to the situation in Thessalonica: "Therefore comfort one another with these words" (v. 18). The Thessalonians need not grieve over those who have died in Christ. They can take comfort in the fact that the dead in Christ as well as the living will share in the glorious event of the parousia.

Does Paul, however, teach in verses 15 and 17 ("we who are alive") that he would personally be alive at the parousia? There are several considerations that should caution us before we answer this question affirmatively. For one, it should be noted that what Paul is primarily emphasizing in 1 Thessalonians 4:13–18 is not that he and the recipients of this letter will be alive when Jesus returns. Rather, he is affirming that the dead in Christ will not miss out on the parousia. Accordingly, Paul does not bother to clarify who among those presently living will be alive at the parousia and who will not. Since the contrast lies between those Thessalonians who are dead in Christ and those who are alive, where else can Paul include himself and the recipients of this letter except with those who are alive?

Second, the economy of language used did not permit Paul to clarify the various possibilities that faced him and the Thessalonians. If, simply for the sake of argument, we assume that Paul believed that not all the recipients of this letter would be alive at the parousia (and certainly it is extremely doubtful that Paul believed that no more Thessalonian Christians would die before the Lord returned), how would Paul have worded it? The following by its very nature would have been overly clumsy: "We who are alive, who are left until the coming of the Lord (although, of course, some of us presently alive may not be alive then, but may have joined those who are asleep), shall not precede those who have fallen asleep." Since Paul was primarily concerned with teaching about the dead in Christ, such exactness about the living was unnecessary. A simple deduction on the part of the Thessalonian Christians would have enabled them to add this qualification to Paul's words.

Third, a literal interpretation of Paul's words in 1 Thessalonians 4:15, 17, which claims that Paul taught that he would be alive at the parousia, requires that Paul also taught that all the Thessalonians living at the time of his writing would likewise be alive at the parousia, for the "we" includes them as well. Few scholars, however, would be willing to go this far. It would be absurd to glean from this passage the idea that whereas in the past certain Thessalonian Christians had died, no more of them would die, but they, along with Paul, would remain alive until the parousia. Such an interpretation is necessitated, however, by reading into the "we" of these verses the idea that Paul is affirming that he would be alive at the parousia.

Fourth, it should be noted that the "we" in verse 15 is qualified by the phrase "who are alive, who are left until the coming of the Lord," and in verse 17 by "who are alive, who are left." If Paul were affirming confidently that he and at least the majority of the Thessalonian Christians would be alive at the parousia, why does Paul add this qualification? Why does he not simply say, "We shall not precede" (v. 15) and "We shall be caught up" (v. 17)? Even if we were to say that adding "who are alive" was natural to show a contrast between the living and the dead in Christ, why does Paul add "who are left until the coming of the Lord" in verse 15 and "who are left" in verse 17? It seems reasonable to conclude that Paul by these additions was indicating that he was uncertain as to whether he and the recipients of his letter would be left when the Lord returned, so he qualified the "we" in this manner.

Finally, it should be noted that in 1 Thessalonians 5:10 Paul uses "we" to describe both those who are awake (i.e., living) at the time of the Lord's return and those who are asleep. The fact that Paul does not say, "so that we who are awake and those who are asleep," but rather, "so that whether we wake or sleep," indicates that Paul is not claiming in 1 Thessalonians 4:15, 17, that he will be alive at the parousia.

It would appear, then, that the context as well as the wording of the text does not require us to interpret these verses as an affirmation by Paul that he would be alive at the parousia. On the contrary, it appears that Paul was well aware that he and the Thessalonian Christians might also be asleep at the parousia. Nevertheless, awake or asleep (1 Thess. 5:10) they would not miss out on the parousia but would meet the Lord and live forever with him.

This interpretation is reinforced by several other considerations as well. One of these involves the occasional nature of Paul's letters. We have already alluded to this when we discussed what Paul was seeking to teach in this passage. We should always be careful in drawing out of the text conclusions on issues that the author is not specifically addressing. It is clear that Paul is not seeking in 1 Thessalonians 4:15, 17, to make a statement about who will be alive at the return of the Lord, but rather about the relationship of the dead in Christ to the parousia. We should therefore be careful not to draw any unwarranted conclusions about Paul's relationship to the parousia.

Second, we should note the date of this letter. First Thessalonians was written some sixteen years after Paul's conversion. In 2 Corinthians 11:23 Paul writes that he was often near death. No doubt some of these instances took place in the years before he wrote 1 Thessalonians. Are we to assume that Paul never thought that any one of these episodes could spell his death? Are we to assume that during his stoning at Lystra (Acts 14:19–20) Paul thought that it was impossible for him to die because the parousia had not come? This seems highly unlikely.

Finally, we must remember that Paul was well aware that numerous Christians had died in the Lord. On what basis could he conclude that despite having faced death a number of times he would somehow be excluded from death and would survive until the parousia? If it is suggested that Paul may have believed that God had revealed this to him, we must point out that nowhere does Paul mention or appeal to such a revelation.

Did Paul's theological understanding of the parousia develop? Surely he grew richer in knowledge. No doubt Paul at the end of his life had a greater understanding of the parousia and the implications of this event than he did in his earliest days as a Christian. But did Paul's understanding of the parousia change in the sense that he denied what he once affirmed or affirmed what he once denied? And in particular, did Paul affirm in his earliest letters that he would be alive at the parousia and then deny this later? From our investigation of 1 Thessalonians 4:15, 17, we conclude that there is no reason why these verses need to be interpreted as teaching this. On the contrary, within the text there are a number of reasons for denying that Paul sought to affirm that he would be alive at the time of the parousia. We have no way of knowing what Paul may have personally thought on the issue, but it is clear that in this passage, he does not teach that he would survive until the parousia.

Was Paul a Universalist? (Col. 1:15–20)

Within the New Testament several passages have been called hymns because of their rhythmic balance. One such passage is Colossians 1:15–20:

He is the image of the invisible God, the first-born of all creation; for in him all things were created, in heaven and on earth, visible and invisible, whether thrones or dominions or principalities or authorities—all things were created through him and for him. He is before all things, and in him all things hold together.

He is the head of the body, the church; he is the beginning, the first-born from the dead, that in everything he might be pre-eminent. For in him all the fulness of God was pleased to dwell, and through him to reconcile to himself all things, whether on earth or in heaven, making peace by the blood of his cross.

Although this passage raises a number of issues, the particular issue to be dealt with in this section involves the apparent reconciliation of "all things, whether on earth or in heaven," which has resulted by the death of Christ. Does Paul teach in this passage that everyone and everything will ultimately be reconciled to God irrespective of whether individuals accept or reject Jesus Christ in this life? In other words, does our passage teach the universal salvation of all creation?

Such a view while attractive would seem to oppose numerous clear statements in Paul and in the rest of the New Testament. The traditional position of the Christian church on this matter has been that the destiny of each individual will be determined by whether one places personal faith in Jesus Christ during this lifetime. The result will be either eternal bliss (heaven) or eternal damnation (hell). Evangelical Christians do not hold this view because they desire the eternal damnation of non-Christians. On the contrary, many would love to be universalists in this regard, for they are not eager to believe that friends and relatives whom they love will experience the eternal condemnation of a holy and righteous God. If they could vote on this issue, they would gladly vote a universalist ballot. Theology, however, is not determined by vote! The theological reality of an eternal judgment (or of no eternal judgment) is not determined by ballot. God is not an elected official of a democracy; he is the sovereign King.

Theology therefore does not conduct Gallup Polls of what people believe or want to believe, but seeks to discover what the sovereign God has decreed. Theology ultimately is determined by the exegesis of God's revelation, that is, our understanding of the Bible. Our wishes and desires are ultimately irrelevant.

The reason why the statement concerning the reconciliation of all things in Colossians 1:20 raises problems is that elsewhere in Scripture we come across numerous passages which clearly teach that those who reject in this life the love of God in Christ will experience an eternal judgment. The wicked in their judgment are seen as existing in an unchangeable state of torment (Luke 16:26); Jesus portrays the separation of the goats from the sheep as an ''eternal punishment'' (Matt. 25:46); the fires of hell are described by Jesus as unquenchable (Mark 9:43, 48) and eternal (Matt. 18:8); and the torment of the wicked is seen as continuing ''for ever and ever'' (Rev. 14:11). Paul also teaches in his writings that the judgment of God involves eternal felicity for the believer, but eternal wrath for the unbeliever. Concerning those who do not obey the gospel he states, ''They shall suffer the punishment of eternal destruction and exclusion from the presence of the Lord and from the glory of his might'' (2 Thess. 1:9). He also tells the Thessalonians, ''For God has not destined us for wrath, but to obtain salvation through our Lord Jesus Christ'' (1 Thess. 5:9). (See also 2 Thess. 2:10, 12; Phil. 3:19; Rom. 2:6–10, 12; 5:9.)

In seeking to understand Paul's meaning, we should interpret Colossians 1:20 in the context of his other teachings. Hypothetically, Paul could have changed his views when he wrote Colossians or he could have been inconsistent, but we should assume, unless it is proven otherwise, that a theologian of his stature would be consistent and not make contradictory statements. For the evangelical Christian the doctrine of inspiration and infallibility also argues strongly for consistency in Paul's writings.

One way of understanding Colossians 1:20 which is consistent with Paul's teaching elsewhere involves the meaning of the term *reconcile* in this verse. This term can be understood in light of what Paul says in Colossians 2:15: Jesus has disarmed the principalities and powers and triumphed over them. It is evident from this verse that there exist a serious hostility and animosity between God and all things. The reconciliation of the hostile powers in Colossians 1:20 refers, then, not to a willing rapprochement, but to a reluctant submission such as we read of in 1 Corinthians 15:28 and Philippians 2:10–11. This reconciliation stands in synonymous parallelism with the phrase "making peace." Now peace can be joyously accepted, but it can also be forcibly imposed! Is the peace referred to in our verse the kind of peace that comes when the God of peace crushes Satan under our feet (Rom. 16:20)? The *pax Romana* which existed in the Mediterranean world of Paul's day was of this type. It came through force of arms. But it was peace.

If the reconciliation spoken of in Colossians 1:20 is interpreted in light of Jesus' triumph over the principalities and powers of Colossians 2:15, we should not see this final pacification as a joyous, happy turning to God in faith. More likely we have portrayed here the victory of Christ over his enemies: the powers submit against their wills, bow their knees, and confess with gnashing teeth that Jesus Christ is Lord (Phil. 2:10–11). This forcible subjugation, furthermore, need not involve an eternal state but rather the reconciliation that will take place in the great day when everyone gives glory to God and confesses, willingly or unwillingly, that Jesus Christ is indeed Lord of all. After this the final separation of the sheep and the goats will take place.

A second way of interpreting Colossians 1:20 (it should be pointed out that these two ways are not mutually exclusive but may very well be complementary) is to take into consideration the hymnlike nature of Colossians 1:15–20.

In general, hymns should be interpreted somewhat differently from nonpoetic material. A good example of this is found in Judges 4 and 5. In chapter 4 we have a narrative account of the defeat of Sisera by the forces of Israel led by Deborah and Barak. It is written in prose and should be interpreted literally. On the other hand, we find in chapter 5 a poetic version of the same event. Here we must take into consideration the poetic form and allow for a certain degree of hyperbole and exaggeration, for poetry frequently makes use of these elements to get its point across. It is not surprising, therefore, that in Judges 5 we read that "the earth trembled, and the heavens dropped" (v. 4), "the mountains quaked" (v. 5), and "from heaven fought the stars, from their courses they fought against Sisera" (v. 20). And with regard to an even more familiar incident we have Israel's crossing of the Red Sea described both in narrative and in poetry (Exod. 14 and 15). In the poetic version we read, for example, "the horse and his rider [the Lord] has thrown into the sea" (15:1), "Pharaoh's chariots and his host he cast into the sea" (v. 4), and "thy fury . . . consumes them like stubble" (v. 7).

Even today it is not unusual to find exaggeration and hyperbole present in the songs and hymns of the church. Note, for example, the following verse from Charles Wesley's "Hark! the Herald Angels Sing":

Hail, the heav'n-born Prince of Peace!
Hail, the Sun of Righteousness!
Light and life *to all* He brings [not "offers" but "brings"],
Ris'n with healing in His wings.

Consider also Isaac Watt's "Joy to the World!":

He rules the world with truth and grace,
And makes the nations prove
The glories of His righteousness,
And wonders of His love.

The latter hymn if sung in a Russian gulag would be a confession of faith in the sovereignty of God and his future judgment and rule of the world, but it would also be clearly hyperbolic with respect to the present situation. Yet in hymns and poetry such language does not bother us because we accept the presence of hyperbole, for rhyme and meter often put unique demands on the writer, and the genre itself encourages the use of exaggeration for expression. In this regard we even speak of poetic license.

Is it possible that in a similar way the poetic hymn of Colossians 1:15–20 may be using exaggeration and hyperbolic language because of its rhythmic structure? It is noteworthy that the expression *ta panta* (or "all things") is used four times in this passage, and that other forms of this Greek word occur four more times. The balance of the poetic form should also be noted:

"all things were created *through him* and for *him*" (v. 16b)
"and *through him* to reconcile to *him*self all things" (v. 20a)

Recently one writer has demonstrated that there exist in both Jewish and Greek literature a number of creation statements in which the term *all* appears with unusual frequency. This tendency and the attempt to balance verse 20 with verse 16 may well have led the hymnwriter to practice the same kind of poetic license that the writers of Judges 5 and Exodus 15, as well as later hymnwriters and poets, found necessary for their works.

If Colossians 1:15–20 is understood in the way we have suggested, this passage does not conflict with what Paul and the rest of the Scriptures teach elsewhere, for what we have here is not a confession in prose using literal terminology, but rather a joyous song celebrating the creative and redemptive work of Jesus Christ who is Lord of all.

If We Are Already Dead to Sin, Why the Exhortation? (Rom. 8:9–13)

Within the Pauline Letters we encounter a number of statements and exhortations which, although standing side by side, appear to conflict with each other. One such example is in Romans 8:9–11 and 12–13:

> But you are not in the flesh, you are in the Spirit, if in fact the Spirit of God dwells in you. Any one who does not have the Spirit of Christ does not belong to him. But if Christ is in you, although your bodies are dead because of sin, your spirits are alive because of righteousness. If the Spirit of him who raised Jesus from the dead dwells in you, he who raised Christ Jesus from the dead will give life to your mortal bodies also through his Spirit which dwells in you.

> So then, brethren, we are debtors, not to the flesh, to live according to the flesh—for if you live according to the flesh you will die, but if by the Spirit you put to death the deeds of the body you will live.

Another example of apparent conflict is found in Colossians 3:3 and verses 2 and 5, where Paul's statement, "For you have died, and your life is hid with Christ in God," is preceded by "Set your minds on things that are above, not on things that are on earth," and followed by "Put to death therefore what is earthly in you: fornication, impurity, passion, evil desire, and covetousness, which is idolatry."

The problem raised by these passages and others like them is that the statements made by the apostle in Romans 8:9–11 and Colossians 3:3 seem to conflict with the exhortations found in Romans 8:12–13 and Colossians 3:2 and 5. If Christians are not in the flesh but in the Spirit, why should they be exhorted and warned not to live in the flesh? If believers have died with Christ, why are they commanded to put to death what they have already died to? Or to use the language of Romans 6, why does Paul tell the Christian who was crucified with Christ and has died to sin (vv. 6, 11, 14) not to let sin reign within (vv. 12–13)? How can a person dead to sin commit sin? In Pauline studies this problem is known as the problem of the indicative (the statements) and the imperative (the exhortations). The issue is by no means a minor one, for many additional passages contain this seeming conflict (see Rom. 6:17–18 and 19; 1 Cor. 5:7b and 7a; 6:11 and 9–10; 10:13 and 12; Gal. 5:25a and 25b; Col. 3:1a and 1b; 3:9b–10 and 9a).

Numerous attempts have been made to resolve this problem. One such attempt explains the problem as arising from a conflict between the Pauline ideal, the apostle's conviction that under the impulse of the Spirit the Christian can be nothing but moral (the indicative), and the reality, which caused Paul to give commands (the imperative) to those who failed to live up to this ideal. Another explanation sees Paul as teaching two separate and irreconcilable ethical systems. The one involves a law ethic and is witnessed to by the imperatives; the other is the ethic of the justified believer and is witnessed to by the indicatives. Unfortunately the apostle never brought them into harmony, so that a basic contradiction stands between the indicative and the imperative. A third explanation argues that there is no real connection or relationship between Paul's theology (the indicative) and his ethics (the imperative). They are simply isolated and separate categories in Paul's thinking which he never reconciled. Still another explanation is to see Paul's teaching as inherently paradoxical; accordingly, we should not try to reconcile the indicative and the imperative, but rather should delight in their dialectical antagonism. One advocate of this view argues that Paul taught that believers should "become [in fact] what they are [in principle]." A final explanation argues that Paul overstates and exaggerates the indicative aspect of the Christian's redemption in order to emphasize that Jesus has brought about a radical break with the old life. As a result, the indicatives should not be taken at face value.

Each of these explanations suggests that the problem between the indicative and the imperative in Paul cannot be resolved, and that an irreconcilable contradiction of some sort is present in this material. Yet before we come to such a conclusion, it may be profitable to look at the biblical data. We should note that the indicatives and the imperatives causing our problem are not found in widely scattered portions of the Pauline Letters. On the contrary, they are intimately associated together. In fact they are frequently found in the same passage. It is therefore unlikely that Paul was unaware of the problem or that he has given in the same sentence two totally different and contrasting theories of Christian ethics. It would appear that at least in Paul's mind the indicative and the imperative were interconnected, belonged together, and made sense.

We should also note that the imperative rests on the indicative and that the order is not reversible. In other words the exhortations of the apostle are based on the reality of the statements. The exhortations do not bring about the truths stated in the indicatives but are built on the reality of the indicatives. We are not exhorted to put the sin in us to death in order to die with Christ. On the contrary, it is because we have died with Christ that we are told to put to death the deeds of the body, that is, sin in us. We are not commanded not to let sin reign in our mortal bodies in order to die to sin. Quite the reverse—it is because we have died to sin that we are told not to let sin reign in our mortal bodies. It is only because Christians have died to sin that they are able to resist it. It is important in this regard to note such words as "so then" in Romans 8:12, "therefore" in Colossians 3:5, "if" in Colossians 3:1, "for" in Colossians 3:3, and "as" in 1 Corinthians 5:7. These passages indicate that the imperative is based and built on the reality of the indicative.

We should note further that there is no textual evidence which suggests that Paul believed that the indicatives were overstatements of some kind. On the contrary, he truly believed that Christians have died, been buried, and been raised with Christ. Probably the key to understanding Paul's teaching here (as well as when he speaks of being in Christ or in Adam and when he depicts the church as the body of Christ) can be found in the concept of corporate solidarity. According to this concept an individual can be so associated with a group or another individual that what is said of the one can also be said of the other. So when Achan sinned (Josh 7:1), it could be said that all "Israel has sinned" (7:11–12). Note also the solidarity between the people who came out of Egypt and their descendants in Joshua 24:6–7, where the writer speaks of the present generation, most of whom were not alive at the time, as having been delivered out of Egypt. In the New Testament we read that if "one member [of the church] suffers, all suffer together; if one member is honored, all rejoice together" (1 Cor. 12:26). In a similar manner, because we are in Adam we experience death through our association with him, yet because we are in Christ we experience life through our association with him.

The apostle sees the church as united to Christ by faith in such a way that what Christ has experienced has also been experienced by the members of his body. Because Christ died, so have they. Because Christ rose, so have they. For Paul this is not some sort of fiction but an actual reality. Believers, because they are in Christ, can be said to have died to sin and been raised with Christ. Viewed from the perspective of the believers' unity with Christ, all these realities, even if not yet fully realized, are theirs. Because Paul views believers from the perspective of all that they are in Christ, he is able to say what he does in his indicatives. Viewing Christians from the perspective of all that they are in Christ involves not just where they are at the moment, but what they have been, are, and will be; and as a result the indicatives are absolutely true. Believers in Christ are not only forgiven, saved, and justified, but glorified, rendered dead to sin, and raised in newness of life. While it may be true that at the present they do not possess all of their inheritance in Christ, all these blessings are theirs nonetheless. In the light of eternity all these are true of Christians. There are no ifs. Believers can be accurately described as forgiven in Christ, saved, justified, glorified, rendered dead to sin, and raised in newness of life. In the indicatives Paul views Christians from the perspective of eternity, which involves a "not yet" dimension, and not simply from the momentary situation in which they now exist.

On the other hand, the imperatives view and deal with Christians in light of their present situation, that is, the "already now." The imperatives deal with what believers have presently realized and where they are at the moment. They view the Christian on this side of the second coming where sin is still a reality and the resurrection still future. The indicatives deal with believers from the viewpoint of what they are in the light of eternity. It is because of what we are in Christ eternally that Paul makes his indicative statements. It is because of what we are in time and on this side of the second coming that he exhorts us to set our minds on the things that are above and not to let sin rule over us.

A story concerning one of the kings of England well illustrates our point. While he was a boy and his father was still alive, he was, of course, the heir to the throne. He was not yet the king, but he would be on his father's death. Accordingly, the boy's tutor would time and time again exhort him with the words, "You are the king, and kings do not behave that way." Now, of course, he was not yet the king, but he was the future king, so he was exhorted to live in light of all he was and would be. Paul in a similar way reminds Christians that they must view their lives in light of all that they are in Christ, and this involves not just the present time but eternity itself. In light of eternity (not yet) and in light of our kingly inheritance already received (now), Paul exhorts us to live like the kings we really are.

Should the Church Hand an Offending Member Over to Satan? (1 Cor. 5:1–5)

Discipline is not a favorite subject in the Christian church today. In evangelical settings there is much interest in following the apostolic teaching and preaching, but there is considerable uneasiness in following the apostles in their practice of church discipline. This is often most difficult to carry out and rightly so, for we do not always possess the clarity of insight that the apostles possessed in their practice of church discipline. Furthermore, we are constantly aware that we need to take heed to ourselves (Gal. 6:1) and be careful that we not fall (1 Cor. 10:12).

Church discipline, however, should not be understood as an act of judgmental vengeance but rather as an act of love for God, his church, and the individual. The command to ''judge not'' (Matt. 7:1) warns against being judgmental in nature, that is, being critical of others with the aim of hurting them or of making us feel better by making others look worse. Yet to neglect church discipline is to deny the keys with which the church has been entrusted (cf. Matt. 18:18 with what precedes). It is interesting to note in this respect that some of the Reformers, especially Ulrich Zwingli and the Anabaptists, saw the marks of a true church as being not only the true preaching of the Word of God and the right administration of the sacraments, but also the faithful exercise of church discipline.

One of the most troubling passages in the New Testament which deal with church discipline is in 1 Corinthians 5. Paul has heard, perhaps from Chloe's messengers (1:11), about an example of gross immorality in the church. A member of the church was living sexually with his stepmother (''his father's wife''). Such behavior was prohibited in the Old Testament (Lev. 18:8; 20:11), and marriage between a man and his stepmother was also forbidden by Roman law. This is why Paul states that this immorality is ''of a kind that is not found even among pagans'' (1 Cor. 5:1). It seems that whereas the man himself was a Christian, for the church was directed to take action against him, his stepmother was not, for no church discipline was to be exercised toward her.

After a brief rebuke of the church for its overly high opinion of itself, Paul states in verses 3–5:

> For though absent in body I am present in spirit, and as if present, I have already pronounced judgment in the name of the Lord Jesus on the man who has done such a thing. When you are assembled, and my spirit is present, with the power of our Lord Jesus, you are to deliver this man to Satan for the destruction of the flesh, that his spirit may be saved in the day of the Lord Jesus.

Paul, even though not in Corinth at the time, feels compelled to judge this particular matter, since the Corinthians, who ought to have disciplined the man, have not done so. Although Paul is not physically present, he is nonetheless present in spirit (cf. Col. 2:5), and so he passes judgment. Clearly Paul sees the need for discipline in this matter. It is to the shame of the Corinthians that he had to write them and command them to take action. They should have done so on their own.

A number of questions arise with regard to what the phrase "in the name of the Lord Jesus" modifies. Does it go with "assembled"? With "deliver"? With "pronounced judgment"? Or does it go with "has done such a thing"? The last-mentioned may not be as farfetched as it first appears, for the man may have claimed that his action demonstrated that he was free in Christ and no longer under the law. The New International Version (NIV) favors "assembled in the name of the Lord Jesus," while the Revised Standard Version (RSV) favors "pronounced judgment in the name of the Lord Jesus." We cannot be certain, but in light of the fact that Paul usually associates this particular phrase with a finite verb rather than a participle, the RSV reading should be favored (in the original Greek the word translated "pronounced judgment" is a finite verb, while the word translated "assembled" is a participle; cf. 1 Cor. 6:11; Phil. 2:10; Col. 3:17; 2 Thess. 3:6; but note Eph. 5:20). Another question involves the phrase "with the power of our Lord Jesus." Does it go with "assembled" or "deliver"? The NIV and the RSV both favor "assembled" in this instance, the RSV reading, "When you are assembled... with the power of our Lord Jesus."

In verse 5 we come across additional difficult questions which affect our understanding of this passage even more. What does "deliver this man to Satan" mean? What does "for the destruction of the flesh" mean? Finally, what does "that his spirit may be saved" mean? With regard to the last two phrases the RSV reproduces the ambiguity of the Greek text better, while the NIV has eliminated much of the ambiguity and chosen a particular interpretation ("so that the sinful nature may be destroyed and his spirit saved on the day of the Lord").

What does Paul mean by "deliver this man to Satan"? He seems to be referring to expulsion from the church (note v. 2). Although we should not read into the text later doctrines of excommunication, we have here a command to expel the offender from the fellowship of the church. Since this means that the man will leave the fellowship of God's people, where God rules, and be forced out into the world, where the devil rules (Eph. 2:2–3; 2 Cor. 4:4; John 12:31; 16:11), he is in effect to be handed over to Satan. Expelled from the community of God's people, the offender is to be delivered to the realm where the ruler of this age works in those who are disobedient (Eph. 2:2; cf. Col. 1:13).

The offender is to be handed over to Satan "for the destruction of the flesh." This has been interpreted to mean "for the mortification or putting to death of his sinful lusts." This is how Origen interpreted the expression and is the preferred reading in the NIV. Romans 8:13 is seen by some as expressing the same idea, but there Paul speaks of putting to death the "deeds of the body" and not the "flesh." Colossians 3:5, which refers to putting to death evil desires, is likewise not an exact parallel. According to the alleged parallels, one is to put to death evil deeds or desires, but not the flesh. Furthermore, these commands are given to Christians in good standing, not to one about to be expelled from the Christian community for gross sin. The question can also be raised at this point whether Paul really thought that destruction of the flesh or sinful nature can be achieved in this life. Finally, it should be noted that Paul never uses the term flesh (*sarx*) elsewhere in 1 Corinthians to refer to sinful lusts, so that it does not appear likely that he would use it in this way here (see 1 Cor. 1:26, 29; 6:16; 7:28; 10:18; 15:39, 50).

A second possible interpretation holds that Paul is referring to physical suffering. Some scholars see a parallel in 1 Corinthians 11:30–32, where Paul explains that some of the congregation are sick and some have even died as a result of improprieties at the Lord's Supper. It is hoped that through such suffering repentance will result and the offenders will be restored to fellowship. We note, however, that this passage is referring to members *within* the Christian community, whereas the offender in 1 Corinthians 5 is expelled from and stands *outside* the Christian community.

A third explanation is that the destruction of the flesh refers to physical death. Being handed over to Satan means to be handed over to death. Some see death in this case as remedial, that is, through death the offender would atone for his sins, while others see it as purely punitive. The idea that death has some sort of atoning significance is found in rabbinic literature, but it is absent from the New Testament. It seems best to interpret "the destruction of the flesh" as referring to physical illness and even death that the offender will face outside the community of faith.

With regard to the clause "that his spirit may be saved," it should be noted that the word *his* does not appear in the Greek text. Literally Paul states, "in order that *the* spirit [or *the* Spirit] might be saved." The basic issue here is whether Paul sees the discipline of the church as being primarily remedial and for the sake of the offender (in order that *his* spirit may be saved in the final day), or whether he sees such discipline as being purificatory and for the sake of the church (in order that *the* Spirit's presence may remain unhindered, i.e., unquenched, until the final day). In favor of the latter interpretation are the lack of any reference to repentance in our passage and Paul's evident concern for purity within the community (see v. 13). We have a similar example in Ananias and Sapphira, who died for their sin (Acts 5:1–11). Their death was punitive and perhaps purificatory but certainly not remedial, for there was no opportunity for repentance. There are a number of arguments, however, in favor of the former interpretation. One is the use of the term *saved*, which seems far more appropriate for the human soul than for the Holy Spirit. How is the Holy Spirit "saved"? Furthermore, Paul uses the term *spirit* in verses 3 and 4 to refer to his own spirit rather than to the Holy Spirit. It is more likely, then, that he is referring to the human spirit in verse 5 than to the Holy Spirit.

Another passage that helps us determine whether Paul envisions discipline here as remedial or purificatory is 1 Timothy 1:20, where Paul speaks of having "delivered [Hymenaeus and Alexander] to Satan that they may learn not to blaspheme." Once again we find the same terminology ("delivering [someone] to Satan") followed by a statement of purpose ("that they may learn not to blaspheme"). Although the verb "learn" (*paideuthōsin*) can refer to punishment, in the New Testament it is almost always positive in nature. Even when it is used in reference to chastisement, the hoped-for result is positive. In 1 Timothy 1:20 the main reason for delivering Hymenaeus and Alexander to Satan may be punitive and purificatory, but there is also in view a hoped-for repentance as well. Only through repentance and restoration to the community will the expressed purpose that they learn not to blaspheme be fulfilled. If the discipline is merely punitive, how will they learn this? Certainly the ruler of this age will not teach them not to blaspheme. On the contrary, they will be all the more free to do so. Only if there is the possibility of repentance and restoration to the community can the offenders learn not to blaspheme.

Although there may be difficulties and ambiguities with certain aspects of Paul's teaching in our passage, this should not blind us to what we can clearly know and understand. Paul did believe and teach that in certain cases (such as the immorality described in 1 Cor. 5) members of the Christian community were to be expelled (lit., "delivered to Satan"). During this period, since they were no longer within the protected community, they were more liable to experience physical trials (see 1 Cor. 11:30) and even death (lit., "the destruction of the flesh"). Furthermore, such discipline was concerned not only for the community and its relationship with God, but also for the offender. His salvation (lit., "so that the spirit may be saved") was also in view. In the light of this and other passages the church today should clearly rethink its attitude of indifference toward church discipline. If we love God, we must exercise discipline within the church, for he has commanded us to do so; if we love the church, we must be concerned for its purity; and if we love the offender, we must be concerned for his eternal soul.

Is Paul's Teaching on the Law Consistent?

One of the most important and yet confusing areas in the writings of the apostle Paul is his teaching on the law. Despite the vast amount of effort that has been put into the study of this area of Pauline theology, no consensus exists. Not only does Paul use this term to designate different entities, but at times he appears to say contradictory things about the law. It is important to note that the term "law" (nomos) possesses a range of meanings in Paul's writings. It can refer to the Ten Commandments ("if the law had not said, 'You shall not covet,'" Rom. 7:7), to the Pentateuch ("the law and the prophets," Rom. 3:21), or even to the whole Old Testament (note 1 Cor. 14:21, where "in the law it is written'' is followed by a quotation from Isa. 28:11–12; see also Rom. 3:19 with the quotations that precede it). The term can refer to a principle (''I find it to be a law that when I want to do right, evil lies close at hand,'' Rom. 7:21) and perhaps to Roman civil law (Rom. 7:1–3), and can serve as a synonym for ''works of the law'' (cf. Gal. 3:10 and 11), which refers to the keeping of the law in order to gain or retain one's salvation. That the term *law* has a broad semantic range in Paul should not surprise us and should keep us from trying to assign a single meaning to the term wherever it appears in his writings.

In addition to the problem of multiple meanings, there are a number of places in Paul's letters where he seems to be saying contradictory things about the law. One scholar in fact claims that there are five major contradictions. Before investigating two of the areas in which Paul supposedly contradicts himself, it may be wise to reflect for a moment on what we think of Paul's capability as a theologian. It is, of course, possible that Paul did in fact say contradictory things about the law. Yet it is also possible that Paul was an extremely logical thinker. If this is the case (and, if anything, we have grossly understated the apostle's intellectual ability), then he certainly would have seen the contradictions and rectified them, especially since some of the supposed contradictions are found not only in the same letters, but even within the same sections and arguments. We should, then, attribute to the apostle a reasonable degree of intelligence and try to make sense of his various statements concerning the law. It may be that a single harmonious understanding may result. On the other hand, Paul's teachings on the law may ''defy attempts at harmonization,'' as one scholar has claimed; but we should, out of courtesy to Paul, at least make an attempt to see if the supposed inconsistency lies with him or is a result of our own misinterpretation.

One of the areas where a contradiction is said to exist is in Paul's opinion of the value of the law. In a number of places Paul clearly states that the law is good: "So the law is holy, and the commandment is holy and just and good" (Rom. 7:12); "we know that the law is spiritual" (Rom. 7:14; see also Rom. 3:31; 7:7, 13, 16; Gal. 3:21; 5:14). For Paul the law was always the "law of God" (Rom. 7:22). Such statements are not at all surprising from a man who was raised as a Pharisee (Phil. 3:5). Since the law ultimately comes from God, what else can it be but good?

Yet Paul does appear to say a number of negative things about the law as well. In Galatians 3:13 he speaks of the "curse of the law." Indeed, "cursed be every one who does not abide by all things written in the book of the law, and do them" (Gal. 3:10, quoting Deut. 27:26). Our inability to keep the law perfectly brings a curse on us. The law brings universal condemnation, for it comprises a series of "Thou shalt nots," which we all have in fact broken. So for those seeking to establish their standing before God by works of the law there is nothing but condemnation, for any attempt to attain righteousness must meet the requirement of perfect obedience to the commands of the law, which no one can achieve (see also James 2:10). The problem, however, does not lie with the law, but rather with us as human beings. Whereas the law is spiritual, "I am carnal, sold under sin" (Rom. 7:14). With the mind I can approve the law and even desire at times to keep it, but "with my flesh I serve the 'law' [i.e., the rule] of sin" (Rom. 7:25). The law, weakened by our flesh (Rom. 8:3), is not able to make us righteous. It can prescribe what we should do, but it does not contain within itself the power to bring about what it prescribes.

Nevertheless, the law serves a positive function in all this. When Paul talks about the curse of the law, he is not contradicting what he has said elsewhere about the law's being good. The law serves a positive function here in that through it we become aware of our sin (Rom. 3:20; see also

Rom. 4:15; 5:13, 20). The law reveals to us our condition of sin: "if it had not been for the law, I should not have known sin" (Rom. 7:7). For some people this means that Paul views the law as essentially condemnatory, a supposed conflict with what he says elsewhere about the law's being good. Yet is an X-ray machine good or evil when it reveals that the patient has cancer and requires radical surgery for healing? In a similar way, is the law evil because it reveals the cancer of our sin and the need for radical surgery by the Great Physician?

The perfection of the law cannot help revealing our imperfections, and in so doing it serves a good and positive function. It drives those who desire spiritual health, that is, righteousness, to seek, as a gracious gift from God, the righteousness which comes through faith in Christ. Since the law reveals to sensitive people the inadequacy of their own attempts to keep the law, it serves positively by pointing to God's way of righteousness, which is through faith in Christ. Therefore, instead of seeking to create our own righteousness, which cannot help falling short (Rom. 3:23), we joyously submit to the righteousness of God which is in Christ Jesus (contrast Rom. 10:3). Because the law serves as a kind of X-ray machine which reveals our desperate need of God's remedy, it functions positively; it is good in that it leads us to seek the gift of justification which comes through faith in Christ (Eph. 2:8).

A second area in which scholars see a contradiction in Paul's teaching concerning the law involves the relationship between the keeping of the law and justification. On the one hand, Paul states that "no human being will be justified in his [God's] sight by works of the law" (Rom. 3:20); that "a man is not justified by works of the law" (Gal. 2:16); and that "if justification were through the law, then Christ died to no purpose" (Gal. 2:21; see also Gal. 3:11, 23–25; Rom. 4:15). On the other hand, the apostle also seems to argue that justification and its opposite, condemnation, are based on whether or not one keeps the law. One such passage is Romans 2:13–15:

> For it is not the hearers of the law who are righteous before God, but the doers of the law who will be justified. When-[ever] Gentiles who have not the law do by nature what the law requires, they are a law to themselves. . . . Their conscience also bears witness and their conflicting thoughts accuse or perhaps excuse them.

It should be noted that in the middle part of this quotation Paul is not saying that the Gentiles do in fact keep the law, but rather that "whenever" or "on those occasions when" some Gentiles keep or do the law, they reveal a knowledge of God's law written on their hearts. The use of the present subjunctive "do" (*poiōsin*) with "when[ever]" (*hotan*) reveals that Paul is referring to occasional acts of keeping the law, and that these occasional instances of obedience to what the law teaches in no way disprove that the Gentiles in question are nonetheless sinners in need of the grace of God. We cannot read this statement without noting what Paul has just said about the condition of the Gentiles in Romans 1:18–32. What Paul is saying is that the Gentiles are not without a witness to God's law and that their occasional keeping of the law reveals that they possess within them some knowledge of the will of God. In the day of reckoning they will be judged according to this knowledge.

With regard to the statement that it is the doers of the law who will be justified (Rom. 2:13), we must remember that this remark is made in the context of establishing that Jews are as much in need of the grace of God in Christ as are Gentiles. Jews, to be sure, possess the law of God, but possession is not enough. One must keep the law of God, for not the hearers of the law but the doers of the law will be justified. But who are the doers of the law? Surely we are to think here of those whom Paul describes in Romans 8—those who are in Christ, who are justified by faith and walk according to the Spirit. There is no conflict, then, between Romans 2:13–15 and what Paul says elsewhere about the law.

Still another passage which is frequently seen as conflicting with the Pauline doctrine of justification by faith is Romans 2:26–27:

> So, if a man who is uncircumcised keeps the precepts of the law, will not his uncircumcision be regarded as circumcision? Then those who are physically uncircumcised but keep the law will condemn you who have the written code and circumcision but break the law.

Again we should note that this passage appears in the section of Romans (2:1–3:19) in which Paul is arguing that the Jew, just like the Gentile, stands in need of justification by faith. In this diatribe against a hypothetical Jewish opponent Paul argues that simply being the physical offspring of Abraham is not enough. Circumcision and possession of the law are insufficient. We must do what the law demands. Breaking the law makes one's circumcision irrelevant (Rom. 2:25). On the other hand, if someone who is uncircumcised, that is, a Gentile, keeps the law, he is in God's sight circumcised in the true sense, that is, one of God's covenant people. A true Jew is not one who is externally or physically a Jew, but one who is a Jew internally (2:29), that is, he is circumcised in heart and possesses the faith of Abraham (Gal. 3:7–9). What, however, does it mean to keep the law? In Galatians 3:10 the implication is clear that no one keeps the law perfectly. How, then, can Paul speak of the Gentiles' keeping the law? Do we not have a contradiction here?

There is a sense in which Paul claims both that no one keeps the law and that the believer does in fact keep the law. With regard to keeping the law perfectly in every respect, Paul clearly teaches that "all have sinned and fall short" (Rom. 3:23). In the sense of absolute obedience to the law, "None is righteous, no, not one; . . . All have turned aside, . . . no one does good, not even one" (Rom. 3:10, 12). Yet there is a sense in which Paul speaks of the Christian's keeping the law. To trust in Jesus Christ and walk in the Spirit is to keep the law. In so living, the just requirements which the law demands are fulfilled in us (Rom. 8:4), for believers love their neighbors and thus fulfil the law (Rom. 13:8). Through being loving servants to one another we fulfil the whole law, which says, "You shall love your neighbor as yourself" (Gal. 5:13–14). The believer who has become a new creature in Christ and is filled with the Spirit can truly love God and neighbor as the law teaches.

Paul makes a clear distinction between the keeping of the law as a believer and the keeping of the law as an attempt to gain a right standing before God. Seen legalistically as a means of achieving salvation or as a means of remaining in a saved state, the law can only condemn. For anyone who tries to establish a relationship with God on the basis of keeping the law there is nothing but condemnation, for "cursed be every one who does not abide by *all things* written in the book of the law, and do them" (Gal. 3:10, italics added). Paul agrees with James that "whoever keeps the whole law but fails in one point has become guilty of all of it" (James 2:10). Seeking one's own righteousness by keeping the law can lead only to failure, for no one abides by and does all the things written in the book of the law. It can also, because of pride in a false sense of self-achievement, lead to a hardness of heart which refuses to submit to the only way to true righteousness—the righteousness of God which comes through faith in Christ (Rom. 10:3).

The Old Testament law never taught such a legalistic self-righteousness. The law was given in grace to a people already redeemed from their bondage, and it contained provision for sins. The law was given to the covenant people of God who had been delivered out of their bondage in Egypt. The law, furthermore, not only revealed the sovereign will of the holy God, but it led the devout believer in times of failure to seek the grace of God by the sacrificial system and ultimately in the Lamb of God who would take away the sins of the world. But for those who misunderstand the law and seek to establish their standing before God on the basis of their own works of the law, it can only condemn. Paul's argument in Romans and Galatians is not directed against the Old Testament law properly understood, but rather against a misunderstanding of it and a use for which it was never intended—as a legal code through which one earns righteousness and places God in one's debt (Rom. 4:4–5). Paul was not an antinomian; he was not opposed to the law or the commandments of God. Rather, it was his view that as believers walk in the Spirit they keep the commandments of God. Through the Spirit not only do they keep the commandments externally, but they do so with a renewed heart. In this way their righteousness exceeds that of the scribes and Pharisees (Matt. 5:20).

Perhaps nowhere does Paul teach about the Christian's relationship to the law and its requirements more clearly than in Romans 8. "There is therefore now no condemnation for those who are in Christ Jesus" (v. 1) is a favorite verse for many Christians. Yet it is frequently quoted with no regard for its context. In verse 2 Paul gives the reason for the absence of condemnation. Note that he does not say it is because we are justified by faith. Rather he states, "For the law of the Spirit of life in Christ Jesus has set me free from the law of sin and death." There are numerous exegetical questions surrounding this verse; one of the most important involves the referent of the word *law*. We do not need to resolve this issue here, but we do need to note that the absence of condemnation in verse 1 is based or grounded on the freedom achieved by the "law of the Spirit" referred to in verse 2. This in turn is grounded or based on the fact that "God has done what the law

. . . could not do . . . he condemned sin in the flesh, in order that the just requirement of the law might be fulfilled in us, who walk not according to the flesh but according to the Spirit" (vv. 3–4). Ultimately the absence of condemnation spoken of in verse 1 is grounded on the fact that the Christian, who walks according to the Spirit, fulfils the just requirement of the law. Frequently this reference to the fulfilment of the just requirement of the law has been understood as a reference to our being justified by faith and being granted the righteousness of Christ. Paul, however, is not speaking here of the position of righteousness which has been granted to us by faith, that is, the forensic or legal standing which the Christian possesses before God. This is clear from verses 5–6, which speak about the believer's life or living in the Spirit rather than a righteous standing before God. Paul is referring in verse 4 to the fact that believers in Christ, while possessing a forensic standing, are also now walking by the Spirit and thus can truly love God with the whole heart, soul, and mind, and their neighbor as themselves. He is referring to the fact that believers now keep the law as the Old Testament meant it to be kept—in faith, in trust, and in constant dependence on the grace of God for forgiveness and cleansing. To use Pauline terminology, we can say that the believer lives by a faith working through love (Gal. 5:6), and in so doing keeps the law.

Although Paul saw the ceremonial law as no longer binding (Rom. 7:1–4) but as only a shadowy portrayal of what was to come in Christ (Col. 2:17), he could at times surrender his liberty in Christ and voluntarily place himself under the ceremonial demands of the Old Testament law in order not to hinder his witness to his Jewish kin (Rom. 14:13–23; see also Acts 21:19–26; 16:1–4). While Christians are not under the law in the sense of having to achieve or maintain their salvation legalistically, Paul claimed that Christians nevertheless keep the intent of the law, for they are able to love God and neighbor as God intended and thus fulfil the law (Rom. 13:8; Gal. 5:14).

It is, of course, true that the believer will many times fail and fall, for we are sinners not merely by choice but also by nature, and until the resurrection we will fall short of the glory of God time and time again. But the Lord has taught us to pray, "Forgive us our debts" (Matt. 6:12); and we have the promise of Scripture that "if we confess our sins, he [God] is faithful and just, and will forgive our sins and cleanse us from all unrighteousness" (1 John 1:9). So we delight in the law of God and meditate on it day and night (Ps. 1:2). We also keep the law, ever mindful that we do not do so in order to establish a relationship with God, for we are already justified and stand before him by faith alone. Rather, because the law is a reflection of the will of God for us, we seek to keep the law in order to be pleasing to our heavenly Father. Born again through God's Spirit, we can in our innermost being love God and neighbor and keep the law as God has commanded his sinful, fallen, but redeemed people. We do not keep the law perfectly, but we keep it in our new nature as we never could before and in constant dependence on the heavenly Father's grace and forgiveness. Understood in this manner, Paul's teaching on the law is not contradictory.

Every serious interpreter of the Scriptures has heard at some time or other a statement like, "Read it in its context," or "Keep in mind the context." This is good advice. Authors surround words and sentences with other words and sentences which they hope will provide clues in the interpretative process. It is foolish indeed not to make the most of these clues which an author provides to the reader. Time and time again difficulties and problems in interpretation are resolved when we pay careful attention to the context of the author. After all, what better commentary is there than that of the author, who surrounds a verse with clues that help reveal its meaning? Therefore we should read the words and their grammatical construction in their authorial context.

11

Considering the Context
Other Biblical Books

In past generations the unity of the Bible was assumed as a given by the majority of Christians. This view was built on the belief that the Bible was uniquely inspired by God and thus could not contradict itself. At times the reverse was also argued: the unity of all its parts was one of the evidences of the inspiration of the Bible. Because of this presumed unity the Reformers developed a hermeneutical principle called the analogy of faith, which affirms that all biblical teachings are part of the revelation of God and thus any one part can and should be interpreted in light of the whole. This view is not as universally held as it once was, and some would minimize using the writings of one author of Scripture to cast light on the writings of another. It would appear, however, that completely apart from the matter of inspiration, one part of the Bible can prove quite useful in shedding light on another part. After all, the writers of the New Testament were well versed in the thoughts of the Old Testament; it was, in fact, their Bible! As a result, passages in the Old Testament may prove quite useful in interpreting parts of the New Testament dealing with similar themes. Furthermore, despite differences on various issues and in emphases, there was a great deal of commonality in the beliefs of the first-century Christian church. Whatever the differences, Christians certainly had more in common with one another than with other religions and philosophies. It seems only reasonable, therefore, to assume that there was a certain degree of common practices and beliefs, and that what one author reveals about a particular belief may help us to understand what another author, supposing his readers already knew it, did not explicitly mention. Our first example builds on the view that there was a great deal of agreement among the writers of the early church (and of course believers in general) concerning Christian baptism.

Is Baptism Necessary for Salvation?

One of the most common problems we encounter in the interpretation of the Bible is our tendency to understand the text in light of our own experience. This is especially true of passages which deal with doctrine and practice, or with the sacraments. A good example involves the numerous passages in the New Testament which speak of Christian baptism. Since most interpreters investigating these passages have experienced some form of baptism, it is not surprising that each has a tendency to interpret them, whether consciously or unconsciously, within the framework of his or her own experience.

In this section we will look at a number of New Testament passages on baptism which cause Baptists (as well as many pedobaptists) serious problems when they are understood in the light of the reader's personal experience of baptism. We shall then posit a thesis which will make sense of these passages by interpreting them in the light of what the first-century writers meant by them. Some of the most difficult passages are:

> And such [i.e., unrighteous] were some of you. But *you were washed*, you were sanctified, you were justified in the name of the Lord Jesus Christ and in the Spirit of our God. [1 Cor. 6:11, italics added]

> He saved us, not because of deeds done by us in righteousness, but in virtue of his own mercy, by *the washing of regeneration* and renewal in the Holy Spirit. [Titus 3:5, italics added]

> We were *buried therefore with him by baptism* into death, so that as Christ was raised from the dead by the glory of the Father, we too might walk in newness of life. [Rom. 6:4, italics added]

> *Baptism*, which corresponds to this, *now saves you*, not as a removal of dirt from the body but as an appeal to God for a clear conscience, through the resurrection of Jesus Christ. [1 Pet. 3:21, italics added]

Numerous attempts have been made to reconcile these passages with a traditional nonsacramentalist interpretation which claims that baptism has no immediate relationship to becoming a Christian, but comes either later, when one confesses saving faith by undergoing the rite, or earlier, when one is presented for baptism by one's parents. In this regard, it is usually denied that 1 Corinthians 6:11 and Titus 3:5 refer to baptism, and the term *washing* is seen as a metaphor which has nothing to do with Christian baptism. The burial with Christ in baptism of Romans 6:4 is seen as referring to a symbolic acting out in baptism either of what actually happened earlier when a person believed in Christ and was born again, or of a faith which is to come later. And 1 Peter 3:21 is sometimes interpreted as referring not to Christian baptism but to a ''Spirit baptism.''

While it is true that "washing" in 1 Corinthians 6:11 and Titus 3:5 is a metaphor, it does call to mind baptism, which involves the experience of being dipped into water. It should also be noted that in Titus 3:5 this experience of washing is intimately associated with renewal in the Holy Spirit, which calls to mind the tie between baptism and renewal in the Holy Spirit in the expression "the baptism of the Spirit." The Greek term translated "washing" (*loutron*), furthermore, was used by several non-Christian religions of that day to refer to baptism and was frequently used by the early church fathers to describe Christian baptism. In addition, the Greek verb translated "washed" in 1 Corinthians 6:11 is used only one other time in the New Testament: "And now why do you wait? Rise and be baptized, and wash away your sins, calling on his name" (Acts 22:16). Washing away one's sins is here clearly connected with baptism and with calling on Jesus' name. Calling on his name is likewise closely associated with baptism in Acts 2 (see vv. 21 and 38), and the related expression "in the name of Jesus Christ" appears to be a baptismal formula (Acts 10:48; see also 1 Cor. 1:13–15).

As for the reference to being buried with Christ through baptism, would it be legitimate to add to Romans 6:4 the parenthetical comment, "Of course we are not talking about baptism, but about the experience of conversion, which may occur years earlier or later and is symbolized by baptism"? There is not the slightest hint in this passage that Paul is referring to an experience which may occur weeks, months, or years before or after baptism. Nor is there any hint that the term *baptism* is to be interpreted symbolically. Finally, any attempt to fit 1 Peter 3:21 into our experience by explaining "baptism" here as some sort of "Spirit baptism" drowns in the flood waters mentioned in verse 20!

How, then, should we interpret these passages dealing with baptism as well as a passage like John 3:5, which refers to being "born of water and the Spirit"? Perhaps the simplest way of proceeding would be to formulate a thesis of how baptism and conversion are related, taking into consideration the teachings of the whole New Testament:

> In the New Testament, conversion, that is, becoming a Christian, involved five dimensions or aspects, all of which took place at the same time, that is, on the same day. These five dimensions were repentance, faith, confession, regeneration (or the receiving of the Holy Spirit), and baptism. To separate any of these in time does violence to the New Testament pattern.

Two major arguments can be advanced in support of this thesis: (1) the New Testament portrays various combinations of these dimensions in intimate association, and (2) each of these dimensions is said to bring about salvation.

We turn first to the various New Testament combinations of repentance, faith, confession, regeneration, and baptism:

1. At times faith and baptism are associated together. Paul says, "But now that faith has come, we are no longer under a custodian; for in Christ Jesus you are all sons of God, through faith. For as many of you were baptized into Christ have put on Christ" (Gal. 3:25–27). Note that Paul uses faith and baptism interchangeably in these verses. This is no problem if faith and baptism occurred at the same time, but if we separate them in time, the passage becomes difficult to interpret. Another example is Colossians 2:12: "And you were buried with him in baptism, in which you were also raised with him through faith in the working of God, who raised him from the dead." Here again baptism and faith are seen as occurring at the same time, for being buried (baptism) and being raised (faith) are a unity (see also Acts 16:31–33; 18:8).

2. At times faith and regeneration, that is, the reception of the Spirit, are associated together. In seeking to demonstrate to the Galatians that they were justified by faith alone, Paul asks, "Did you receive the Spirit by works of the law, or by hearing with faith?" (Gal. 3:2). The answer,

of course, is that they received the Spirit when they believed (see also Gal. 3:14; Eph. 1:13).

3. At times baptism and regeneration, that is, the receiving of the Spirit, are associated together. Titus 3:5 is an
illustration. We might also mention the New Testament
references to the baptism of the Spirit (Matt. 3:11; Mark
1:8; Luke 3:16; John 1:33; Acts 1:5; 11:16), each of which
makes an explicit comparison between the baptism of John
the Baptist and that of Jesus. John's baptism was one of
repentance, whereas Jesus' was to be a baptism of the
Spirit. We see no reason for the term *baptism* in this contrast
to refer to two separate things. On the contrary, what we
have here are the water baptism of John, which is associated with repentance, and Christian water baptism, which
is associated with the coming of the Spirit. This lends
support to the view that baptism and regeneration occurred on the same day.

In Romans 6:4, although the Spirit is not explicitly mentioned, baptism is associated with dying with Christ and
walking in "newness of life." Since Romans 7:6, in the
only other New Testament use of the term translated
"newness" (*kainotēti*), speaks of "the new life of the
Spirit," it seems reasonable to conclude that "newness of
life," which is associated with baptism, and "the new life
of the Spirit" are synonymous (see also the association of
baptism and regeneration in Acts 9:17–18; 10:44–48).

4. At times faith and confession are associated. Here all
we need to do is quote Paul's well-known words, "If you
confess with your lips that Jesus is Lord and believe in your
heart that God raised him from the dead, you will be
saved" (Rom. 10:9).

5. At times baptism and confession are associated. In
Acts 22:16 Ananias tells Paul, "And now why do you wait?
Rise and be baptized, and wash away your sins, calling on
his name."

6. At times faith and repentance are associated. At the
beginning of Jesus' ministry he states, "The time is

fulfilled, and the kingdom of God is at hand; repent, and believe in the gospel" (Mark 1:15). To this we can add Paul's words reminding the Ephesian elders that he did not shrink from preaching to them the entire counsel of God, "testifying both to Jews and to Greeks of repentance to God and of faith in our Lord Jesus Christ" (Acts 20:21).

7. At times repentance, baptism, and regeneration are associated. A good example is found in Acts 2:38. When Peter is asked by his audience as to what they should do, he replies, "Repent, and be baptized every one of you in the name of Jesus Christ for the forgiveness of your sins; and you shall receive the gift of the Holy Spirit." Here repentance and baptism are associated with the gift of the Spirit, that is, regeneration, which comes when one repents and is baptized. Another example is found in Acts 11:15–18. When Peter recounted to the Jewish Christians in Jerusalem that he had baptized a Gentile named Cornelius because he had received the Spirit, "they glorified God, saying, 'Then to the Gentiles also God has granted repentance unto life.'"

8. At times faith, baptism, regeneration, and repentance are associated. In Acts 19 Paul encounters some disciples in Ephesus, but notices that something is wrong. He then asks a simple yet clear question to determine whether they are Christians or not, "Did you receive the Holy Spirit when you believed?" (v. 2). When they answer in the negative by stating that they have not even heard of a Holy Spirit, Paul knows that they are not Christians. To his follow-up question, "Into what then were you baptized?" (v. 3), they reply that they were baptized into the baptism of John the Baptist. Paul responds, "'John baptized with the baptism of repentance, telling the people to believe in the one who was to come after him, that is, Jesus.' On hearing this, they were baptized in the name of the Lord Jesus. And when Paul had laid his hands upon them, the Holy Spirit came on them; and they spoke with tongues and prophesied" (vv. 4–6). Here we should note that in

verse 4 Paul recognizes not only the need for repentance as preached by John, but also the need for faith in Jesus Christ. In verse 5 we read of the disciples' being baptized, and in verse 6 of their receiving the Spirit.

It would seem reasonable to conclude that all five of these dimensions (repentance, faith, confession, regeneration, and baptism) were understood as being involved in the experience of conversion. At times one or more of them may, according to the particular emphasis of the writer, be omitted from the account, but although omitted they are both assumed and implied. When Peter says, "Repent, and be baptized every one of you in the name of Jesus Christ for the forgiveness of your sins; and you shall receive the gift of the Holy Spirit" (Acts 2:38), he does not mention the need for faith. Yet certainly it must be assumed that faith is also required for his listeners' conversion. To deny this would mean that Peter is saying, "To receive the gift of the Holy Spirit you do not have to believe so long as you repent and are baptized." By any New Testament standard this is clearly absurd. Likewise, when Paul says, "If you confess with your lips that Jesus is Lord and believe in your heart that God raised him from the dead, you will be saved" (Rom. 10:9), he is not saying that we are saved by an act consisting exclusively of confession and faith. Regeneration, baptism, and repentance, although not mentioned, must be assumed. It seems clear, therefore, by the varied groupings of these dimensions throughout the New Testament that the experience of conversion was understood to involve all five of them and that they took place on the same day. As a result, when we read an account or come across a passage in which one or more of these aspects are missing, we ought to presume that although not mentioned, they are assumed by the speakers or writers.

We turn now to the argument that each of the five aspects is said to bring about salvation:

1. At times salvation is said to come about through

repentance. A good example of this is found in 2 Peter 3:9: "The Lord is not slow about his promise as some count slowness, but is forbearing toward you, not wishing that any should perish, but that all should reach repentance" (see also 2 Cor. 7:10; Luke 13:3; Acts 3:19; 11:18).

2. At times salvation is said to come about through faith. There are numerous examples of this, one of the most familiar being where Paul tells the Philippian jailor, "Believe in the Lord Jesus, and you will be saved" (Acts 16:31; see also Eph. 2:8–9).

3. At times salvation is said to come about through confession. After Paul declares that whoever confesses that Jesus is Lord and believes that God raised him from the dead will be saved (Rom. 10:9), we read, "For, 'every one who calls upon the name of the Lord will be saved'" (10:13).

4. At times salvation is said to come about through regeneration. Regardless of how we interpret Titus 3:5 with regard to the question of baptism, one thing is clear— salvation comes about "by the washing of regeneration." This is similar to Jesus' words in John 3:3, 5, where the expression "kingdom of God" is used as a synonym for "salvation." To enter the kingdom of God, that is, to acquire salvation, one must be born again of the Spirit.

5. At times salvation is said to come about through baptism. Here once again we can mention 1 Peter 3:21, where baptism is clearly said to save. The only way that we can separate baptism from salvation in this statement is by attributing to the word *baptism* a meaning different from what it usually bears.

Other blessings which are said to be brought about by baptism as well as by faith are forgiveness (cf. Acts 2:38 and 22:16 with Acts 10:43 and Rom. 4:3–8), union with Christ (cf. Gal. 3:27 with Eph. 3:17), and sonship with God (cf. Gal. 3:26–27 with John 1:12).

From all that has been said it would appear that our thesis has been demonstrated: In the New Testament, conversion involved five dimensions or aspects, all of which took place at the same time, that is, on the same day. These five dimensions were repentance, faith, confession, regeneration (or the receiving of the Holy Spirit), and baptism. To separate any of these in time does violence to the New Testament pattern, which involved three parties: the individual, who repented of sin, believed in Christ, and confessed Jesus as Lord; God, who gave his Spirit and brought about the individual's rebirth; and the church, which baptized the individual.

At this point we must note that although baptism was part of the process and necessary for becoming a Christian in New Testament times, it did not automatically bring about regeneration. Paul in 1 Corinthians 1:13–17 and 10:1–6 indicates rather clearly that baptism does not magically bring about a person's salvation or regeneration. Individuals were born again or saved because upon repenting, believing, and confessing their faith, God graciously forgave them and through the gift of his Spirit made them a new creation. Baptism was the visible sign which God ordained as the initiation rite for entrance into the Christian faith. Hypothetically, it is true that one could enter the kingdom of God apart from baptism (the thief on the cross is a pointed example). But the normal manner by which one became a Christian involved being baptized on the same day. To refuse to be baptized was unheard of, and such a refusal would have exposed an unwillingness to repent and submit to what God had ordained. (That it was the refusal to submit to baptism rather than the lack of baptism which would damn is clearly the view of the postbiblical addition found in Mark 16:16, which reads, ''He who believes and is baptized will be saved; but he who does not believe will be condemned.'')

Perhaps an illustration will help. If in our culture the act of placing a gold ring on the third finger of the left hand were reserved exclusively to the marriage ceremony, and everyone who married did so, it is quite easy to see how a gold ring on the third finger of the left hand would become intimately associated with getting married. The question, "When were you married?" could even be reworded to, "When did you put the ring on your finger?" In fact, getting married could easily be referred to as "putting on the ring," even though other things such as obtaining the marriage license, the repeating of certain vows, and the sexual consummation, would also be involved in the process. In like manner, baptism in the New Testament is so intimately connected with becoming a Christian that becoming a Christian (getting married) can be referred to as being baptized (putting on a wedding ring). But, and this is no small but, it is always assumed that baptism is accompanied by repentance, faith, confession, and regeneration (a wedding license, vows, the sexual consummation).

Problems would, of course, develop if certain people began to place gold wedding rings on the third finger of their left hands in anticipation of a future marriage (i.e., before the wedding) or perhaps on their fifth anniversary (i.e., after the wedding). The original meaning of the gold wedding ring would be shattered, and its intimate connection with getting married would be destroyed. "When did you put the ring on your finger?" would no longer be synonymous with "When were you married?" Furthermore, comments made when gold wedding rings were put on only at the time of marriage would now tend to be misunderstood, for the later situation and practice conflict with the earlier.

In a similar way the present-day practices of baptizing people long before faith (pedobaptism) or after faith (believer's baptism) make it difficult to understand the new Testament teaching on the subject in that we tend to interpret these passages in light of our own experience. In the Book of Acts, however, baptism is intimately connected with conversion. With few (if any) exceptions it occurred on the same day. The Philippian jailor was baptized the very night of his conversion (Acts 16:33); the Ethiopian eunuch was baptized immediately (Acts 8:36–38). Baptism for them was less a testimony and confession to the world than part of the process of becoming a Christian.

The basic purpose of our discussion has not been to recommend how baptism should be practiced today. This is properly the task of a systematic theologian. Rather, the basic purpose has been to offer help in interpreting the New Testament passages dealing with baptism. Instead of interpreting them in terms of our own experience and trying to make their meaning conform to it, we need to understand how the New Testament writers viewed the relationship between baptism and conversion and what they meant to say in those passages we find difficult. By looking at the entire biblical context on this subject we are able to acquire an overall conception of baptism and make sense of many troublesome individual passages.

What Does It Mean That Paul Speaks and "Not the Lord"? (1 Cor. 7:10, 12)

In 1 Corinthians 7:10 and 12 we find two statements which have caused interpreters serious difficulties in that it appears as if the apostle Paul is denying that what he says comes from God. In verse 12 he states:

> To the rest I say, not the Lord, that if any brother has a wife who is an unbeliever, and she consents to live with him, he should not divorce her.

The problem this verse creates is heightened by the fact that in verse 10 Paul has just said:

> To the married I give charge, not I but the Lord, that the wife should not separate from her husband.

It appears, at first glance at least, that Paul in verse 10 is claiming divine authority for what he is saying in that it comes from the Lord, whereas in verse 12 what he is saying is not from the Lord at all, but simply his own view.

Is Paul in 1 Corinthians 7:12 claiming that what he says stands in opposition to what God has proclaimed to be his will? Or is Paul saying that he knows that what he has said in verse 10 comes from God, but that he is unsure of whether what he says in verse 12 is the will of God? In either instance we have a problem, for how can we accept verses 12–16 as the Word of God if they conflict with what God says elsewhere or if Paul is simply expressing his own uninspired opinion?

This problem is more apparent than real, however, for when we understand what Paul means in verse 10 the problem disappears. There is a parallel to verse 10 in 1 Corinthians 9:14, where Paul states, "In the same way, the Lord commanded that those who proclaim the gospel should get their living by the gospel." For each of these verses there is also a parallel in the Synoptic Gospels. Luke 10:7, the parallel to 1 Corinthians 9:14, reads, "For the laborer [the preacher of the gospel] deserves his wages"; Mark 10:11–12, the parallel to 1 Corinthians 7:10, reads, "Whoever divorces his wife and marries another, commits adultery against her; and if she divorces her husband and marries another, she commits adultery" (see also Luke 16:18). Note that the words of the Lord which Paul gives in 1 Corinthians 7:10 and 9:14 closely resemble words spoken by the Lord Jesus during his ministry (see also 1 Cor. 11:23–26 and Mark 14:22–24).

What Paul means in 1 Corinthians 7:10 is that the statement concerning divorce which he is about to make comes from Jesus' teachings. Although Paul is writing ("to the married I give charge"), ultimately his teaching comes from Jesus ("not I but the Lord"). Jesus had taught that wives should not divorce their husbands and vice versa, and Paul is quoting this dominical tradition here. However, Jesus in his ministry never dealt with the issue of mixed marriages in which one partner is a believer and the other is not, so Paul states that on this issue he has no word from the teachings of Jesus that is applicable (1 Cor. 7:12).

As a result he now gives his own apostolic teaching. (Cf. 1 Cor. 7:25, where Paul states, "Now concerning the unmarried, I have no command of the Lord, but I give my opinion as one who by the Lord's mercy is trustworthy.") That Paul does not doubt his divine authority in what he says in 1 Corinthians 7:12–16 is evident from verse 40: "And I think that I have the Spirit of God."

A second problem that is raised by 1 Corinthians 7:12–16 is the apparent conflict we find here with Jesus' teachings on this subject as recorded in Mark 10:11 and Luke 16:18. The Markan and Lukan accounts give no grounds whatsoever for divorce. Paul, however, seems to permit divorce in the case of desertion by the non-Christian partner (1 Cor. 7:15). Moreover, in Matthew 5:32 and 19:9 we have the famous exception clause which permits divorce in the case of adultery. The problem can be worded simply as follows: "Did Jesus forbid divorce absolutely as it appears in Mark 10:11 and Luke 16:18, or did he permit divorce in the case of adultery as we find in Matthew 5:32 and 19:9, and in the case of desertion by the unbelieving partner as we find in 1 Corinthians 7:15?"

This question has been debated for centuries, and all the arguments and views cannot be presented here. Instead, we will suggest a solution which we hope will do justice to all the evidence. It appears that what is found in Mark and Luke is closer to the actual words of Jesus than are the Matthean accounts. One evidence of this is that the Markan and Lukan forms are more difficult: it is easier to see why Matthew would add an interpretive comment (the exception clause) than why Mark and Luke (and Paul in quoting Jesus in 1 Cor. 7:10) would have made the saying more difficult. Second, we have three independent witnesses (Mark, Luke, Paul) who record a form of Jesus' saying which does not have the exception clause; only Matthew includes this clause.

Assuming that Jesus did not give any exception in his prohibition of divorce, how are we to explain what Matthew has done in 5:32 and 19:9, and Paul in 1 Corinthians 7:15? One feature of Jesus' teachings that we frequently encounter is his use of hyperbolic language. For example:

> If any one comes to me and does not hate his own father and mother and wife and children and brothers and sisters, yes, and even his own life, he cannot be my disciple. [Luke 14:26]

> You blind guides, straining out a gnat and swallowing a camel! [Matt. 23:24]

> It is easier for a camel to go through the eye of a needle than for a rich man to enter the kingdom of God. [Mark 10:25]

> If your right eye causes you to sin, pluck it out and throw it away; it is better that you lose one of your members than that your whole body be thrown into hell. [Matt. 5:29]

We could cite many other examples, but it is sufficiently clear that Jesus did use hyperbolic language in his teachings. No doubt he did so for mnemonic purposes, that is, to help his hearers remember his teachings, for the use of hyperbole creates a deep impression and is easily remembered. Another reason Jesus used such language was to reveal the intensity which he felt for the subject. This is certainly true with regard to the matter of divorce.

In the context of Mark 10 Jesus is asked to enter into the rabbinic debate concerning the legitimate causes for a man to divorce his wife (Mark 10:2). In the debate over what constituted an "indecency" and thus legitimized divorce according to Deuteronomy 24:1–4, various positions were taken. Rabbi Shammai and his followers took a more conservative stance and argued that only unchastity on the part of the wife was a legitimate reason. Rabbi Hillel and his followers, however, took a much more liberal approach and argued that divorce was legitimate if a wife burned the evening meal or if the husband found someone more attractive. When Jesus was asked what constituted a legitimate ground for divorce, he protested strongly against this whole attitude and pointed out that divorce was contrary to the divine pattern and goal, and that God had from the very beginning intended a lifelong monogamous relationship between a man and a woman (Mark 10:3–9). In affirming the divine pattern for marriage—that marriage was to be "until death us do part"—Jesus had no intention of giving a hypothetical situation in which divorce was permissible, for if he did (we are assuming for the sake of argument that he knew of one or two), the focus of attention would fall on the possible exceptions rather than on the divine plan and pattern, which was that marriage should not be "put asunder" (v. 9). As a result, he used an overstatement to express his view.

How do we know that Jesus was using a hyperbole in this instance? By noting that Matthew in the two instances where he presents the same material found in Mark 10:11 and Luke 16:18 adds his exception clause. This indicates that in Matthew's understanding Jesus was not laying down an absolute law which would cover all circumstances. With divine authority the Evangelist interprets Jesus' words as a forbidding of divorce but not in an absolute sense. Having the mind of Christ, he is aware that the horror of adultery does pose a legitimate ground for divorce. Even as surgery is never a good thing but may be the lesser of two evils, at times divorce is less evil than a union in which adultery has taken place.

That the apostle Paul was also familiar with Jesus' basic teaching on divorce is evident from 1 Corinthians 7:10. Yet Paul, too, was aware of a situation when divorce is permissible, namely, when "the unbelieving partner desires to separate" (1 Cor. 7:15). Such an action was never to be initiated by the Christian (note vv. 12–14), but if the unbelieving partner "desires to separate [divorce]," then the Christian "is not bound." ("Not bound" almost certainly means "free to remarry," since separation in the sense of simply no longer sharing bed and board is a later idea.) So Paul, possessing the Spirit of God (1 Cor. 7:40), interprets Jesus' teaching as not excluding divorce in the case of desertion.

Does Paul's teaching in 1 Corinthians 7:15 conflict with Jesus' teachings? The answer is no! He, like Matthew, knew well Jesus' teaching on the subject and interpreted it as a strong prohibition of easy divorce and a strong affirmation of the divine pattern given at creation. For both Paul and Matthew divorce is an evil. There is no such thing as a good divorce. The divine pattern is for marriage to last until death parts the one-flesh union. Jesus' abhorrence of divorce is clearly revealed by the way in which he condemned it. One tends to use exaggerated language when one feels strongly about a subject, for such language tends to impress and persuade. The few exceptions where divorce is the lesser of two evils Jesus did not wish to elucidate. Both Matthew and Paul, however, faced specific issues in their church communities which needed to be resolved. In dealing with these specific instances (adultery, and desertion by an unbelieving partner) they follow Jesus in affirming the divine pattern of marriage, but they also acknowledge two situations in which divorce is permissible as the lesser of two evils. In so doing they possess apostolic authority and the mind of Christ.

What Is the Standard for Orthodoxy?
(1 John 4:2–3)

The New Testament contains a number of letters which were occasioned by a major theological problem. The book which most obviously fits into this category is Paul's letter to the Galatians; another is 1 Corinthians. Yet another letter which emerged out of a major theological controversy is 1 John. It is somewhat unclear as to exactly what the problem was, but Irenaeus writing around A.D. 180 states that it centered around a Gnostic named Cerinthus, who taught that Jesus was not born of a virgin but was the natural son of Joseph and Mary, and that the Christ descended upon him after his baptism and withdrew from him just before his suffering and death. Associated with this view was a dualistic philosophy which viewed matter (and thus the body) negatively. The incarnation was denied in order to save the divine Christ from being contaminated with a body. That this error involved both ethics (1 John 1:6, 8, 10; 2:4) and Christology (1 John 1:1–4; 4:1–6; 5:6; cf. 2 John 7) is evident.

How did John deal with this christological issue? In 1 John 4:1 he writes, "Beloved, do not believe every spirit, but test the spirits to see whether they are of God; for many false prophets have gone out into the world." John tells his readers that they should stop believing (the imperative is in the present tense, which implies that his readers should cease doing something they are presently doing) every spirit, that is, every utterance or person supposedly inspired by the Spirit. On the contrary such spirits are to be continually tested (again a present imperative). The reason for this is evident. There are both true and false prophets. If one does not test their interpretations, one will not be able to distinguish between the true and the false, between the divine and the satanic. A childlike trust in the divine promises is praiseworthy, but a childlike faith in the demonic is not. Before we make a leap of faith we must be sure that we are leaping into the hands of God rather than Satan.

John therefore tells his readers that they should test the various views that they are hearing concerning the Savior. No doubt the reason for this was that a false view about him was circulating among the churches, a position that had its roots not in divine revelation but in the "spirit of antichrist" (1 John 4:3). Yet how were John's readers to make such a test? How were they to distinguish truth from falsehood, orthodoxy from heresy? Speaking from what he himself has witnessed (1 John 1:1–4) and using his apostolic authority, John gives a test. Even as the color of a piece of litmus paper reveals immediately if a solution is an acid or a base, so the apostle provides a test by which his readers will immediately be able to tell if a christological view is true or false: "By this [test] you know the Spirit of God: every spirit which confesses that Jesus Christ has come in the flesh is of God, and every spirit which does not confess Jesus is not of God" (4:2–3a).

Although the exact nature of the christological problem is unclear, it is evident from the test given by John that it involved the denial of the humanity of the Son of God and his oneness with Jesus. This is confirmed by 2 John 7, where the apostle states, "For many deceivers have gone out into the world, men who will not acknowledge the coming of Jesus Christ in the flesh." The christological heresy John was combating denied that the Son of God truly became a man. It may have even separated the human Jesus from the Christ, claiming that the Christ descended on Jesus later and was never identical with him. Here then was the test for orthodoxy. Here was the litmus paper which could be used to determine truth from error. A person who confessed belief that Jesus Christ, the Son of God, came in the flesh, was of the truth. And whoever denied the true humanity of Jesus Christ, the Son of God, that is, whoever denied that Jesus took on himself real flesh, was heretical and of the evil one.

In 1 John 5:6 John adds that Jesus, the Son of God, "came by water and blood . . . not with the water only but with the water and the blood." The twofold reference to water and blood is probably best interpreted not as a reference to Jesus' baptism and the Lord's Supper, nor to the incarnation in general, nor to Jesus' baptism and death, but to the death of the Son of God. The closest parallel to this is found in John 19:34 (which was either written by the author of 1 John or well known by him): at the death of Jesus "blood and water" flowed from his side. This would fit well the statement of Irenaeus that one of the problems facing John was the view that the Christ-spirit descended on the human Jesus only after his baptism and departed before his death. No, says John, Jesus Christ, the Son of God, came in water and blood. The Jesus Christ who has come in the flesh truly died!

The test for orthodoxy, then, was the confession ''Jesus Christ has come in the flesh.'' But is this really *the only* test for orthodoxy? It is important at this point to distinguish between the original meaning of our text and its present-day significance. John clearly meant that this belief was to be *the* test for orthodoxy *for his readers*. In the context in which John wrote his letter the litmus test for orthodoxy was clearly the confession that Jesus Christ had come in the flesh. This was not simply a test of a better theology. It was the test of true or false religion, of a divine revelation or a human philosophy. To deny the humanity of Jesus Christ was heretical and still is. But while the incarnation is a test for orthodoxy, is it still *the only* test for orthodoxy?

Whereas the particular issue confronting the readers of 1 John involved denial of the humanity of Jesus Christ, so that confession of the humanity of the Son of God could be *the* test for orthodoxy, today this is not the primary issue facing the church. Relatively few people today would deny the true humanity of the one whom the Bible calls Jesus of Nazareth. Both believers and unbelievers are willing to accept the true humanity of Jesus. (We shall leave aside the question of whether some theologians of our day are essentially Docetic and deny in principle the humanity of Jesus Christ.) Since even unbelievers are willing to acknowledge the humanity of Jesus Christ, this clearly cannot be *the* test for orthodoxy today.

The situation today is different from that faced by 1 John, for the kinds of errors which the modern church faces are different. And even more significant is the fact that we do not have an apostle like John to formulate a test to cover today's problems. On the other hand, while we may lack an apostolic authority, we do possess a canonical authority. We have in the Scriptures the only infallible rule for faith and practice. The variety of revelation in the Bible and the fact that it is not a catechism nor a systematized collection of theological beliefs remind us, however, that if we should attempt to establish canonical tests for orthodoxy, we must do so only with great care and reverence—with care lest we read into the Scriptures our own personal biases, and with reverence lest we make God a liar! With such caveats ever in view, it may at times be helpful, in light of certain false teachings, to establish out of the teachings of Scripture a litmus test which will enable the church to judge truth from error.

In the past such tests have served the church well. In the christological debates of the early church, *homoousios* (Jesus is the same as the Father in essence) and *homoiousios* (Jesus is like the Father in essence) separated orthodoxy and Arianism. "Justification by faith alone" was the central test during the Reformation. At the turn of the twentieth century some evangelical Christians formulated a platform of five "fundamentals" which were to distinguish evangelical from liberal Christianity. These five were the inerrancy of the Scriptures, the deity of Jesus Christ, the virgin birth, the substitutionary atonement, and the bodily resurrection and imminent physical return of the Lord. Such tests while helpful should not be considered as the sum total of the Christian faith. They were useful and helpful at the time, but are not to be isolated from the rest of the teachings of Scripture, for their effectiveness may become dated with the rise of other issues in the church.

It is necessary for the church to test the spirits continually (1 John 4:1). Christians are not to believe every message or interpretation that they hear. Furthermore, truth is not dependent on which preacher or teacher is proclaiming the message or interpretation, for fame and reputation are not tests of the truth. The evangelical claim has always been that the Bible is the only infallible rule of faith and practice. No true spirit will conflict with the Scriptures; all true teachers will welcome any use of the Word of God to test their messages. Even historical creeds and confessions are not infallible but are true only to the degree that they agree with the Scriptures.

The church needs both to test the spirits (1 John 4:1) and to be nonjudgmental (Matt. 7:1–5). Each of these practices can become dangerous in isolation from the other. Many a local church and denomination have suffered from over-zealous guardians of orthodoxy who are continually seeking out error and finding heresy lurking behind every bush. Eventually this mentality becomes so divisive that only two individuals remain, and each of these is not too certain about the other! On the other hand, there is also a danger of being oblivious to the Scriptures' warnings of fierce wolves (Acts 20:29–30), false prophets (Matt. 7:15), and false Christs (Mark 13:22) who will come and not spare the flock. These two concerns of the church must be held in tension; regard for truth should arise out of a love for God and for his people.

Once Saved, Always Saved? (Heb. 6:4–6)

Within the New Testament there are a number of passages which believers throughout the history of the church have found comforting and reassuring. These give assurance to Christians that they need not worry about the future, for as God's people they have nothing to fear. We are God's children, and as his children we can be confident "that he who began a good work in [us] will bring it to completion at the day of Jesus Christ" (Phil. 1:6). As Christians we know that God is for us and that Christ shall be our advocate in the day of judgment (Rom. 8:31, 34).

> Who shall separate us from the love of Christ? Shall tribulation, or distress, or persecution, or famine, or nakedness, or peril, or sword? . . . No, in all these things we are more than conquerors through him who loved us. For I am sure that neither death, nor life, nor angels, nor principalities, nor things present, nor things to come, nor powers, nor

height, nor depth, nor anything else in all creation, will be able to separate us from the love of God in Christ Jesus our Lord. [Rom. 8:35–39]

These are precious words indeed, and on the basis of these and similar passages and considerations some have argued that Christians are eternally secure, that is, that once they have been saved they can never lose that salvation. On the other hand, there are also passages in the New Testament which appear to warn believers lest they become apostate and lose their place among the people of God. A most important passage in this respect is found in Hebrews 6:4–6:

> For it is impossible to restore again to repentance those who have once been enlightened, who have tasted the heavenly gift, and have become partakers of the Holy Spirit, and have tasted the goodness of the word of God and the powers of the age to come, if they then commit apostasy, since they crucify the Son of God on their own account and hold him up to contempt.

As might be suspected, this passage is interpreted quite differently by those who hold to a doctrine of eternal security and by those who deny it. Frequently such views are described as Calvinism and Arminianism respectively, although both of these theological systems involve far more than just this one issue. As might be imagined, an Arminian interpretation tends to see in these verses a rather straightforward teaching that Christians who have at one time truly repented of their sins and been born again into the family of God (and thus "have become partakers of the Holy Spirit") can become apostate and lose the salvation they once possessed.

On the other hand, a Calvinist usually interprets this passage in one of two ways. One way is to claim that the persons spoken of in these verses were never true Christians. Whereas they had become involved in the Christian community, had been illuminated by the Holy Spirit so that they both knew and were convinced of the truth of the gospel message, and had even witnessed God's power and might, they had never truly become Christians. They had never been born again. As a result they could not have lost salvation in that they never possessed salvation. This is the way that John Calvin interpreted this passage. The second way in which this passage has been interpreted, although Calvin rejected this explanation, is to lay great weight on the "if" in verse 6. (Although the "if" is not in the Greek, the participle rendered "commit apostasy" [*parapesontas*] can be translated conditionally.) This interpretation argues that the passage refers to a purely hypothetical situation which in reality could never take place. The main problem with this interpretation is that the situation envisioned in this passage is clearly real and not simply imaginary.

The warning in these verses does not stand alone in the Book of Hebrews. We find similar warnings in 3:12–19; 10:26–31; and 12:25–29. The fact that the author often repeats this warning clearly reveals that we are not dealing simply with an imaginary, hypothetical situation. The author tells us six things about the people described in 6:4–6: (1) They professed *repentance*. Note that in verse 1 of this chapter repentance from dead works is associated with faith toward God. (2) They had been *enlightened*. This term is used once more in 10:32, where it refers to those who, in contrast to those who shrink back and are destroyed, "have faith and keep their souls" (10:39). (3) They have *tasted the heavenly gift*. Although some have suggested that this refers to participation in the Lord's Supper (as enlightenment allegedly refers to baptism), probably the best interpretation is to see the expression as a general metaphor for tasting the kindness (1 Pet. 2:3) and goodness (Ps. 34:8) of God. (4) They have *become partakers of the Holy Spirit*. The Greek term translated "partakers" is also used in 3:1 ("who share") for the readers who are further defined as "holy brethren," and in 3:14 ("we share"), where we find a similar warning. (5) They have *tasted the goodness of the Word of God*. Probably this can best be interpreted to mean that they have tasted the good Word of God. (6) Finally, they are described as *having tasted the powers of the age to come*. This apparently refers to the signs, wonders, and miracles which accompanied the preaching of the gospel message they heard (2:4).

It is evident that when we interpret a passage of Scripture, we do so in light of the overall understanding which we bring to the text. Whether this is good or bad is irrelevant. It is simply a fact. We interpret any portion of Scripture by means of our existing understanding of the Scripture as a whole. At the same time, however, our understanding of the particular part of Scripture is helping shape our understanding of the Scripture as a whole. Here we encounter once again the phenomenon of interpretation referred to as the hermeneutical circle. We cannot interpret any passage of Scripture without at the same time having our general understanding of Scripture (our theological system) play a major role. On the other hand, our interpretation of any particular passage is also helping shape our general understanding of the teachings of Scripture. Since our theological understanding is not infallible, since we know only in part, our system must always be open to change. At times we may come across a passage that does not seem to fit our system. A single such passage is seldom sufficient to refute it, but if we come across other passages which appear to contradict our system, we shall have to make certain modifications and changes to fit the new evidence.

In actuality the doctrine of eternal security is usually less dependent on individual passages of Scripture than on the overall theological system which one brings to these passages. This is not always recognized, but it is nevertheless true. (It may be less true, however, for lay people than it is for theologians.) In this regard I remember a television evangelist who in the same sermon vigorously condemned (actually damned as originating in hell) the theological system called Calvinism and those who deny the doctrine of eternal security. The irony in all this is that the doctrine of eternal security stems for the most part from a Calvinistic theological system. It was due to Calvin's belief in the doctrine of predestination and unconditional election that he came to believe in the doctrine of eternal security. And the fact is that he was far less convinced of the latter than the former! Calvin realized that if the doctrine of eternal security was to be based on something more than mere wishing on our part, it required the system of theology which we call Calvinism. The only sure basis for the eternal security of the Christian is the sovereign predestination of God. (For those familiar with the five cardinal points of Calvinism this means that eternal security, i.e., the perseverance of the saints, is dependent and based on the doctrines of total depravity, unconditional election, limited atonement, and irresistible grace.)

At this point it may be helpful to define such expressions as "eternal security" and "once saved, always saved." These are not the best ways to describe this theological concept. A far better expression is the "perseverance of the saints." Here the thought is that the believer will persevere in faith until the end. This is a much more biblical way of expressing the concept. If it is understood in this manner, there is little practical difference between a Calvinistic and an Arminian view on this subject. Calvinism argues that by God's grace true believers will continue in faith until they meet the Lord. From this it is concluded that someone who does not persevere in faith never had true faith, that is, never truly was a Christian. First John 2:19—"They went out from us, but they were not of us; for if they had been of us, they would have continued with us; but they went out, that it might be plain that they all are not of us"—is often used as an illustration. A person who does not persevere is lost and in fact was never saved.

On the other hand, the Arminian position also states that Christians must by God's grace persevere in the faith. If they do not persevere, they have become apostate, have rejected the faith, and are now lost. Whereas once they were saved, now they are lost. Note that the result is the same for both the Arminian and the Calvinist: whoever does not persevere in the faith is lost! Whether the individual once had saving faith and lost it (Arminianism), or never had saving faith to start with (Calvinism), both systems ultimately agree that the lack of a persevering faith means that the individual is lost in sin. Both agree that "he who is of God hears the words of God" (John 8:47), and that "by this we may be sure that we know him, if we keep his commandments" (1 John 2:3).

With regard to Hebrews 6:4–6 it is clear that any one of the six characteristics found in these verses can be interpreted as referring to someone who is not a true Christian, but when all six are grouped together, such an interpretation becomes much more difficult, if not impossible. As one who has always believed in the doctrine of eternal security, I must confess that this passage does indeed conflict with such a view. I have much less of a problem, however, with the more biblical concept of the perseverance of the saints. Yet in discussing this passage we must not lose sight of what the writer is saying. He is urging his readers to pay closer attention to the gospel message lest neglecting so great a salvation they receive a just retribution (Heb. 2:1–3), to take care lest there be within them an unbelieving heart leading them away from the living God (Heb. 3:12), to avoid the fearful prospect of judgment (Heb. 10:26), and to confirm their call and election (see 2 Pet. 1:10). Whether we are Calvinists or Arminians, the writer of Hebrews would urge us to pray with Bernard of Clairvaux, "Lord, let me never, never outlive my love to Thee."

We should interpret every passage of Scripture in its

context. This is especially true in cases where the passage seems to conflict with teachings found elsewhere in the Bible. The contexts to be kept in view as we interpret a passage include (in order of importance):

the immediate sentence in which the words are found

the paragraph in which the sentence is found

the chapter in which the paragraph is found

the letter in which the chapter is found

other writings of the same author

the New Testament

the Old Testament

The last two contexts have often been abused in the past; it is not uncommon for people to try to interpret a verse in Romans primarily through a verse in Revelation or in Genesis instead of through the verses which immediately precede and follow. This is, of course, a mistake, for the writers of Genesis and Revelation cannot contribute clues to the meaning of this verse to the degree that the author himself can by the immediate context. The chapter and the book in which the verse appear are likewise more valuable than the Psalms or Isaiah.

Nevertheless, we should not lose sight of the fact that at times an author, because of the very nature of his letter, may not provide clues which are important for understanding his meaning. He may not have had to provide such clues for his first-century readers, for he was able to build on a common knowledge and understanding which often came through personal acquaintance with the author. Unfortunately, today's readers lack that common knowledge and understanding, and so at times, as we have illustrated in this chapter, it is helpful to interpret a passage in light of the New Testament context. This is true even if all the members of the first-century church did not believe exactly alike. Whatever the diversity may have been in the early Christian community, there was, nevertheless, a greater unity of thought and values among believers than among the world at large. Knowing something of that unity, and for that matter also the diversity, provides us clues in understanding the meaning of an author. These clues are never as good as the clues that the author himself may give, but they are helpful.

We should also remember that the Old Testament was the Bible of the early church. Here, too, there was no doubt diversity in understanding and interpretation, but there was also a common world which was shared as the early church read and searched the Law, the Prophets, and the Writings. Someone like Paul would have been especially well versed in the Old Testament. Thus it is far more helpful to look for clues in the Old Testament than in such places as the mystery religions, various pagan cults, and later Gnosticism.

Some other contexts that may prove useful include the Jewish literature of the intertestamental period, the writings of the earliest church fathers, and contemporary Greek authors. These, however, are seldom as useful as the biblical materials themselves. We will not go wrong if we follow the Reformation principle of the analogy of faith: each Scripture is to be interpreted in light of the rest of Scripture.

12

Two Difficult Passages
A Comprehensive Approach

In the previous chapters we have discussed how to go about seeking to understand some of the difficult passages in the Epistles of the New Testament. The basic principles we set down are fundamental principles of biblical interpretation. More often than not, difficult passages can be resolved when we interpret them properly and discover what the authors meant by their words. We pointed out that a correct interpretation requires a correct understanding of the basic building blocks of literature—the words. First, we must obtain a correct understanding of the key words that an author uses in his writing. Second, we must then seek a correct understanding of how the author relates these words to one another. For this we need to know the syntax or grammatical relationships in which the author places these words. Neither of these steps can be isolated from the other, for there is a circular process in which the meaning of the sentence informs us as to the meaning of the individual words, and at the same time

357

the meaning of the individual words informs us as to the meaning of the sentence.

In the third chapter we examined the importance of the authorial context. The circular process involved in interpretation continues beyond the sentence, for the meanings of the paragraph, the chapter, the book, and the other writings of the author provide us with clues to the meaning of the sentence, which is at the same time informing us of the meaning not only of the words, but also of the paragraph, chapter, book, and other writings. This hermeneutical process sounds much more complicated than it really is, for the mind is able to do all this simultaneously. It is, nevertheless, important for the interpreter to understand the logical procedure which is being followed. In chapter 4 we pointed out that at times the clues provided by the authorial context may be insufficient and that the larger context of the whole Bible may provide assistance as to the meaning of a text.

In this chapter we will look at two additional passages. The first will serve as an example of all the principles discussed in the preceding chapters; the second will raise the issue of difficult passages which may, at least for the present, elude resolution.

What Is the Sin unto Death? (1 John 5:16)

Within all of Scripture there is probably no single passage which causes more individual problems of interpretation than does 1 John 5:16. Whereas usually one particular problem in this passage receives the most attention, there exist numerous other difficulties as well. The passage reads:

> If any one sees his brother committing what is not a mortal sin, he will ask, and God will give him life for those whose sin is not mortal. There is sin which is mortal; I do not say that one is to pray for that.

In this verse various exegetical problems are encountered, the first two of which have to do with the understanding of key words:

1. Is there any difference in meaning between the words "ask" (*aitein*) and "pray" (*erōtan*)? Probably not. It seems best to see in the use of these two different but related terms a favorite Johannine stylistic device. John is fond of using synonyms. A good example of this is found in John 21:15–17, where John uses interchangeably two different words for "love" (*agapan* and *philein*) and the words *sheep* and *lambs*.

2. Another problem we encounter in our text involves the meaning of "mortal" (lit., "unto death"). Is this a reference to physical death as a result of sin? Here we might think of the example of Ananias and Sapphira (Acts 5:1–11) or of those who abused the communion table (1 Cor. 11:30). And when Jesus says, "This illness is not unto death" (John 11:4), he is referring to physical death. But since the nearest antecedent of the "life" which is prayed for in 1 John 5:16 is spiritual or eternal life (5:11–13), it would appear best to see the death being referred to here as spiritual death.

3. A third problem arises in the area of syntax (grammar): Who is it that gives life to the brother who has committed what is not a mortal sin? Is it the person who prayed for the sinner or is it God? While the Revised Standard Version reads, "God will give . . . life," there is a note in the margin which points out that the Greek text actually says "he." In favor of the view that "he" refers to the person who prayed is the fact that God is not mentioned. The verb *will give* is preceded by the verbs *sees* and *will ask*, and the subject of both these verbs is the believer who is praying for his brother. The subject of the next similar verb ("pray") is once again the believer. Grammatically, therefore, it makes good sense not to see any change in the subject of these verbs, for John does not indicate that there is such a change.

On the other hand, a point in favor of seeing "God" as the subject of "will give" is the theological fact that no human being can give eternal life to another human being. This is something God alone can do. Probably the best way of resolving this question is to recognize that the ultimate source of eternal life is God, but that the believer by prayer may act as a mediate cause in the sinner's receiving of life. Even though God alone brings healing to the sick, yet the prayers of faithful believers serve as the instrumental means of this healing (James 5:14–15). The believer can serve in a parallel capacity in regard to those who have committed a nonmortal sin.

4. A fourth problem that arises can be resolved by investigating the authorial context. Whose soul is saved by the believer's asking? Who is the "him" to whom God will give life? Is it the one praying or the sinner being prayed for? Actually the grammar permits either possibility, but the general flow of the argument indicates that it is the sinner who is granted life. This finds support in verses 14–15, which speak of God's hearing and granting believers' requests; and in this particular case, of course, the request involves the situation of the sinner. (See also James 5:15, where prayer saves the sick man from death.)

Other problems raised by 1 John 5:16 can be solved by looking to the biblical canon:

5. Whereas the person described as committing a nonmortal sin is clearly referred to as a "brother," that is, a Christian, what kind of a person is it who commits the sin unto death? Is this individual likewise a brother or a non-Christian? Our text does not say. The decision we make on this question will be determined by our theological position concerning the perseverance of the saints, that is, eternal security.

6. Is the writer expressly forbidding Christians to pray for those who have committed the sin unto death, or is he simply refraining from urging them to do so? In rare instances in Scripture we find God forbidding believers to

pray for someone or something. Jeremiah is told by the Lord, "Do not pray for the welfare of this people" (Jer. 14:11; see also 7:16; 11:14). There may very well be times when we should no longer pray for certain people since they have already been given up in this life to the judgment of God, and their lot is irreversible. It would appear that this is what John is saying in this verse. In practical terms, however, since we seldom can know if such is the case, we probably should not withhold our prayers in behalf of anyone. Who knows if the present blasphemer and persecutor of God may experience God's mercy in the same manner that Saul of Tarsus did?

7. The final question that we shall raise with regard to this verse, and the one which we shall discuss at length, involves the two kinds of sin mentioned. In particular we want to deal with the question of the "sin which is mortal." Apparently the sin which is not mortal is external, since it can be seen. Yet no attempt is made to describe or define either of these two sins. No doubt these terms were perfectly understandable to John's readers; but, unfortunately, the context in which John wrote and in which this letter was read is not known to us, so that we have great difficulty in trying to understand what John means by these expressions.

The expression "sin which is mortal" is literally "sin unto death." It calls to mind similar descriptions in the Scriptures. In Mark 8:38 Jesus warns that when he comes as the Son of man in all his glory, he will be ashamed of those who in this life are ashamed of him and his words. In Mark 3:29 we read of being "guilty of an eternal sin." This eternal or unpardonable sin is specifically referred to as blasphemy against the Holy Spirit, but, unfortunately, exactly what this eternal sin consists of is unclear. So it does not profit us to define the unclear meaning of "mortal sin" in our passage by the unclear meaning of "eternal sin" in Mark 3:29. We find similar warnings in Hebrews 3:12–19; 6:4–6; 10:26–31; and 12:25–29.

In the history of the church numerous suggestions have been made as to what this sin unto death is. Some have suggested in light of Mark 3:29 that it refers to hardening one's heart so obstinately and so persistently against the influence of the Spirit of God that repentance becomes impossible. Others have suggested that it refers to a permanent rejection of the true faith in favor of paganism. Still others have suggested, in the light of the many exhortations in 1 John to love one another, that the hatred of one's brothers and sisters in Christ is meant. It has also been suggested that the Old Testament references to deliberate or presumptuous sins provide us with a clue. In the case of such sins there was no sacrifice permitted and death was often prescribed (see Deut. 17:12; Ps. 19:13; cf. Lev. 4:2, 13, 22; 5:15). In this regard we might also note that intentional sins resulted in excommunication from the Qumran community, whereas unintentional sins were punished with lesser disciplinary action (1QS 8:20–26).

It may be wise at this point to admit that certainty as to the exact meaning of "mortal sin" is impossible. A *possible* explanation may involve a group who had been members of the community to which John was writing, but who maintained a serious christological heresy and subsequently withdrew from the fellowship. These people were not of God, for they denied the incarnation of Jesus. They denied that Jesus Christ had come in the flesh (4:2–3). When their views were shown to be contrary to what the apostolic eyewitnesses were teaching (1:1–4), they withdrew from the fellowship. This proved that "they were not of us; for if they had been of us, they would have continued with us" (2:19). Here were people who had been brought into the most intimate contact with the people of God and the message of redemption. Yet they made an irreversible decision to reject the Light, preferring darkness instead. They had witnessed the working of God's power, yet in their hardness of heart they rejected the inward working of the Spirit, who sought to lead them to repentance and true faith. When God so reveals himself in power and conviction, there is no longer any excuse left. In referring to his past persecutions of the church, Paul points out that although he formerly blasphemed and persecuted and insulted God, he received mercy because he had acted ignorantly in unbelief (1 Tim. 1:13). Is Paul suggesting that if he had been aware that he was in reality opposing God, he would not have received mercy? Would such activity have been a sin unto death?

At this point we must emphasize that anyone who is in any way concerned about this issue need not fear that he or she is guilty of such a sin. Those guilty of this sin have no such concern and do not care about it at all. The very hardness of heart which leads to such a sin excludes any concern or regret in the matter. We can therefore be assured that if we fear we have committed the sin unto death, we have not committed it.

The Bible never discusses whether it is possible for a Christian to commit such a sin, or how sinful a Christian must be to be guilty of the sin unto death. Scripture is no more interested in discussing how bad a Christian can be and still be a Christian than it is in discussing how unfaithful a marriage partner can be before being guilty of adultery. Love for our marriage partner thinks only of how we can please him or her. Love for God likewise thinks only of how we can please him. The Christian keeps God's commandments (1 John 2:4–5) and does not abide in sin (3:6). The purpose of our text is to serve as an exhortation both to pray for believers whom we see sinning and to be aware that certain sins in this life may cut us off from the possibility of divine forgiveness. Needless to say, every believer like the psalmist of old should pray, "Keep back thy servant also from presumptuous sins; let them not have dominion over me!" (Ps. 19:13).

What Is Baptism for the Dead?
(1 Cor. 15:29)

One of the most baffling statements found in Paul's letters is 1 Corinthians 15:29. In a context of defending the resurrection of Jesus in particular and the resurrection of the dead in general Paul asks, "Otherwise, what do people mean by being baptized on behalf of the dead? If the dead are not raised at all, why are people baptized on their behalf?" For centuries this passage has been a problem for the church, and any good commentary will list a host of suggested interpretations. The problem is due, of course, to the fact that nowhere else in Paul or the entire New Testament do we read of a baptism for the dead. At first glance the passage seems to refer to some sort of proxy baptism for dead people. In other words, it appears that Paul is referring here to a practice of experiencing baptism on behalf of people who have already died. Such a teaching would appear impossible to reconcile with Pauline teachings elsewhere which clearly associate baptism with a personal faith on the part of the individual for whose benefit the rite is performed (see Gal. 3:26–27).

One commentator has counted nearly two hundred different attempted explanations of this difficult passage. Among the more important attempts to explain the passage:

1. The interpretation of the early church explained the expression "on behalf of the dead" as a reference to the future resurrection of the dead; Paul was seen as saying that the people being baptized were baptized with a view to their own future resurrection from the dead. The problem with such an interpretation is that it assumes Paul intended that the words "for their own [future] resurrection" be inserted before the expression "on behalf of the dead." This would be a strange way for Paul to express the thought that those being baptized were being baptized with the aim of achieving their own future resurrection from the dead.

2. Some interpreters have suggested that the Corinthians were *wrongly* practicing a baptism for those who had already died and that, although Paul disagreed with the practice, he used it as an argument in support of his doctrine of the resurrection. In other words, Paul is saying something like, "How can some among you say there is no resurrection [v. 12] and at the same time practice [wrongly of course] a vicarious baptism for the dead?" A major problem with this interpretation is that there is no hint in our text that Paul is disapproving of this practice of the Corinthians, whatever that practice may in fact have been. It is furthermore atypical of Paul to build his arguments on a theological understanding or practice with which he disagrees.

3. Another suggestion is that our passage refers to the practice of vicarious or proxy baptism on behalf of dead Christians who for one reason or another had not been baptized. Some have even suggested on the basis of 1 Corinthians 1:14–17 that a number of the Corinthian Christians had not been baptized by Paul and had subsequently died. Again we encounter a serious problem with this interpretation: Baptism in the early church was so intimately associated with the conversion experience that unbaptized believers were a decided rarity. Conversion, as Acts clearly shows, always resulted in baptism. The claim that this baptism may have been for the stillborn infants of believers assumes among other things a clearly established practice of infant baptism by the 50s in the early church, an assumption which lacks any substantial New Testament support.

4. It has also been suggested that Paul's words should be interpreted as referring to the experience of people who became believers and were baptized because of the love and respect they had for Christians who had died. An example of this might be the promise made to a dying mother or father to become a Christian in order to be reunited in the resurrection day. It is also not at all uncom-

mon for the deaths of godly people to inspire others, even unbelievers, to take their place. The martyrdom of Nate Saint, Roger Youderian, Ed McCully, Pete Fleming, and Jim Elliot in January 1956 at the hands of Auca tribesmen is certainly a vivid example of this. Yet although permitting such an interpretation, our passage does not demand it and does not even suggest it.

5. Some scholars have suggested that Paul's words should be taken literally and that he is referring here to a vicarious baptism for the dead much like that of present-day Mormonism. Apparently such a rite was not unknown to the early church, but it was practiced only by heretics (so says Chrysostom). A major problem with such an interpretation is that it demands a sacramentalist view of baptism. Yet baptism is not regarded by Paul or the New Testament as an act which all by itself can bring salvation. Paul clearly refutes the view that baptism works *ex opere operato* (see 1 Cor. 1:14–17). In the New Testament, personal faith is always a requirement for salvation.

All sorts of other explanations could be listed, but it is clear that our text has withstood a satisfactory explanation over the centuries, and it is unlikely that the future will see any resolution of this difficult passage. In essence the problem lies not so much with what Paul said, but with the form of correspondence he used to say it. Adolf Deissmann demonstrated the essential difference between an epistle and a letter. It is quite common for people to use these terms interchangeably and refer randomly to the Pauline Epistles or the Pauline Letters. Yet there is a critical difference between these two forms of correspondence. In an *epistle* the writer assumes a minimum shared context between himself and his readers. He assumes, of course, their knowledge of the language (or access to someone who knows it), a general understanding of the meaning of the terms and the grammar he uses, and a general knowledge of the world about him which he shares with his readers. He does not assume, however, any special understanding between himself and his readers from which others are excluded.

On the other hand, in a *letter* the writer assumes a special relationship and understanding on the part of his readers to which others have no access. He builds on this knowledge and relationship, so that he does not have to explain certain situations, understandings, and knowledge that they have in common. An example of this occurred in my own life when my wife and I were overseas and received a letter from our daughter. In it she wrote something like, "We went out to eat, but we had fish because there was a fire again." Outside of our family this sentence makes little sense, for it builds on a common experience which our family shared but of which others are ignorant. We had gone out to eat at a Hardee's Restaurant, but there was a flash grease fire in the kitchen. So we went next door to eat at Arthur Treacher's Fish 'n' Chips. Our daughter was simply telling us that she and her brothers had gone through the same experience again. In a letter one builds on a common deposit of knowledge and experience; in an epistle one cannot assume such a deposit, and as a result great care is taken to explain each proposition and presupposition.

Needless to say, not all ancient correspondence can be neatly classified as perfect examples of letters or epistles. Romans is closer to an epistle, for here Paul is writing to a congregation he did not found and had never visited. So he does not build his argument on the assumption that his readers are intimately familiar with his theology. At times, however, he builds on a knowledge of the faith which he believes every Christian would have (see Rom. 6:3). On the other hand, 1 Corinthians is more of a letter than an epistle. It assumes all sorts of common information which Paul and the Corinthians share. It assumes even a previous letter (1 Cor. 5:9) as well as knowledge of Paul's person and ministry (1 Cor. 11:2; 15:1). As Paul wrote 1 Corinthians, he assumed a common core of information and background on the part of his readers on which he could build. Unfortunately, we are not privy to much of this information. In the case of 1 Corinthians 15:29 this is especially unfortunate, for Paul does not explain his reference to baptism for the dead. This problem is compounded by the fact that nowhere else does Paul (or the New Testament) use this expression or refer to such a practice. In fact his teachings on baptism elsewhere seem to conflict sharply with a literal interpretation of these words.

No doubt most Christians today would prefer that the Scriptures had been written as epistles rather than as letters. In the providence of God, however, the Spirit of God often worked through spokesmen living at specific times who wrote to specific congregations concerning specific issues. As a result, we must seek the specific meaning which the authors gave to their words within their particular context. Then we need to discover the implications of that meaning for us today. At times, however, we may lack sufficient information to determine what the author meant. In such instances we ought to be humble and admit that we know only in part. The Scriptures clearly reveal to us all that is necessary for our salvation and for godly living. They do not reveal, however, all that we would like to know. Nor is it possible to understand everything that the Scriptures teach.

First Corinthians 15:29 is one of those puzzling passages. We need to admit that we really do not understand what Paul meant by this verse nor how it fits in with his teachings elsewhere. In concluding our discussion it may be profitable to outline a general approach to take with regard to such passages:

1. We need to be humble and admit that we may not be able to understand the meaning of certain passages of Scripture. Rather than forcing on such a text a meaning which fits neatly into our system, we need to confess that we simply do not know of a satisfactory interpretation.

2. We should be careful not to build theological systems

on unclear passages of Scripture. Obviously it would be foolish to build a system of baptizing for the dead on this single and most confusing passage.

3. We should concentrate our attention and emphasis on the clear teachings of Scripture. The problem for most of us is not the passages of Scripture we cannot understand, but the Scripture which we understand quite well but do not take to heart and obey!

Endnotes

Notes to Indtroduction to Part 1

1. Augustine, *De Consensu Evangelistarum*, in *The Nicene and Post-Nicene Fathers*, vol. 6 (New York: Scribners, 1903), I. vii. 10.

2. Ibid. I. xxxv. 54.

3. John Calvin, *A Harmony of the Evangelists Matthew, Mark, and Luke*, ed., David W. and Thomas F. Torrance (Grand Rapids: Eerdmans, 1972), Introduction.

4. William Newcome, *An Harmony of the Gospels in Which the Text is Deposed After Le Clerc's General Manner* (Dublin, 1778), Preface.

5. Two important works written in the last century are J. H. A. Ebrard, *The Gospel History: A Compendium of Critical Investigations in Support of the Historical Character of the Four Gospels*, which appeared in German in 1841 and in English in 1863; and John W. Haley, *Examination of the Alleged Discrepancies of the Bible*, which appeared in 1984. Recently Gleason A. Archer wrote, *Encyclopedia of Bible Difficulties*, (Grand Rapids: Zondervan, 1982). The latter two works, although not exclusively devoted to the Gospels, deal with numerous difficulties in them.

6. Newcome, *An Harmony of the Gospels*, Preface.

Notes to Chapter 1

1. Augustine, *De Consensu Evangelistarum*, in *The Nicene and Post-Nicene Fathers*, vol. 6 (New York: Scribners, 1903), II.xiv.31.

2. Ibid.

3. Ibid.

4. Ibid., II.xix.45.

5. Andreas Osiander, *Harmonia Evangelicae* (Basel, 1537).

6. For a recent advocate of this view see Gleason L. Archer, *Encyclopedia of Bible Difficulties* (Grand Rapids: Zondervan, 1982), p. 366.

7. Cf. Matthew 7:28; 11:1; 13:53; 19:1; 26:1.

8. Augustine, *De Consensu Evangelistarum*, II.xxxix.86; cf. also II.xiv.29; II.xix.44; II.xxviii.64; II.lxxvii.147.

9. Cf. Psalm 25:16.

10. It is interesting to note that the Qumran community referred to itself at times as the "Congregation of the Poor": 4QpPs 37 2:10; cf.1QpHab 12:3, 6, 10; 1QH 5:22; 1QM 11:9.

11. John Calvin, *A Harmony of the Evangelists Matthew, Mark, and Luke,* ed. David W. and Thomas F. Torrance (Grand Rapids: Eerdmans, 1972), on Matthew 5:3.

12. Augustine, *De Consensu Evangelistarum*, II.xxxvii.85.

13. Calvin, *A Harmony of the Evangelists,* on Matthew 5:1; cf. on Matthew 7:13.

14. For a similar conclusion see Calvin, *A Harmony of the Evangelists,* on Matthew 8:5.

15. Ibid.

16. Augustine, *De Consensu Evangelistarum*, II.xxviii.66.

17. Calvin, *A Harmony of the Evangelists,* on Matthew 9:18.

18. Note also the presence of the same parenthetical comment, "he then said to the paralytic" (Matt. 9:6)/"he said to the paralytic" (Mark 2:10)/"he said to the man who was paralyzed"(Luke 5:24).

19. Calvin, *A Harmony of the Evangelists,* on Matthew 9:1.

20. Cf. Matthew 1:22–23; 2:15, 17–18, 23; 4:14–16; 8:17; 12:17–21; 13:14–15, 35; 21:4–5; 26:54, 56; 27:9–10.

21. See Josephus, *Autobiography* (1) and *Against Apion* (I.7).

22. See the *Babylonian Talmud,* Kethuboth 62b.

23. See J. Gresham Machen, *The Virgin Birth of Christ* (New York: Harper, 1930), pp. 199–209.

24. For a similar approach to these two passages see Calvin, *A Harmony of the Evangelists,* on Matthew 18:12. He assumes that they are the same identical parable and that Matthew and Luke apply the parable to different audiences.

25. Cf. Malachi 4:5–6 with Luke 3:7–9, 16–17.

26. Cf. Calvin, *A Harmony of the Evangelists,* on John 1:21.

27. Cf. Mark 14:16 and Luke 22:15.

28. Cf. John 13:1, 29; 19:14.

29. Cf. 2 Chron. 30:22.

30. Augustine, *De Consensu Evangelistarum*, III.xiii.42.

31. Cf. John 11:9.

32. Calvin, *A Harmony of the Evangelists,* on John 19:14.

Notes to Chapter 2

1. Note Matthew 5:34–37.

2. That the expression *debt* was a common term for sin in late, or post-biblical, Judaism is evident from the Targums. See their translations of Genesis 18:20–26; Exodus 32:31, 34:7; Numbers 14:18–19; and Isaiah 53:4, 12 where they use the Aramaic term for *debts* to translate "sins."

3. Cf. Romans 8:15–17; Galatians 4:4–7.

4. Cf. Luke 11:1.

5. Cf. Sirach 28:2: "Forgive your neighbor the wrong he has done, and then your sins will be pardoned when you pray."

6. Cf. Luke 4:12; Acts 5:9, 15:10; 1 Corinthians 10:9; etc.

7. Cf. Hebrews 2:18, 4:15, etc.

8. Berakoth 60b.

9. Cf. Exodus 34:6–7; Isaiah 43:25, 44:22, 55:7; Psalms 103:3, 104:4; etc.

10. Cf. Acts 2:38, 5:31, 8:22, 10:43, 13:38–39, 28:18, etc.

11. William Barclay, *The Gospel of John*, vol. II (Philadelphia: Westminster Press, 1956), p. 319.

12. Cf. Matthew 25:14–30; 2 Corinthians 5:10.

13. The most recent and serious attempt is S. G. F. Brandon, *Jesus and the Zealots* (New York: Scribners, 1967).

14. See Matthew 5:38–42, especially v. 39, 26:52; Luke 6:27–29.

15. Cf. Luke 10:4f.

16. Cf. the metaphor of the "cross" used in passages such as Mark 8:34.

17. Note: "war" (1 Tim. 1:18; 1 Cor. 9:7; 2 Cor. 10:4); "fight" (1 Tim. 6:12; 2 Tim. 4:7; cf. Heb. 11:34); "being a soldier" (2 Tim. 2:3–4; Phil. 2:25); and even "bearing a sword" (Eph. 6:17; cf. Heb. 4:12; Rev. 1:16; 2:12, 16).

18. For a similar view see John Calvin, *A Harmony of the Evangelists Matthew, Mark, and Luke*, ed., David W. and Thomas F. Torrance (Grand Rapids: Eerdmans, 1972), on Luke 22:36.

19. I. H. Marshall, *Luke* (Grand Rapids: Eerdmans, 1978), p. 823.

20. See Mark 14:26–31, 66–72; Galatians 2:11–21.

21. Compare the following parables in this regard: the wise and foolish servants (Matt. 24:45–51); the two debtors (Luke 7:41–43); the good Samaritan (Luke 10:30–35); the great supper (Luke 14:15–24); the gracious father (the prodigal son) (Luke 15:11–32); etc.

22. Luke 14:16—"A [certain—*tis*] man once gave . . ."; Luke 15:11—"There was a [certain—*tis*] man who had . . ."; Luke 16:1—"There was a [certain—*tis*] rich man who . . ."; Luke 19:12—"A [certain—*tis*]

nobleman went . . ."; compare also Luke 18:2—"In a certain city there was a [certain—*tis*] judge who . . ."

23. Cf. Matthew 6:19–21; 7:21–23; 10:28; 13:24–30, 36–43, 47–50; 25:31–46; etc.

24. Cf. Acts 23:6–8.

25. Cf. Philippians 1:23—"to depart and be with Christ"; 1 Corinthians 15:12–57—"the mortal nature must put on immortality"; 1 Thessalonians 4:13–18—"and so we shall always be with the Lord"; 2 Corinthians 5:1–5—"if the earthly tent we live in is destroyed, we have a building from God, a house not made with hands, eternal in the heavens"; 2 Corinthians 5:8—away from the body means to be home with the Lord; 2 Thessalonians 1:9—the unrighteous "suffer the punishment of eternal destruction and exclusion from the presence of the Lord": Romans 2:5–11—"to those who by patience in well-doing seek for glory and honor and immortality, he will give eternal life"; 2 Timothy 4:6–8; etc.

26. Cf. Hebrews 5:11–14; 1 Corinthians 3:1–3.

27. Deuteronomy 29:29; Psalm 115:16.

28. Cf. Mark 1:1, 11; 3:11; 5:7; 9:7; 15:39; John 3:16; etc.

29. Cf. Mark 2:8; John 2:25, 5:16, 6:64; etc.

Notes to Chapter 3

1. Note Mark 1:16, 22; 2:15; 3:10, 21; 6:14; 7:3; etc.

2. Cf. Mark 6:34, 8:2; Matthew 9:36; Luke 7:13; etc.

3. Cf. Luke 15:1f.; Mark 2:16.

4. Compare the other three instances of this same verbal form in this chapter. In Mark 7:9, 14, 20 they are all dealing with a continuing conversation between the parties involved.

5. Compare Matthew 15:28 where the response of Jesus is, "'O woman, great is your faith! Be it done for you as you desire.'"

6. Cf. Luke 24:39; Matthew 28:9.

7. Note Acts 2:32–33; Romans 1:4; Philippians 2:9–11.

8. C. K. Barrett, *The Gospel According to St. John* (Philadelphia: Westminster, 1978), p. 565.

Notes to Chapter 4

1. Cf. Matthew 16:1–4; Mark 8:11–12; Luke 23:8–9; etc.

2. Cf. Mark 1:40–45, 5:35–43, 7:31–36, etc.

3. Cf. Luke 24:31 where the two disciples on the road to Emmaus say on Easter Sunday, "It is now the third day since this (the crucifixion) happened."

4. Cf. Mark 8:38, 13:26–27; Matthew 25:31; etc.

5. Cf. John 6:35, 51; 8:12; 10:7, 11; 11:25; etc.

6. The *Midrash Rabbah* on Genesis 28:12.

7. Cf. Genesis 28:17 and John 10:7–9; 14:6.

8. Cf. John 3:13.

9. John Calvin, *A Harmony of the Evangelists Matthew, Mark, and Luke*, ed., David W. and Thomas F. Torrance (Grand Rapids: Eerdmans, 1972), on Matthew 10:23.

10. See Matthew 16:27–28; 24:27, 30, 37, 39, 44; 25:31; 26:64.

11. Cf. Mark 13:9/Luke 21:12.

12. Cf. Mark 13:11/Luke 21:14–15.

13. Cf. Mark 13:12–13/Luke 21:16–17.

14. Cf. Matthew 24:21–22; 1 Corinthians 10:13.

Notes to Introduction to Part 2

1. Stephen J. Brown, *Image and Truth: Studies in the Imagery of the Bible* (Rome: Catholic Book Agency, 1955), pp. 45–46, summarizes this tendency: "The Oriental imagination delights in simile, metaphor, allegory, hyperbole and a hundred other figures."

2. T. E. Lawrence, *Seven Pillars of Wisdom* (New York: Doubleday, 1953), p. 38.

3. Claude C. Douglas, *Overstatement in the New Testament* (New York: Henry Holt, 1931), p. xxi.

4. James Barr, "Reading the Bible as Literature," *Bulletin of the John Rylands University Library of Manchester* 56 (1973): 15.

Notes to Chapter 5

1. For a helpful collection of the views of the early church fathers on this passage, see Thomas Aquinas, *Catena Aurea*, trans. John Henry Parker (Oxford: John Henry Parker, 1841), vol. 1, pp. 632–37.

2. Ibid., pp. 193–94.

3. Ibid., p. 378.

4. See b. (Babylonian Talmud) Baba Metzia 38b; b. Erubin 53a; b. Berachoth 55b.

5. G. B. Caird, *The Language and Imagery of the Bible* (Philadelphia: Westminster, 1980), p. 133, comments rather harshly on such attempts to explain this saying: "In this last instance plodding literalists have suggested that the needle's eye was the name for a low gate, like the door into the Church of the Nativity at Bethlehem, or that a camel was a kind of rope. But the Semitic bravura of Jesus' speech resists all such pathetic attempts to tame it." See also P. C. Sands, *Literary Genius of the New Testament* (Oxford: Clarendon, 1932), p. 77.

6. See Ian T. Ramsey, *Religious Language* (London: SCM, 1957), p. 95.
7. See Robert H. Stein, *The Method and Message of Jesus' Teachings* (Philadelphia: Westminster, 1978), pp. 8–12, for additional examples.

Notes to Chapter 6

1. Other passages which picture the worm as an agent of judgment include Deut. 28:39 and Isa. 51:8. For unquenchable fire see Isa. 34:10; Jer. 7:20; 17:27; Ezek. 20:47–48.
2. MATT. 5:48 should be compared with its entire context and the parallel in LUKE 6:36.
3. August Tholuck, *Commentary on the Sermon on the Mount*, trans. R. Lundin Brown (Edinburgh: T. & T. Clark, 1860), p. 164, states, "The correctness of the interpretation of a sentence and an isolated clause must be determined by the consistency of that interpretation with the idea of the whole work."
4. Teachers do, of course, change their minds at times, but in such instances the teacher is under obligation to make clear to his pupils that what he says now should not be interpreted in the light of the previous context.
5. Claude C. Douglas, *Overstatement in the New Testament* (New York: Henry Holt, 1931), p. 90, rightly states, "Either we must admit that here [Matt. 23:2–3] Jesus greatly exaggerates the facts or else he contradicts himself."
6. That the antitheses in Matthew were not understood by the Evangelist as doing away with the teachings of the Old Testament is evident from the context. The antitheses must be interpreted in the light of Matt. 5:17–20. Here Jesus states that he has not come to destroy the Old Testament ("the law and the prophets") but to fulfil it. To relax even one of the least important of its commandments is to make oneself least in the kingdom of heaven.
7. C. S. Lewis, *Fern-seed and Elephants and Other Essays on Christianity* (Glasgow: William Collins Sons, 1975), p. 112.
8. Tholuck, *Sermon on the Mount*, p. 165. Chrysostom's twenty-third homily on the Sermon on the Mount is still profitable reading for a proper interpretation of MATT. 7:1.

9. In 1 Cor. 7:10 Paul's words, "To the married I give charge, not I but the Lord," are best understood as referring not to a revelation from the risen Lord, but to a teaching of the historical Jesus. On the other hand, the material in vv. 12–13 is a revelation from the risen Lord ("To the rest I say, not the Lord," is to be understood in the light of 1 Cor. 7:40b—"And I think that I have the Spirit of God").
10. The present writer remembers a somewhat similar incident in his

own life when he, for emphasis, also used exaggeration to present his view. In a discussion of situation ethics various individuals were speculating as to when it is all right to engage in sexual activity with someone other than one's spouse. All sorts of different hypothetical situations were being suggested, some of them extremely unrealistic and unlikely. Lost in the discussion were the divine rule and normal, usual situations. When asked my views, I responded that there is never a right occasion for adultery. Now hypothetically there might be an occasion when adultery is the lesser of two evils, but my concern was to bring the discussion back to the plan and purpose of sex as God has ordained it. As a result I gave the universal divine rule which is applicable at least 99.99999 percent of the time. I can easily see why Jesus reacted in a similar manner to a debate on acceptable reasons for divorce.

11. Compare here Rom. 3:6, where Paul argues that God must be just since he will judge the world. The certainty of this fact (God's judgment of the world) proved for Paul that God is just.

12. The very fact that Christians accept the truth of both MATT. 7:7–8 and James 4:3 indicates that they understand the former to be an overstatement. Qualifying a statement in any way indicates that we believe that statement to be an exaggeration. Any statement which we accept on the assumption of certain unstated qualifications is by definition an exaggeration.

13. G. B. Caird, *The Language and Imagery of the Bible* (Philadelphia: Westminister, 1980), p. 57, correctly points out that "it is characteristic of Semitic style to express ideas absolutely and to leave the listener to fill in for himself the implicit qualifications."

14. Origen *On First Principles* 4. 18.

15. Douglas, *Overstatement*, p. xiv.

16. Walter C. Kaiser, Jr., *Toward an Exegetical Theology* (Grand Rapids: Baker, 1981), p. 230, states concerning proverbs, "It is the nature of proverbial speech to assume that *ceteris paribus* ('all other things being equal'), this then is true."

17. For our purposes we shall not make any distinction between prophecy and apocalyptic literature.

18. Caird, *Language and Imagery*, pp. 56–57.

19. That the poet was aware of the actual facts is evident from 5:26 (cf. 4:21).

20. Joachim Jeremias, *New Testament Theology*, trans. John Bowden (New York: Scribner, 1971), pp. 15–16.

21. Robert H. Stein, *The Method and Message of Jesus' Teachings* (Philadelphia: Westminster, 1978), pp. 27–32.

22. Recognition of the exaggerated nature of poetry may also be helpful for understanding some of the pre-Pauline hymns. The hymnic nature of Col. 1:15–20 is generally conceded by all Pauline scholars. Is it possi-

ble that the universal quality of this hymn ("to reconcile to himself all things") is due more to the exaggerated nature of poetry than to an attempt to teach a universal salvation? Compare 1 Cor. 15:22, which at first glance also seems universalistic but must be interpreted in the light of the next verse, which speaks of "those who belong to Christ."

23. For a discussion of both the difficulty involved in defining a parable and the kinds of material that fall under its domain see Robert H. Stein, *An Introduction to the Parables of Jesus* (Philadelphia: Westminster, 1981), pp. 15–21.

24. Josephus *Antiquities of the Jews* 17. 318.

25. For examples of paired terms see Mitchell Dahood, "Ugaritic-Hebrew Parallel Pairs," in *Ras Shamra Parallels,* ed. Loren R. Fisher, Analecta Orientalia 49 (Rome: Pontificium Institutum Biblicum, 1972), vol. 1, pp. 71–382; Peter C. Craigie, "Parallel Word Pairs in the Song of Deborah (Judges 5)," *Journal of the Evangelical Theological Society* 20 (1977): 15–22.

26. See also Isa. 13:16; Hos. 10:14; 13:16; and Nah. 3:10, where, however, a different Hebrew verb is used.

27. Othmar Keel, *The Symbolism of the Biblical World,* trans. Timothy J. Hallett (New York: Seabury, 1978), p. 9. Keel points out that the reference to the destruction of the children, who "concretize the continuation of the unrighteous kingdom," should be understood as a figure symbolizing the complete destruction of that kingdom. Keel includes two illustrations (plates 341 and 342) of a ruler sitting on a throne and holding his son on his lap. Subject peoples are depicted beneath the *child's* feet. Dashing little ones against the rock, then, suggests the total destruction of Babylonian rule: both ruler and heir encounter divine judgment.

28. Cf. the description of the judgment of Babylon in Isaiah 13 with the specific historical circumstances. Some of the language used is clearly nonliteral and eschatological. See especially vv. 9–10, 13.

29. To pose Jesus as an exception here is to lose sight of the context of Rom. 3. Paul is referring to all flesh (Rom. 3:20), i.e., all who are in Adam (Rom. 5:12), both Jews and Greeks. He does not include Jesus among those who are in Adam. Note carefully the wording of Rom. 8:3: the Son did not come "in sinful flesh," but "in the likeness of sinful flesh." It is clear that, in Paul's view, Jesus Christ was sinless (2 Cor. 5:21).

30. The number of such universal statements in the Bible should be noted. Douglas, *Overstatement,* p. 7, states that the term *all* is used 5500+ times in the Bible; and when we add such terms as "any," "none," and "every," the number swells to over ten thousand!

31. See note 13.

32. See pp. 61–63.

Notes to Chapter 7

1. The writer is indebted to G. B. Caird, *The Language and Imagery of the Bible* (Philadelphia: Westminster, 1980), pp. 7–36, for much of the terminology used in this section. Caird subdivides referential language into informative and cognitive language, and commissive language into performative, expressive, and cohesive language.

2. Philip Wheelwright, *Metaphor and Reality* (Bloomington: Indiana University Press, 1962), p. 38.

3. There is also a pun here—the Aramaic word for gnat was *galma* and for camel was *gamla*. See Robert H. Stein, *The Method and Message of Jesus' Teaching* (Philadelphia: Westminster, 1978), p. 13.

4. Claude C. Douglas, *Overstatement in the New Testament* (New York: Henry Holt, 1931), p. 3, states, "In general hyperbole increases in proportion to the intensity of the emotion experienced by the speaker or writer."

Scripture Index

392 Scripture Index